HOW TO GROW
A GROWN UP

D0896801

To Simon and Jack, and Jason, Tom and Jack.
This book is for you, with love.

HOW TO GROW A GROWN UP

Prepare your teen for the real world

DR DOMINIQUE THOMPSON
AND
FABIENNE VAILES

Vermilion
LONDON

1 3 5 7 9 10 8 6 4 2

Published in 2019 by Vermilion an imprint of Ebury Publishing,

20 Vauxhall Bridge Road,
London SW1V 2SA

Vermilion is part of the Penguin Random House group of companies
whose addresses can be found at global.penguinrandomhouse.com

Copyright © Dominique Thompson and Fabienne Vailes 2019

Dominique Thompson and Fabienne Vailes have asserted their right
to be identified as the authors of this Work in accordance with
the Copyright, Designs and Patents Act 1988

First published by Vermilion in 2019

www.penguin.co.uk

A CIP catalogue record for this book is available
from the British Library

ISBN 9781785042782

Typeset in 10.5 /15 pt Sabon LT Std
by Integra Software Services Pvt. Ltd, Pondicherry

Printed and bound in Great Britain by Clays Ltd, Elcograf S.p.A.

Penguin Random House is committed to a sustainable
future for our business, our readers and our planet.
This book is made from Forest Stewardship Council®
certified paper.

Contents

CONTENTS

Introduction

Imagine one of those pictures made of coloured dots ... If you look at the individual dots you can't make out what you're looking at, but if you let your eyes relax and take a step back, suddenly an image comes together. We want this book to be like an image coming into focus for you, bringing together all the different elements of your teenager's or young adult's life, to make sense of what they experience, examining the changes they go through and suggesting what you might do to support them.

This is a book written to help you grow and develop an independent and resilient teenager or young adult. All the advice within will make your job as a parent a little easier, knowing that young people are more likely to feel stressed (or even have mental health issues) these days, and recognising that you may be parenting in a world that is very different to the one you grew up in, and that is changing constantly. Our aim is to help parents and carers raise young adults who will feel well and who will function effectively in a complex world, preparing them for careers and jobs that may be very different from those we aspired to when we were young.

WHO WE ARE

B etween us, we bring years of experience to this book. Dominique is a GP with a special interest in mental health, and has spent 20 years caring for university students, as well as working to improve mental health awareness and care for students at a national strategic level. You can google her TEDx Talks – 'What I learnt from 78,000 GP consultations with university students' and 'Understanding the why' – which capture some of her ideas about what might be underlying the rise in mental health issues and how to approach young people's challenging self-destructive behaviours. Dominique now works with universities internationally to improve services supporting students' mental health and well-being.

Fabienne is an educator (also with 20 years' experience), a university insider, working as French Language Director in the School of Modern Languages of the University of Bristol, author of *The Flourishing Student* and Director of Flourishing Education Ltd. She is currently researching and promoting how to embed well-being in the curriculum to create flourishing institutions with flourishing students and staff.

Speaking to our academic colleagues in a wide range of universities it became apparent that many students today are unprepared for university life, and are also feeling an increased need for emotional support. In our professional lives, in our consulting or tutorial rooms, we too have spent many hours advising students and other young people about their health and well-being. This is a trend not a blip, and it isn't just at university that young people are struggling; half of young people enter the workplace or an apprenticeship scheme directly from school, and it is just as important to prepare them well for life outside the cocoon of home.

TODAY'S CHANGING WORLD

We are often asked what is the one reason behind the difficulties encountered by young people today, and it would be great if we could find a simple answer to explain the issues! Can't we simply point the finger at technology, mobile phones, education or sleep? The answer, sadly, is no, which means that, unfortunately, there is no silver bullet and no 'one-size-fits-all' solution that will solve everyone's problems.

Though there will be challenges that teens share with others – and for some it might be a couple of stressors that affect them while for others it will be many – we are all unique (just like our DNA and fingerprints) and so are the challenges and experiences our children will have over their lifetimes. This is where we hope this book will help in a different and unique way. Bringing together all the contributing factors that have been researched and reported to positively or negatively impact our children, we will put this evidence under the microscope and outline how we can support young people from childhood through to their mid-twenties, as we know that the problems don't stop when they turn 18. For a multitude of reasons, students and other young adults appear to be suffering from more stress or mental health issues than in the past, leaving parents and carers in desperate need of reliable information, reassurance and guidance about what to watch for, when to seek help and where to access support. We have noticed that more parents are going to doctors' consultations *with* their adult children, and more are phoning counselling and health centres (including in the USA and Australia) to express concern about an adult 'child', or to ask for advice.

Where is this increased mental health demand coming from? What is causing it? How have things changed so much from our own experiences as young adults? Are the younger generation less 'resilient' in some way? Difficult, possibly unfair, questions are now being asked. So what has changed? *We are raising and educating a culturally different generation.* This statement may seem obvious as, by definition, generations are characterised not just by the years in which people are born, but by the culture or society in which they are immersed and which shapes them. Each generation will be different, so how is this new generation being defined? What has happened over the past 30 years to create such an 'emotionally different' generation? As we will describe, our children are being raised in a significantly more competitive culture, with the additional pressures of new technology to manage and a 24/7 drive to be 'on' and at their best. These factors, among others, may be affecting their mental health.

Those born before the mid-eighties may struggle to understand the increasing concerns of the younger generation, and find themselves comparing their childhoods, often characterised by the comfortable 'benign neglect' of their own parents – when, as kids, they would disappear off to play out of sight and out of mind for hours, returning only for food – with the upbringing of our current young people. But they are not comparing like with like, so it is unsurprising that the results are also vastly different – their carefree childhoods were so different from those of the stressed kids we see today.

HOW THIS BOOK CAN HELP

In today's world, parents seem to have much less of a background role and are less incidental to their child's existence than we might have been accustomed to as children ourselves, and they take a much greater and more active part in the life of their offspring. There even seems to be a greater pressure to be a 'perfect' parent and, in some more extreme scenarios,

4

there is an air of competition in the frantic arena of parenting. And yet, while there are multiple resources and services to refer young people to and, increasingly, school and university staff have policies to follow when met with the daily crises, anxiety or suicidal thoughts of their students, and many workplaces have well-being programmes firmly in place, there was a gaping hole in terms of advice and support for the parents or carers of the young people we were seeing, who were coming forward in increasing numbers asking for help. Parents felt anxious, confused and sometimes overwhelmed, but were doing their very best to support their young adult. The more we spoke to parents and carers of children aged 16–25 in particular, the more we realised what an enormous gap there was in practical support. This is where this book comes in.

We wrote this book to advise the parents of teens and 'tweenagers' (11–13-year-olds) about what to expect, and to learn from those parents who had gone before them, as well as to hear from professionals ready to share their experience and knowledge.

This book will start by offering some suggestions about what societal changes might explain the higher number of children and young adults feeling stressed and under pressure now, and how we can better support our younger generation in the twenty-first century wherever we live in the world. These factors may even go some way to explaining the rising mental health problems that we are noticing and are relevant to many cultures. We will go on to cover topics which undoubtedly have an effect on our children's well-being, from parenting, education and technology, through to relationships, and the wider world they live in now. We will then look at how you can create independent and resilient young adults, ready for university and the world of work. We will finish by carefully reviewing the mental health problems that can arise in young people, give advice on what support parents can offer, and there is a separate chapter on mental health crises and what to do, should you ever need that level of help. The overarching message of the book is to know that there is plenty that you can do as a parent or carer to build independence, resourcefulness and resilience in your young adult, and while the earlier you start the better, it is never too late. Whether your child is a tween, a teen or in their twenties, we want you to find tips and strategies to help foster their inner strength and ability to deal with whatever life throws at them.

IS THIS BOOK JUST FOR PARENTS?

No. In this book we will use the term 'parent' to encompass all of you who are significant carers, such as grandparents and foster parents, not just biological parents, and who are parenting a young person through their life. Families come in all shapes and sizes, so to avoid confusion or repetition please be assured that the word 'parent' will include all of you who are parenting; who love, care for and support emotionally, practically and financially, the young people in your lives.

There is no single way of doing things right in life, and least of all when parenting or caring for young people, but we hope that this book, based on the latest evidence and years of experience, will boost the confidence of parents, carers, grandparents, teachers, lecturers, social workers and anyone else who works with young adults, in knowing how best to guide and advise them in a fast-changing world. We will use the terms 'child', 'teenager', 'young adult' and 'young person' throughout the book, but we will try to be consistent where we can, to avoid confusion. We use the abbreviation 'LGBT+' to encompass all those who identify as lesbian, gay, bisexual, transgender and other sexualities. We hope the book will not feel too UK-centric, as our experience and liaison with overseas colleagues tells us that the issues and our suggested solutions will apply in many parts of the world.

Throughout the book we have highlighted 'Parent Pointers' – top tips specifically designed to build the resilience and independence your children may need to thrive in the twenty-first century. The checklists at the end of each chapter will provide a quick review of the main points, which you can revisit over the years when you haven't got time to read the whole book again.

This book won't make you 'down with the kids', and you will still be embarrassing to them sometimes (which, as you will read, is actually a vital part of the growing up process), but it will hopefully allow you to better understand the world your young adult inhabits and support them to be ready for what lies ahead.

Finally, bear in mind the advice given by author Kahlil Gibran in his book *The Prophet*:

Your children are not your children.
They are the sons and daughters of Life's longing for itself.
They come through you but not from you,
And though they are with you yet they belong not to you.
You may give them your love but not your thoughts,
For they have their own thoughts.
You may house their bodies but not their souls,
For their souls dwell in the house of tomorrow which you cannot visit, not even in your dreams.
You may strive to be like them, but seek not to make them like you.
For life goes not backward nor tarries with yesterday.
You are the bows from which your children as living arrows are sent forth.

PART 1

SOCIETY'S CULTURE SHIFT

CHAPTER 1

Understanding Generation Z

If we are going to communicate, connect and work with our younger generation effectively we need to understand them better; the better your dialogue with your young person the more they will open up to you when things get tough. So much is written about Millennials, Generation Z, iGen, Digital Natives and, sometimes (more disparagingly), 'Snowflakes' or Generation Sensible, that it is hard to get our heads around who they really are. But their culture is not impenetrable; it may just take time and a little effort to 'get' it.

First of all let's separate out the generations, and make sure we are all talking about the same kids and young adults. Labels aren't always helpful, but for the purposes of this book, the generation we are mainly concerned with is Generation Z – young people between the end of primary school through to those in their early twenties (born after 1995). Millennials, on the other hand, were born after 1981 and many of the oldest are actually now approaching 40! So when the media uses that name as a blanket term for young people, they are in fact describing a population who are now in their mid-twenties to late thirties.

Children and young adults born since 1995 are the most culturally and racially diverse, socially aware, digitally competent, educated, but also risk-averse, generation the world has ever known.[1] They feel both powerless (often too young to vote) and powerful (they know the future is theirs and they *own* technology). They are 'children of meme culture', raised by the Internet, hyperaware of what is going on in the world, yet they struggle to get their voices heard. They worry about becoming a 'grown-up', with the perceived list of achievements (having a steady job, owning property, paying bills) that being a grown-up seems to require. They are funny, bright, and politically engaged but frightened, often all at once. They are constantly connected, to each other but also to the world around them, to traumatic events as they occur, and to a constant bombardment of new information. This has upsides and downsides, as they can find information instantly, feel connected to friends and family wherever they are in the world, but can also immerse themselves in terrible world events, such as school shootings, as they happen, which can be traumatic. Their beliefs and values are shaped by society and advertising, and they are generally very socially responsible, environmentally friendly and keen to be associated, and later work with, organisations that have a social conscience or responsible attitude.

An example of the younger generation's awareness of ethical living and willingness to live by their beliefs is in the dramatic rise in veganism. Young people are driving this principled approach to eating, with most being females under the age of 35.[2]

THEIR VALUES

Having a purpose is fundamental to human well-being. Knowing where you are going and what you are getting up for each day is key to our functioning, and the next generation are driven by wanting to make a positive difference in the world.

They share and they care

The idea of helping each other out while being efficient really appeals to young people, and participating in the 'sharing economy' (where skills or belongings are shared in return for others' skills or belongings) is commonplace and unremarkable to them. They will use their personal assets, such as living space or cars, to earn income. The rise in food sharing apps (such as OLIO) brings the food bank ethos closer to home and neighbours, by allowing people to advertise spare food direct from their cupboards and fridges to share it locally, before it goes out of date. Such altruism mixed with practicality is very attractive to a caring generation.

They worry about the planet and sustainability, with school kids going 'on strike' for the planet all over the world (#FridaysforFuture), making their voices heard where their options to do so are limited.[3] In the UK a quarter of British schoolchildren have avoided buying certain products because of the conditions under which they were produced, so when your teenager tells you not to buy products containing palm oil despite the fact that they *love* chocolate hazelnut spread, you should respect their environmental awareness and altruism![4]

They are tolerant, visual and 'woke' (socially aware)

They expect a significant digital innovation every year (rather than every few years as we might have done), and they will build their 'personal brand' in a way we never considered (it wasn't a thing in our day). Their attention span may be seemingly shorter (although the evidence for this is thin, and it may be more about the number of distractions they now have) and their learning will be hugely visual, with YouTube being a favourite source of tutorials and information.[5] One of the things they love most about being a twenty-first-century teen is having access to learning about any and all subjects at the touch of a screen.

And they are a remarkably tolerant bunch, fluid around roles, gender and identity, and open-minded towards those around them who challenge stereotypes. They are the most likely generation to have friends who are of different races from them (81 per cent compared with 69 per cent of Millennials in one survey).[6]

But being born since 1995, and in most cases knowing only a world of stock market crashes or austerity (and university fees), they worry more about debt and family finances, and, like Millennials before them, may never be able to afford to buy a house.[7] Money, or lack of it, is a source of constant and unavoidable stress to many.

They put family first

The book *Gen Z @ Work* explains how for Generation Z 'family comes first' – 73 per cent of the teenagers said they enjoyed spending time with their parents and 91 per cent felt that their parents were involved in their lives.[8] Many are close to their parents, and their parents may consider them as friends, which can have pros and cons (as we will see in Chapter 3). Reassuringly (you may be surprised to hear this!), their families are more important to them than social media or their phone.[9] However, their Internet connection *is* more important to them than going to the cinema, getting pocket money, attending a sporting event or watching TV.[10]

The protectiveness that this parental closeness may engender can potentially lead to parents monitoring their offspring at all times, sometimes using technology to do so. Whether it's monitoring their location through apps on their phones or setting up

'Nest Cams' in the home, some families are taking drastic measures to keep track of their children and their behaviour.[11] This 'surveillance' is taking extreme parenting to a whole new level.

PARENT POINTERS

- The need to be in control and watching over your children at all times may reassure you initially and make you feel that you are parenting them to the best of your ability. However, it may be worth considering whether building trust in them to be where they say they will be or do what they say they will do is a more productive and healthier route in the longer term. Though it won't give you the quick-fix of checking an app (or, God forbid, a camera!), it will develop their independence and your faith in them.
- Building trust with your child can be one of the most effective ways to care for them while guiding them to an autonomous future (see Chapter 7 for more on this).
- A five-minute 'check-in' a day will keep the communications open with your teenager and let them know you are interested, available and engaged. This is not constant hand-holding; just a gentle low-key enquiry.

They volunteer

Young people volunteer in their local communities in large numbers with almost half of UK 14–16-year-olds giving their time to help in the local community in the last two years, and many spending their holidays or gap years making a difference to others at home or abroad.[12]

Whether they choose to improve literacy rates by joining reading projects for local children, participate in litter picking outings, campaign against period poverty, visit the elderly who are lonely or fundraise to build toilets in developing countries, there are endless opportunities for young people to volunteer, help out, gain some life experience, give back to the community and, as a bonus, have something to put on their CV. They are a generation prepared to step up and help out, engaged with their communities and happy to give back.

They speak out

Prejudice towards LGBT+ (Lesbian, Gay, Bisexual, Transgender +other) people, racism and gender inequality concerns this generation more than it did the generations that came before them.[13] Previous generations were also politically active of course, but while it can feel easy to dismiss this generation (and many do) as 'overly sensitive, safe space seeking, trigger-warning-demanding snowflakes', it is important to remember that our young people are compassionate, tolerant of difference, but perhaps less likely to endure the nasty bits of life that we have long accepted or lived with.[14,15]

They campaign against transphobia, sexual harassment and racism, and for refugee or animal rights, and, in some countries, they fight for gun control (#NeverAgain). Often they risk their own personal safety to raise awareness of the issues, putting their heads above the parapet and speaking up for those less able or willing to do so. Campaigns such as #MeToo are beginning to define our era, and vocal, brave young leaders are at the forefront, alongside celebrities and experts in the field. In the UK we have seen them strike for climate change and campaign for better mental health services. One group of young people in Cumbria set up the advocacy group 'We Will' to try to get better mental health support for themselves and their peers, when NHS help was too slow coming.[16] They are engaged, motivated and not afraid to speak up.

ANTI-RACISM

The #BlackLivesMatter movement, which started in 2012 after the shooting of Trayvon Martin in Florida, was led from the beginning by three young Millennial women. In their footsteps came black American teenagers Sophia Byrd, Eva Lewis, Natalie Braye and Maxine Wint (all aged 16 or 17 at the time), who organised a huge silent march in Chicago in July 2016.[17] The movement is now supported by 43 per cent of Americans.[18]

ANTI-GUN

The young American anti-gun campaigners who rose up after school shootings in the USA are heroes to their peers all over the world, and rightly so. Such passion and energy should make all of us feel more optimistic about the future and world politics.

ANTI-SEXUAL HARASSMENT

Young people are in the midst of several social revolutions, and most of them embrace that and are proud of their peers campaigning for justice or fighting inequality. They are particularly proud of the social progress made with the anti-sexual harassment campaigns, from #EverydaySexism to #MeToo, which have allowed people everywhere (especially young women) to feel able to push back, and speak out about inappropriate sexual behaviour.[19]

Generation Z will likely break down stigma around sexual assault, participate in hashtags and campaigns, and support each other non-judgementally, but we still need to act (by educating them) to prevent assaults in the first place.

They are compassionate

Claire Fox (a British libertarian writer and political activist) coined the derogatory term 'Generation Snowflake' to describe young people who are obsessed with their psychological well-being, who are easily offended by criticism of their views or 'triggered', and who, she postulates, have adopted a 'cult of victimhood'.[20] Her criticism of the young generation has been echoed by others, including Jonathan Haidt and Greg Lukianoff (authors of *The Coddling of the American Mind*), who argue that we have created a generation unable to cope with the everyday stresses of life, and for whom disappointment, stress and frustration are no longer part of growing up but create mental illness.[21] From our decades of experience speaking with and caring for young adults daily, we would argue differently.

We see a generation that is breaking down the stigma of mental health, talking about topics that have long been taboo, and raising awareness of conditions such as anxiety or depression in a bid to support help-seeking and action. They firmly believe that it is 'okay to be not okay' and are compassionate to

PARENT POINTER

- We can prepare our children for a challenging world, and we can teach them how to manage the views they find offensive, and how to counter those views, but we need to understand that they are much more Generation Compassion than Generation Snowflake.

others, which encourages conversation. All of this is much more about caring for others and getting help when needed, than about self-obsession.

THEIR POLITICS

It has always been the case that fewer young people than older people vote, which may be down to apathy, disillusionment or lack of real choice, but the 2017 general election in the UK saw the highest turnout for 20 years, with 54 per cent of eligible voters in the 18–24 age group voting.[22] It is easy to dismiss young people as 'disengaged' or not exerting their right to vote, but they can and do, despite sometimes feeling that their vote won't make any difference or they don't like any of the candidates. They may also not vote because they have not registered or it feels too time-consuming.[23]

You can encourage your young adult to vote, and be politically engaged, in many ways, and not just by making sure they do the paperwork. You may be able to support their political engagement by making sure that they see you voting, by encouraging them to vote whenever they have an opportunity, to ask questions about issues, to challenge their MPs and to listen to different views (they can get stuck in their social media 'echo chamber', hearing only views that are similar to their own), and they can learn to debate with those whose views do not align with their own, for example at university or school political or campaign events. Take them on marches or demonstrations from a young age, so that they can see peaceful democracy at work. They love feeling that they are part of something and making a difference, so let them suggest other ways to do so, at school, uni or in the wider community, creatively and engagingly, leading the social revolution from the front.

The rise of 'no platforming'

'No platforming' is the term given to the boycotting of persons or organisations by removing their 'platform' to speak. In UK universities there have been several examples of this happening, with attempts to ban speakers such as Germaine Greer and Peter Tatchell, a gay rights activist, for what were considered 'transphobic' or 'racist' views. Rather than embrace free speech and the opportunity for impassioned debate, the students called for the guest speakers to be 'no platformed', in other words for their platform to be taken away. This has been one of the more disappointing approaches taken by some in a generation that generally responds positively to challenge. When talking with your own children, it may be helpful to discuss such actions and bring up the possibility that (apart from doing themselves no favours and appearing precious) the students missed an amazing opportunity to debate with highly experienced, world-class speakers, on a topic they clearly felt passionately about, and to potentially win over their fellow students. Freedom of speech is a glorious right, which can of course be abused, but learning to embrace it, leverage it and influence others to their own ends may be a healthier and more useful approach than banning speakers you don't agree with.

Learning to debate and argue your case in a calm and balanced manner is certainly a skill worth developing, and may be one to practise over the dinner table with your teenager or young adult.

GENERATION SENSIBLE?

Adolescence is known as a time of taking risks and trying new experiences, even potentially dangerous ones. The stereotypical recklessness of youth is well known, but in recent years there has been a particularly shocking trend ... according to the media (and the statistics) the youth of today are becoming more 'sensible'!

Or are they?

While rates of binge drinking, drug misuse, teenage pregnancy, smoking and being arrested have plummeted in the UK, and in the USA the proportion of accidents leading to death in those aged 15–19 years has plunged over the last 20 years, is it because the young are becoming more 'sensible' or are they in fact becoming more *risk-averse*?[24,25] In other words, are young people now *too* careful, too worried about their health, and in some cases just too anxious to take the usual teenage risks and try the traditional methods of teenage rebellion? Is it fantastic news that they care about their health more, especially mental health, and even know that the real evil is sugar, not (unsaturated) fat, or is this part of a bigger picture of rising health anxiety?[26] Should we be rejoicing, along with our Public Health colleagues, that young people are participating in fewer risky behaviours, or should we ask what else they're also missing out on? Should we sit back and relax with a satisfied 'job done' as our teenagers curl up on the sofa close to us, or should we be talking to them, ensuring that they still have an interest in trying new things (not necessarily smoking!) and are not completely afraid of the unknown?

In the words of Katherine O'Brien, head of media and policy research at the British Pregnancy Advisory Service who carried out a study of 1000 young people:

Our research reveals that this is a generation who are focused on their education, aware of economic challenges but determined to succeed regardless and many of whom enjoy time with their families as much as with partners and friends. They seem to place significant value on responsibility and maturity, particularly when it comes to alcohol consumption and sex. We believe that young people themselves are making different choices about the way they live their lives.[27]

Being responsible is of course to be applauded, but are young people still prepared to take measured, interesting 'risks' (with an element of the unknown to stretch them), like travelling in their holidays or gap years, meeting new people in unfamiliar situations or trying activities such as coasteering? Despite being designed biologically to take risks, young people appear to be taking fewer of them.

Yet, there are physical and biological reasons why teenagers normally take risks. Their brains are designed to get a buzz from risk-taking. Scientists believe that teenagers take risks because they have a 'reward centre' (in the limbic region of the brain) which is activated and 'lights up' and is hypersensitive in the adolescent years, more than in adults, and also because their 'impulse control zone' (in the prefrontal cortex of the brain) is one of the last areas to develop in humans.[28] There is therefore a mismatch in adolescence when the reward centre is lighting up like a Christmas tree and the 'off switch' (impulse control) has not yet fully matured.[29] Teenagers *can't* always control themselves.

Young people are more likely to take risks when with friends than alone, which illustrates the fact that they can control themselves more in certain situations, but their risk-taking is magnified when with friends, or at a party and excited, compared with at home, doing something domestic.[30]

If such a milestone can exist (bearing in mind that everyone is an individual), the age at which young people make the greatest proportion of risky choices is 14.38 years![31] This may be because this is the age at which they get the most buzz from their reward centre with the least 'brake' applied by the control centre.

Young adults need to take 'good risks' with their work and with their studies, to ask questions in classes or seminars, and to try modules and topics that are unfamiliar to them. In a world of perfectionism, they can be very reluctant to try a new subject or skill, worried that they might not be brilliant, with their worst-case scenario being that they might fail.

The importance of taking risks

Unless we try new things in life and stretch ourselves, we will not grow and develop as humans. Risk is a fundamental part of human existence and evolution. We didn't evolve by sitting in our caves waiting for lunch to be delivered by an 'Early Man Uber Eats'! We went outside the cave, probably terrified, and took the risks necessary to feed ourselves and our families. As a result, we discovered that fortune favours the bold. Risk-taking is an evolutionary necessity.

As parents we can provide opportunities throughout life that provide what one dad described to us as 'secure insecurity', in other words, safe places and circumstances in which our children can take measured risks and learn from their experiences. When they are little this is about letting them toddle off within a boundaried space to explore, as young children they might roam a play area without you, with the possibility of hurting themselves or falling over, but unlikely to be badly hurt; as tweenagers this might mean cycling or walking to the park alone to meet friends; as teenagers it may be going out on a Friday night to someone's house with location and time boundaries pre-agreed. Managing risk is a vital part of growing up, and parents have a central role to play in helping their children learn how to assess it and then deal with it.

THINKING POINTS

Generation Z worry about the future, about political issues, hate, discrimination, the environment and global warming.[32] Their world sometimes feels chaotic and uncertain, but they feel part of a global community. They are less patriotic than previous generations and more likely to see themselves as citizens of the planet, as well as protectors of it.[33] This may mean that they feel resentful of those who have made choices or decisions that have led to the world's problems today. But they are also the generation that can fix it.[34,35] They are keen to vote and are politically engaged. They are motivated, optimistic and ready to tackle the planet's ills, living their beliefs, many of them activists from a young age and keen to make a difference.[36]

Here are a few things to consider:

- They are a generation concerned but ready to step up and fix things so encourage this and have conversations to build independence and resilience.
- Respect their ethical choices (but if they become vegan, keep an eye on their approach and ensure they are not losing weight – see page 273).
- Build trust and don't over-monitor their activity.
- Make time for regular check-ins, especially with teens living at home whom you might see less often.
- Engage them on political matters, debate with them in a constructive way, and show them how to counter difficult views, without blocking free speech.
- Encourage them to vote.
- Educate them about taking interesting 'good risks'.

CHAPTER 2

Twenty-first-century Pressures

Welcome to the twenty-first century, where even the homely art of baking has become competitive, the once clunky telephone is now a smooth extension of our arm, the idea of owning your own home has become only a distant possibility and where many of the jobs our kids may dream of will probably be done (at least in part) by artificial intelligence. This chapter aims to guide you through, and help you to understand, this increasingly competitive and challenging world your children are growing up in, so that you can support them to navigate it successfully. Only by having a better understanding of the world they are immersed in, of the wallpaper of their lives, will you be able to be of most practical and relevant help to your children.

It is no longer enough to understand and notice *what* the differences are, in parenting, in education and in technology; we need to also understand *how* these might affect the well-being of the younger generation. Young people are significantly shaped and conditioned by the environment they live in, the people they spend time with, the online world they interact with and their educational experience. Much of the time these have a positive impact, but occasionally these interactions stress or distress them, leading them to struggle with life. As parents and carers you are in a unique position to influence, for the better, their ability to cope with what life throws at them; to teach them pragmatism, insight, empathy, compassion, resilience and independence. You want them to know what to do and how to react in a *healthy* way when the going gets tough. Young people need to have the tools and resources to do so, and, if you are to help and support them effectively, so do you. Understanding their world is the first step towards growing a capable, creative, thoughtful and robust grown-up.

In talking to young people in our work, and in researching this book, we were struck by the feeling of 'pressure' they all mentioned. They perceived an oppressive sense of expectation, from themselves but also from parents and other authority figures. They felt that, from a very young age, they had to know what they wanted to do and where they wanted to go in life, and that they had to work very hard to get there, with little emphasis on fun or enjoyment. They felt the world was not friendly to them or interested in their views, although they felt strongly that they wanted to be heard. They were passionate and kind, funny and ironic, thoughtful and politically aware, keen to make a difference and matter, but frustrated with a society that wasn't listening to them. They mentioned multiple twenty-first-century influences and pressures that characterised their lives, whatever their backgrounds, which are outlined below.

HOME LIFE

Young people are growing up fast but 'adulting' later – 25 is the new 18. There has been a striking change in the age at which young people start to engage in what are considered 'adult' behaviours or life skills. Research shows that young people around the world are now delaying not only marriage, but also driving, pregnancy and leaving home.[1,2]

'Delayed adolescence' is a concept that has been on psychologists' radars for a while, but in fact the phenomenon seems to be more accurately described as *prolonged* adolescence.[3] The reasons for this may lie in an increasingly health-and-safety-conscious parenting climate, the 'soft play culture' that our young now grow up in, or in well-meaning parents doing more facilitation and path-clearing ('snowplough parenting') for this generation than our parents did for us. However, as one counsellor said to us: 'Might we help them more by teaching them problem-solving skills, rather than problem-solving *for* them?'

Eye-opening work by American psychologists in 2017 revealed that, over the last 40 years, young people in the USA have delayed their adulthood significantly, preferring instead the safety of home until their mid-twenties, and avoiding the responsibilities and activities that have traditionally arrived with legal coming of age.[4] The young people in the study were dating less, having less sex, drinking less, driving less and less likely to have a job than 40 years before. As you will see, this trend is now being mirrored not just in the UK, but in Europe and Australia too.

This idea – that adolescence now lasts from the age of 10 until 25, instead of 19 – explains, in part, why young people attending our universities, workplaces and doctors' consulting rooms are now so often accompanied by parents, deferring to them to ask the questions.[5] Some parents are even accompanying their offspring to graduate job interviews!

So why is this generation different? Are they, like Peter Pan, afraid to grow up, or are we, as parents and older adults, preventing them from doing so? Why are young people delaying independence and indulging less in traditional 'risky' behaviour? Having spoken to young adults while researching this book, they frequently told us of their fear of 'adulting' or the seemingly overwhelming responsibilities (as they perceived them) involved with being a 'grown-up', but they were still keen to be encouraged to be independent and to take on those responsibilities. They hated being infantilised (by the government, by people in authority, by universities, by family members), but were also stressed by what they viewed as the long list of achievements that being an adult would require them to check off. They hadn't yet realised, and no one had told them, that very few of us have it 'all figured out' or that there is no 'checklist', but that we all find our way and muddle through, and then one day we may realise that we have a job, a mortgage or rent to pay, bills to stay on top of and perhaps children, and we are officially an 'adult'. Many young people named specific tasks that they associated with being an adult, and that they felt unqualified for or unable to achieve, such as changing a tyre, filling out a tax return or fixing a broken toilet, but they didn't seem to realise that plenty of adults can't do these things either!

As parents we can reassure our children that there is no single recipe for success (nor a checklist of 'adulthood') and that it takes time to feel like a 'responsible adult'.

Sex, drugs and alcohol

Our teenagers are becoming more risk-averse, with studies in the UK mirroring the steady drop in the USA in alcohol, smoking and drug use over recent years.

In 2014 England recorded the lowest level of smoking in 11–15-year-olds since surveys began in 1982, with fewer than 1 in 5 saying that they had smoked at least once (although the numbers vaping are rising in the UK, mirroring the *increase* in teens vaping in the USA in 2018).[6,7,8] Two in five had tried alcohol at least once – the lowest proportion since the survey began. The frequency of drug use had declined between 2001 and 2010, with only 1 in 6 in 2016 stating that they had ever used drugs. In other words, the numbers of English teenagers using drugs halved in a decade. A Scottish government report in 2015 demonstrated similar trends in declining alcohol and drug use.[9]

Teenage pregnancy rates in England and Wales have followed the downward slope carved by smoking, alcohol and substance misuse, with the most recent under-18 pregnancy rates being the lowest since comparable records began in 1969.[10] The USA has seen similar reductions in teenage pregnancy and drug and alcohol misuse, according to a 2016 report.[11]

However, we shouldn't be too complacent as a UK survey in 2017 discovered that almost half of sexually active under-25s 'never used a condom with a new partner', and about 1 in 10 had never used one at all.[12] It seems that the fear of unplanned pregnancy is somewhat greater than that of sexually transmitted infections; they are prepared to use other, less 'messy', forms of contraception it seems, but not condoms! As the message about unplanned pregnancy seems to be getting through we now need to focus more on them avoiding chlamydia!

Learning to drive

Looking beyond sex, drugs and alcohol, something that surprises many parents is that young people are not learning to drive until much later, perhaps because they are chauffeured by parents more, the cost is prohibitive or public transport and firms such as Uber are improving. The result is that 'Mum and Dad's taxi' is driving well into their offspring's mid-twenties. The average age for passing the UK driving test is now 26 years, despite it being legal from 17.[13] By delaying this adult milestone young people may be choosing to infantilise themselves for longer, so missing out on the independence and experiences that come with the freedom to drive.

SCHOOL LIFE AND BEYOND

L ife, and our society, have become increasingly competitive, not just via the traditional methods by which humans have always challenged each other (sport or academic prowess), but even the fun stuff has been made competitive. From baking cakes, photography and poetry to robot building and dating, more often than not, 'fun' is now a competitive activity. And before you say 'But *life* is competitive, so they need to compete!', we agree, life is, but *fun* doesn't need to be!

Competitiveness (or success by any means necessary)

Young people feel a huge pressure to be successful, to look a certain way, to do things 'right', to achieve certain grades, to know what they want to do with their lives (they really hate this one), to meet targets to keep their parents happy (and their teachers out of trouble) and to tick the boxes that society dictates are necessary for 'success', whether that's extracurricular activities, clubs, sport, volunteering, music and dance or school awards. Many of them feel there is less time for playing, for creativity, and those who love the arts sometimes feel ashamed as these subjects are prized less highly by the 'establishment'. Young people talk about feeling as if they are being educated in a factory where the sole aim is to pass exams and go to university or take a well-trodden career path. Their teachers talk of an 'arms race of qualifications' which continues at university. As parents you may even feel that parenting itself has become increasingly competitive.

Young people are competing against each other in a world that has become all about 'winners' and 'losers', rather than valuing creativity, individuality and non-academic skills. We are giving a very strong message that it is not enough to enjoy these activities or even be any good at them – instead you have to be the best. Try not to ask how their peers did either; while tempting, this just adds to the pressure. Asking about how their friends are, and if your young person helped anyone that day, or did something they were happy about, may be a more supportive conversation to have after a day at school or uni.

PARENT POINTERS

- Challenge this competitiveness where you can and ask the school, the clubs and the teachers, 'Does this activity really need to be competitive or can they just do it for fun, to try something new, to stretch themselves?'
- Many kids won't take part nowadays if they can't win, such is the culture of 'winner or loser', so if we remove the competitive element, they are much more likely to 'give things a go' and they might even enjoy it and discover a new talent.
- Push back on the competitiveness in some environments. That can only be good for your child's well-being!

And it's not just our leisure time that is increasingly competitive, but the job market too, with huge numbers of graduates flooding it as many more young people go to university (half of UK school leavers).[14] The concept of university for all is a great idea, but it also adds to the anxiety and concern that students regularly report.[15] 'If there are more students with degrees, there is more competition for the same jobs and graduate schemes. How are we going to get a job if it is so competitive?' said Lucy, a final-year student we interviewed.

Technology advances and artificial intelligence then add a new edge to the situation. When final-year students used to come to the doctor for 'stress' many years ago, they were mainly worried about passing exams and their potential performance in oral tests, but they were relatively confident of a job once in possession of a degree or qualification. It is now not uncommon to see *first*-year undergraduates worrying about the job market, anxious not just about getting their degree, but achieving a First. International research has shown that one in three first-year university students reports mental health symptoms, so we know that young people from Australia and Mexico to South Africa and Northern Ireland are feeling the pressure.[16]

As increasing numbers of students now obtain a First in the UK (one in four), the stakes have risen, and the pressure is on to apply for Masters and PhDs, to help graduates stand out in an increasingly crowded marketplace.[17] There may be long-term 'added value' financially in obtaining a university qualification, but at what cost emotionally?

Some of our super-competitive young generation now feel the pressure so much that they will use almost any means at their disposal to achieve what *they* view as necessary for success. Some are even cheating in increasing numbers, with studies from the UK and Australia demonstrating an increase in the number of students using 'tech', such as ear pieces and smart watches, for exams or engaging private companies ('essay mills') to write their essays and dissertations.[18,19]

While parents may have strong feelings about such behaviour, it is also worth reflecting on a society that drives young people to try such extreme measures. Do we really want young people to be achieving success by *any* means necessary? Would we do better to encourage them to do *their* best, not try to be *the* best?

COMPETING WITH YOUR KIDS

A final word of advice on the topic of competition. Be wary of not entering into unhealthy competitive behaviour with your children. It is not uncommon for young adults to comment that when they report an achievement to their parents, something which has been hard won and taken significant effort, their parents acknowledge it but then add a comment about their own achievements. This can be very undermining and difficult for children to hear, when they have been so keen to impress and please their parents, when they know how much their parents do for them or how hard they have worked to provide for them. Comments along the lines of, 'Well, that's not bad, but come back to me when you've set up your own business from scratch/written a book/won an award' can be devastating to a young person who never feels they are good enough. It may be unintentional, or even meant humorously, but if there is a grain of truth in it they will feel it like a laceration, and will ultimately feel like a failure even if they have objectively done well. Competing with their parents is one pressure young people can certainly live without.

The rise in perfectionism

We are witnessing an 'epidemic of perfectionism'.[20] A landmark study by British academics in 2017 reviewed over 40,000 students from the USA, Canada and Britain and showed that perfectionism had risen dramatically in the student population worldwide over the last 30 years.[21] In other words, students are increasingly worried about what others think of them, as well as *setting themselves* increasingly high standards which they are then struggling to meet.

What do we mean by perfectionism? The trait is present in all of us to a greater or lesser degree, like kindness or honesty. Some of us are much higher on the perfectionism scale than others, and it means striving for flawlessness, expecting perfection while criticising yourself if you don't achieve it. It means that you set yourself goals but, when you achieve them, you derive little satisfaction or happiness, so you instantly set new, higher goals.

It can also mean worrying that you need to be perfect in the eyes of others, or that you expect others to be perfect. This can lead to high levels of shame and guilt, which get worse if you are driving yourself to be perfect and believe others need you to be.

The super-competitive society (at school, online, at home, at university and in the workplace) we have described may drive this perfectionism (especially the type where we worry about what others think of us). So, too, do young people's unrealistic expectations, which we'll explore further later (see page 37), and parental pressure to succeed.

But does perfectionism matter? Might a streak of perfectionism in a student be a good thing in a demanding and ever-changing world? The answer to this lies in the *degree* of perfectionism. There is a significant difference between someone who checks their work, corrects every typo or reference once, then hands it in, and someone who cannot meet their own impossibly high standards, rechecking multiple times, changing their work, rewriting it, then deleting it and starting again – or even being so panicked about doing a bad piece of work that they have trouble even starting. Ironically for perfectionists this can lead to them being *late* handing work in, which piles on even more pressure. The perfectionist's self-critical eye is unforgiving and such young people have an abnormal ('maladaptive') reaction to what they perceive as 'failure' or substandard work. They work even harder to correct it, getting into a downward spiral that continues until they are exhausted, despairing but never happy with what they achieve, even if objectively it is brilliant. They may even withdraw from trying altogether. Many overly perfectionist people will simply give up if they can't be the best or 'win'.

This level of self-criticism and perfectionism is relentless and undermining, and most importantly, it is strongly associated with mental health illnesses such as obsessive compulsive disorder (OCD), anxiety, eating disorders, self-harm and depression. It is also strongly associated with burnout. This mental health link is why perfectionism (and trying to counter it) matters so much.

SPOTTING PERFECTIONISM

You may recognise perfectionism in the young person who, on scoring 95 per cent on a challenging test, will spend hours analysing the missing 5 per cent, tormenting themselves with their 'failure' and working even harder next time. Such behaviour can start in childhood, and escalate as the child grows up, and the schoolwork mounts, with ever-increasing targets and exams. Parental pressure will make this worse. Asking (even as a joke), 'What happened to the other 5 per cent?' will not help, and will reinforce (even subconsciously) the fact that the question had crossed your mind. The young person will sense an expectation from their parent on top of the pressure they are applying to themselves, and may use it to justify their own harsh academic standards. Parents can reduce this 'toxic' perfectionism by supporting 'good enough' rather than perfect.

In Chapter 6 we will discuss the impact of social media as well as suggesting techniques for challenging perfectionist behaviour constructively, to help young people to manage 'failure' positively, and learn from mistakes.

PARENT POINTERS

- By being more aware of the rise in perfectionism, and by being alert and on the lookout for it in your own children, you can potentially counter some of the undermining thoughts that may arise, or any distressing behaviours related to perceived failure or the idea that their work is not 'good enough'.
- You can help them to set realistic and reasonable standards and challenge the critical internal voices that they may be developing. As parents and carers we can focus on supporting them to do *their* best, but not necessarily have to be *the* best.

The meritocracy myth

Our young people are being sold a myth: that if you just try hard enough you can achieve anything, the life of your dreams. 'I just don't understand,' say our young adults, 'I've worked so hard, been captain of the rugby/chess club and spent my summers interning at local firms. I couldn't have done more. Why haven't I got the job/placement/academic position I dreamt of?' We are then left trying to encourage them not to give up, to keep at it, to try again, while cursing the myth that they have been sold since childhood, in all their favourite TV programmes, music and films, that if you do your best, work hard enough, become the school football captain or prom queen, then success will be yours. You will have riches, happiness and success in everything you do, and you will live happily ever after. You can be anything you want. If you work hard enough you will deserve it. This is the delusion of meritocracy – aka 'The American Dream'.

However, as most of us know, or realise pretty quickly, life isn't like that in reality. Achieving success can be as much about luck, being in the right place at the right time and having advantageous family or social connections ('It's who you know, not what you know') as it is about hard work. This is a tough lesson to learn for our young people who have worked so hard to do well.

A colleague, Jodie Zada, who is Director of Student Services at one of Australia's (and the world's) top universities, shared her view that resilience can be developed:

We see many students that experience a relatively benign challenge or setback in their studies (such as a poor mark on an assignment) and this becomes a major issue and impacts significantly on their well-being. To some extent this seeming overreaction is a characteristic of the developmental stage that these young people are at, still grappling with the challenges of assuming more control over their lives.

The good thing is that resilience can be developed. Part of developing it involves taking a self-compassionate approach to setbacks. Such an approach fully acknowledges the nature of the setback and the difficult feelings that arise, but also reminds students that such setbacks are normal and to be expected and are not a sign that the student is damaged or that they are being maliciously targeted. The feelings are real, but the student's explanation of the feelings might be incorrect. The focus is then on the practical actions the student can take to address or fix the situation, or prevent it happening again.

PARENT POINTERS

- Be pragmatic along the way – remind your young adult that life won't always go their way; that, despite their best efforts, they won't always get the job (even if they are the best candidate), or the university place (even with those great school results), or indeed marry their soulmate despite their seemingly perfect relationship (because actually their soulmate takes a job halfway across the world).

- Countering some of the messages that they hear incessantly in popular culture might go some way to mitigating the broken hearts and disappointment, and develop their resilience for the future, whatever adventures it may bring.

- Understanding that hard work matters, but that it is not *enough* in and of itself to achieve their dreams, is important. Young people need to understand that persistence, tenacity, connecting with people, having a wide network, being prepared to try new things and take opportunities and sometimes risks, are also really important in achieving success, and that success may not always look as they expected.

- It is important that young people understand that you can be happy in the 'middle' and unhappy at the top.

- Tell your children stories of famous people we all know about who didn't succeed the first time, where talent and hard work alone weren't enough to reach the top, but who persevered and adapted: Walt Disney, who was sacked from his first job for 'lacking imagination' and 'having no original ideas'; Steve Jobs, who was famously fired from Apple, but when he came back brought them even more success with his creation of the iPod, iPad and iPhone; and Oprah Winfrey who was fired from her role as a news reporter (she got too emotionally involved with her stories apparently) but made it big in daytime TV despite that setback.

- Praise them for having a go – for taking the test, doing the audition, giving the talk – and remind them even when they are weeping that they are the kind of person who picks themselves up after a knock-back, thinks about what they have learnt and moves on, ready to have another go, on another day.

The happiness myth

We need to remind our children that life is not about being constantly 'happy' and things 'going well' for us. This myth risks setting standards that are unachievable. Life is like a roller coaster; some days, things might go well for us and on others everything goes wrong. It isn't right or wrong – it just *is*.

You could draw this as a graph when you share this with your teen or young adult:

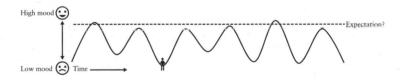

The undulations represent the ups and downs of life, just like a heartbeat on a heart monitor trace. But often young people seem to expect a flat, steady and even line of constant happiness. If the line on a heart trace was flat, it would be bad news as it would mean that we were dead. Using this analogy with your young adult may help them to understand that failures and challenges can lead to better end results.

It is in our lows that we learn the most about ourselves and from these lows we 'grow and expand'. Dr Stan Kutcher (an internationally respected Canadian Professor of Psychiatry) reminds us that difficult times can be short-lived like a 'bad hair day' (or sometimes a little prolonged), but most of the time things will improve for us and, if they don't, this is when we need to seek professional help.[22]

It is by stepping out of our comfort zone (or stretching it) that we learn, discover and become better people. If we teach our children these concepts early on in life, we will enable them to deal with difficulties much more effectively. As a result, they will move away from the victim mentality: 'Why is this happening *to* me' and start thinking that it is 'happening *for* me'. As humans we have an ability to *choose* our response to external events and to accept responsibility for our lives. This may seem obvious to those of us with a little more life experience and a few more wrinkles, but it is often news to young people. It's so important to teach them that they have a responsibility for their response (or 'response ability' as author Jack Canfield calls it in his book *The Success Principles*). Try to share with your children the philosophy that they can control how they feel, and their attitude, in difficult situations. This is not the same as telling people who suffer from a medical condition such as depression that they can 'choose' to feel better, which is extremely unhelpful. This is about how we react to the world around us and our experiences within it.

TECH LIFE

Young people are constantly connected through technology and social media, but is their constant connectedness also having negative effects on their lives, and are they *really* connected?

We know that children live in an intensely stimulating environment with constant access to smartphones, tablets, TVs and laptops, which provide them with information that requires their undivided attention. Young people are spending an increasing amount of time on their devices with one study indicating that 8- to 18-year-olds spent more time with such media than on any other activity besides (maybe) sleeping – an average of more than 7½ hours a day, 7 days a week.[23]

We will look at the impacts (both positive and negative) of social media and connectedness in Chapter 6 but, for now, it is safe to say that academic studies have found that an increase in mental health problems has coincided with the explosion of young people's use of social media.[24] We don't believe that technology and social media are all bad and that we should stop using our devices. After all, as adults we share this world; all our own electronic gadgets are extremely useful and enable us to stay connected. However, it is important to be aware of their effect on our children's lives. Young people themselves, when asked about social media (apart from mocking the older generation and their references to 'on the YouTube'), believe that social media is nothing to be afraid of, though information overload and negative content can create 'bad mental space'. They know that they need to learn how to use it and retain control over what they see to protect their well-being, and they have the power to choose the accounts they follow and the content that they see, most of the time. Social media is neither good nor bad – it is what we make it. Increasing their awareness and having strategies to deal with the relentless pressure to look good, or have a great life, as well as what to do about upsetting posts, and regular 'downtime' is, we believe, extremely important.

Loneliness and isolation in a crowded world

If our children are so connected on their devices, why are they feeling so lonely? A UK study of 10,000 adults in 2018 showed that young adults are more likely to feel lonely than older age groups and that almost 1 in 10 people aged 16–24 were 'always or often' lonely – the highest proportion of any age group, and more than three times higher than people aged 65 or over.[25]

JENNY'S STORY

As they started their Skype conversation and the tutor asked Jenny how she was getting on during her overseas year abroad, Jenny took a deep breath and simply said, 'I feel so lonely. Most of the people I work with are really nice but they are much older than me and we don't have a lot in common. I can see all my friends back home, having a great time at parties and posting photos on social media.'

It is, of course, completely normal to feel lonely at times, particularly when you are in a different country (we will look more closely at years abroad and industry years on pages 184–8), but social media can sometimes compound these feeling of loneliness.

It would appear that loneliness is becoming increasingly important in affecting the well-being of many students and, while social media promises an end to loneliness, it can also produce an increase in solitude and an intense awareness of social exclusion. Texting and other technologies give us more control over our social interactions but also lead to thinner interactions and less real engagement with the world.

Psychologist Dr Tim Sharp moved into the area of positive psychology in the early 2000s, after years of studying depression and anxiety, and is the founder of The Happiness Institute in Sydney. He talks about the importance of small, daily, face-to-face interactions to our overall well-being and longevity: 'A lot of the conversation about mental health focuses on our relationships with family and close friends, but engaging with strangers and acquaintances – the brief, micro interactions we all have on a daily basis – can have amazing benefits as well, with reduced rates of depression.'[26]

Studies have confirmed the importance of small social interactions, including a 2010 report that showed a lack of involvement with the community around us was on a par with smoking in shortening lifespan!

In short, we are humans and we need other humans in our lives to help us stay well and happy.

24/7 LIFE

By creating a 24/7 instant-access world, we have inadvertently created some unfortunate unintended consequences.

We live in a world where we can order pizza, do our online banking and video chat with friends all over the word at 2am. Taxis can be ordered instantly by app, and we can carry out most of our activities 24/7 if we need to. Yet if young people need counselling or medical help, we ask them to book an appointment for two or three weeks' time, sometimes longer, and expect them to understand the implied message – that medical or mental healthcare is less urgent than pizza, banking or socialising, and that they should wait for help. We have created an 'instant response generation' and set up unrealistic expectations of rapid reaction, but we then make them wait when it arguably matters most.

Not unsurprisingly, this creates a significant amount of distress and generates a lot of (not unreasonable) complaints about access to health and counselling or therapy services. Additionally, we are asking our teenagers and young adults to wait for important psychological support at a time when they are still relatively *impulsive* by nature, as their brains are still developing. The prefrontal cortex, right at the front, behind the forehead, the 'mission control' of the brain doesn't fully develop until the age of 25–30, so they may not yet have the biological capability to actually wait patiently for the right help, and rationalise the delay.[27] This combination of biologically impulsive nature and society's system delay in accessing help may be partly to blame for the rise in self-harm and suicidal behaviours in young adults.[28] Young people have always been impulsive, but in creating an 'instant society' an expectation of rapid response is now present, in our experience, in most doctor's and counselling consultations, which in reality cannot be met.

Impulse control

Impulse control (or self-control) is considered to be an essential skill for success in life; for studying, for training hard at a sport, for exam revision and for achieving at work. It is also one of the last behaviours to emerge in adolescence. One of the most famous books about impulse control and our ability to say 'no', or delay gratification and enjoyment, is *The Marshmallow Test* by Walter Mischel.[29] The book is well known for shedding light on this fascinating area of human nature, but it is also well loved for the fact that the main experiment involved putting a single marshmallow in front of individual four-year-olds alone in an empty room, and seeing how long they would last without eating it, having been told that if they waited until the adult came back in the room fifteen minutes later, they would be given two marshmallows!

As you might expect, the children varied in their ability to resist temptation, but a key success factor seemed to be distracting themselves, by swinging on their chair, staring at the ceiling, pushing the marshmallow away or singing to themselves. The really big questions for researchers then followed: could the ability to resist temptation and delay gratification as a child predict *future* behaviour as a teenager or young adult, and secondly, could this self-control be *learnt* if it wasn't innate? The answer to both, it seems from current research, is yes (to a certain extent).

So if your child has so far not impressed you with their ability to control their impulses and behaviour, all is not lost! We can all improve our self-control throughout life, but it takes time. The ability to resist marshmallows (or to have self-control as a child) is associated with many positive behaviour traits in later life. And for those for whom self-control is more of a challenge, techniques such a mindfulness can help to develop it, alongside getting enough sleep, ignoring distractions, moderating stress, using positive affirmations ('I can do this') and, most importantly, having reliable positive experiences when they delay gratification.

Other experiments done since the marshmallow experiment have shown that context (a reliable adult) is essential for learning the skill of self-control.[30] The delay of gratification needs to be consistently rewarded. It has to be seen and experienced as a positive experience. It takes time, but you have to make sure that what is promised is delivered. Then repeat.

PARENT POINTER

- If you say that your child cannot watch TV until their homework is done, you must ensure that this reward behaviour (watching TV) is always delivered. If you change your mind and say they can't watch TV at all, they will not learn self-control. You will have been 'unreliable' and their delayed gratification has consequently been a negative experience.

Over 40 years the 'marshmallow' team studied the children as they grew up and they discovered that those with a greater ability to resist temptation as children went on to have higher school grades, less substance abuse, less obesity, less gum disease, less criminal behaviour and fewer unplanned teenage pregnancies as well as a better response to stress and better social skills.[31] Learning to resist temptation is a behaviour that can therefore help improve long-term physical, mental and social well-being.

Living with 'I don't know' in a world of instant answers

In a culture where young people's first instinct to find an answer is Siri, Alexa or Google, it can be incomprehensible for them to be told that sometimes we just 'don't know'. If they can find facts at the touch of a screen or by calling out to their phone, why can't they have the answers to everything, and instantly? This can create distress and confusion when, instead, there is uncertainty.

A consultant surgeon we spoke to, who both cares for young adults and also trains medical students and junior doctors, told us of the shift she had noticed over the last few years:

> The new generation of doctors is finding it increasingly difficult to live with the uncertainty that is an intrinsic part of medicine. They want to know all the answers about why someone may have become unwell and, even if the test results are normal and the symptoms have settled, they feel uncomfortable sending people home if they can't answer the question 'Why?'
>
> Yet accepting that uncertainty (once you have established that nothing sinister is going on) is part of being a doctor. Sometimes we just don't know 'why' they became ill. This leads the juniors to over-investigate, or keep people in hospital longer, which of course brings its own risks. The younger generation needs to learn that sometimes the answer is, 'I don't know' and that that is okay.

PARENT POINTERS

- As parents you can talk to your young adults about being comfortable with uncertainty. Explain that even Google doesn't have all the answers to questions such as 'Why am I feeling sad?' or 'Why do good things happen to bad people?' In life we all have to learn to live with doubt and ambiguity at times.
- Life can be messy sometimes and learning to live and deal with uncertainty will stand them in good stead for the future.

THINKING POINTS

Life and society have changed dramatically over the last 30 years, affecting young people's development, increasing the pressure they are under and potentially leading to more mental health issues. Rising competition is driving perfectionism, which is in turn intertwined with multiple mental health conditions. Technology, loneliness and parenting approaches are all playing a part in influencing the next generation's well-being and resourcefulness in a changing world. It is important to understand the new culture that our teenagers and young adults are growing up and immersed in, if we are to support them successfully, be empathic and prepare them for adulthood effectively.

One of our main roles as parents, perhaps the most important one, is to prepare our young people for independent living, so that they may thrive and flourish successfully and happily, without our constant involvement and support. Our job is to launch them into adulthood, with the ability to function well and live a rewarding, self-sufficient life. We are not always going to be around to direct operations – we are the launch pad but not the entire mission manager.

As their parents you are perfectly positioned to help your child to grow. We want the grown-ups of the next generation to be encouraged to develop the following life skills:

- To do their best, but not be the best – aim for 'good enough', not perfection.
- To value non-academic, non-competitive activities – to do some things for fun, not prizes.
- To see mistakes and failures as opportunities, and be pragmatic.
- To take (measured) risks.
- To overcome challenges independently.
- To value time spent face-to-face with others.
- To know that hard work does not always bring the 'rewards' they expect.
- To know that pain can be tolerated, and to resist impulsive, harmful behaviour.
- To slowly learn self-control and delayed gratification as their brains mature and they develop awareness.
- To manage uncertainty – learn to live with 'I don't know'.
- To develop independence.
- To be resilient.

CHAPTER 3

Parenting: Tough, Inconvenient, Surprising and Delightful

'Parenting is not what it used to be.'

'The way our parents raised us in the eighties was very differ-ent. We had far more "downtime", freedom to explore and roam around our neighbourhood and far less technology.'

'Parenting is tough, especially with all the tech that you are judged for letting your kids use.'

'As a parent, doing all of it for the first time is a minefield. It was much easier for our parents, maybe even our grandparents.'

These are some of the comments from the mums and dads we interviewed for this book.

Some of you might also feel this way or might have heard similar statements, but has parenting really become more chal-lenging over the last few decades and, if so, why?

WHAT IT MEANS TO 'PARENT'

'To parent' was used as a verb as early as 1663. However, its current use and meaning was extremely rare before the late twentieth century. Parenting has become a defined skill, to be learnt and judged by others, done well or 'badly' – it's become 'a Thing'.

Parenting these days is undertaken by a wide and diverse mix of people, many of whom will not have a 'biological link' to a child, but who will be step-parents, carers, foster parents, supporters and others who love and raise a child. There are as many unique ways of parenting as there are different children, and each will choose to follow one parenting style or another.

One of the most important roles of parents is to model the behaviour and attitudes that they would want to see in their children. Young people will mimic us throughout their lives; from the toddler repeating swear words they have overheard, to the young adult treating a receptionist or other professional as they have seen their parent do before them. The net result is that parenting, and its impact on the future of our children, is the source of much angst, as well as a topic of many articles, courses, websites, blogs, books and conversations. You may have noticed that over the last 20 years parenting has become more commonly associated with expressions such as 'parenting classes' or 'how to parent well', and online searches for these terms have clearly shown an increase over the years.[1]

If you're reading this book you are likely to be one of those parents who takes the role seriously.

PARENT POINTERS

- Reflect on what type of role model you want to be. As a parent you can influence your child and set standards for them.
- Your influence, through your behaviour and attitudes, will have a lifelong impact and define who your child becomes.

It is only in the last 50 years that having children has truly become a choice. Before, it was a given that we would simply follow what our parents and grandparents had done before us: be a child, grow up, find a partner, get married, have children, grow old and eventually die. With changes in culture, working practices and science in recent years, having children has now become optional for many of us.

Could it be that with this choice comes a feeling of moral commitment and a strong desire to do the best for our children? Has choice influenced how we raise our children? Are we more involved and 'buying into' their childhoods more because we opted in? But if we decided to become parents does it mean that we must now also accept all the consequences, many of which we could never have contemplated? Many of us have undoubtedly at times said in frustration to ourselves or to our partners, 'Remind me why I chose to have children?!' despite how much we love them. Choosing parenthood can be tough as well as hugely rewarding.

With access to the Internet comes a deluge of advice on parenting methods, guidelines and options. And being a parent today is not just about bringing a child into our home and raising it to the best of our abilities, hopefully creating a balanced, healthy and educated adult. From the minute we have a child we have to navigate our way through countless articles and books (which sometimes provide contradictory information) on what we should feed them, how much they should sleep, what to do and say, and, as they get older, how much time our children should use their screens, which school they should attend, and so on.

The pressure and stress that we place ourselves under is enormous. Some parents we interviewed for this book told us how overwhelmed they felt at times because they felt obliged to try things they had read about in parenting articles or that other parents in their antenatal classes or at school were doing. There can be a pressure to define ourselves as parents, when actually we want to be defined as and by many other things too, so it is important not to lose sight of these on the parenting highway.

PARENT POINTERS

- Remember that you are unique and so is your child and your family. While articles and information can be extremely useful, it is important to remember that you know what works best for your family because you understand them the most (and spend the most time with them). 'You are the expert on your child' as one teacher reminded us.
- Remind yourself occasionally that you are more than 'just' a parent, and it is important to invest time in activities that are completely unrelated to raising children.

The vulnerable child

The notion of the 'vulnerable child' appeared in the twentieth century; children started to be thought of as more fragile and needing special care and handling. And the responsibility for this rests mainly with us, their parents. Unfortunately, the advice provided online and by experts seems to have intensified parental anxieties, rather than eased them. As concern for children's 'vulnerability' has spread, parents have become more concerned about all aspects of their children's lives. Parents are being blamed for mistakes they have made or things they haven't done, which they then believe result in their children experiencing problems. Have the experts, books and theories made parenting more difficult, not less?

Alison – mum to a 15- and 17-year-old – brought our attention to this point when she mentioned that she had become acutely aware of how worried she was about her children's issues, in comparison to how she recalled her own parents to be when she was a teenager herself: 'My mum and dad didn't seem to concern themselves with as many things, or worry as much, if I was upset. They didn't see it as their responsibility.'

There are many theories about what will shape the adult that your child will become, and we will take a look at parenting styles and behaviours on pages 58–65. But first, as parents you need to start by giving yourselves a break and accepting that you might not always get it right.

Be kind to yourselves

It is so important that as parents we look after ourselves and practise self-compassion. Just as in an emergency on a plane you would put your own oxygen mask on before attending to your children, so you need to care for yourself in order that you can then care for others.

Sophie, who is mum to a 13-year-old, told us that she experienced higher stress levels than usual last year because of difficulties at work. She also mentioned that she noticed it had a clear impact on her daughter's response to her: 'My daughter seemed much more unsettled and snappier than normal and would respond more negatively to what I said or asked her to do.' What Sophie had noticed has been proven scientifically. Researchers at the University of Calgary have discovered through work with mice that the stress we experience is not only contagious, it can actually change the brain of the person it is transmitted to, in the same way as their own stress does.[2] So, if we are stressed, anxious or overwhelmed we will be unable to provide our children with what they need the most: a safe haven and a loving home.

However, there is good news too. We also know that we can avoid toxic stress and its negative effects if we help our children grow in an environment that is nurturing, stable and engaging. Research carried out on stressed-out lab pups who were handled by humans for 15 minutes before being returned to their mothers who then licked them extensively (nurtured them),[3] were far more resilient and very difficult to stress in later life. This clearly shows how we can, as parents, have long-lasting beneficial effects on our children. By trying to avoid spreading our own stress to our children, and by nurturing and caring for them if they are stressed, we can make them more likely to deal well with stress in later life (we will suggest tips for dealing with anxious or stressed adolescents in Chapter 14). Nurturing builds resilience, but as we shall see, healthy nurturing does not mean wrapping them in cotton wool.

'HEALTH AND SAFETY' PARENTING

Our children seem to be growing up in an increasingly 'soft play culture', protected and shielded from perceived danger in everyday life. There is a commonly accepted belief that society has in some way become more dangerous for children. It's fair to say that some of the dangers may have increased, such as from the Internet, but is it really riskier for a child to go outside alone these days?

If you are a parent who encourages your primary-school-aged child to walk or cycle to school alone you are now significantly in the minority, but in 1971 eight out of ten eight-year-olds were allowed to walk to school alone.[4] Thirty years later it was fewer than one in ten.[5] Is it an interesting coincidence that 1971 was also the year that the 'stranger danger' campaigns were launched in the UK (as a reaction to the Moors murderers' case), as today's parents were being raised? Have we been ingrained with the fear of abduction by a stranger, when the reality is that the greatest danger to children's safety has sadly always been from those closest to them?[6] We all tend to focus on shocking cases and worry about similar happenings to our own children, but the fact is that under-16s are least likely to be the victims of homicide (apart from babies under one year, who are tragically at high risk, mainly from their families).[6] 'Being a victim of crime' was UK children's biggest fear in 2017, so it is important to discuss this with your child and give them the facts and context.[7]

In implying that the world is a dangerous place, by restricting their movements and freedom to roam (or walk to the park or cycle to swimming club) we pass on our anxiety to our children.[8] We risk reducing their horizons and increasingly rely on them to entertain themselves at home or with the electronic babysitter, which may be playing a part in the rise in childhood obesity.[9]

We are in a position to take positive action, to prevent what has been called nature-deficit disorder, and get our children outside and active on a day-to-day basis.[10] To develop outdoor independence you should discuss options with your child, not force them into activities they feel worried about, and do trial run-throughs (such as cycling a route together) if helpful. The National Trust published a survey in 2016 that showed that children were spending half the amount of time outside than their parents did, just four hours a week.[11] Another survey in the same year found that three-quarters of UK children were spending less time outside than prison inmates (less than 60 minutes a day)![12]

Some of this may be driven by factors more related to new technology, of course, but some will be related to fear of strangers, abductions, road accidents, paedophiles and generic 'others' – 'It's not *you* I'm worried about, it's *others*'. (There has actually been a significant decrease in the number of children killed as pedestrians in road accidents over the last 10 years – 22 in Great Britain in 2017.[13]) We need to consider the risks calmly, talk to our young people, teach them about safety and risk assessment, and then slowly build their confidence to venture out alone, trusting them to make reasonable decisions and become more independent.

Could we try to encourage our children to build their independence by teaching them to walk safely to the shops or to their friend's house? Should we actually be teaching them to walk (or scoot) to school in pairs or small groups once they are 10 or 11, as they do in many other countries, in order to develop their confidence and give them some exercise?

Depending on the maturity of your child, it might be reasonable for them to take the bus to school alone (or with friends) from the age of 11, catch a train alone from 13 and be unaccompanied on a plane at 14–16 (airlines have policies on this). Going on holiday with friends (without adults) depends on maturity as well as location, but 16 is not unreasonable, though 17–18 is more common. In the UK, while there is no specific law about what age a child can be left at home alone, the law states that: 'It is an offence to leave them at home alone if doing so puts them at risk.'[14] The NSPCC has an online 'Home Alone' guide which may be useful.

It may take persistence and a cultural shift, but allowing your child more independence in this way will pay off and they will develop and grow to become confident, independent young adults, able to navigate their route and the roads. Going out alone will also teach them about potential safety issues in a balanced and realistic manner.

PARENT POINTER

- With your support, your children should be able to travel to school independently, get to friends' houses and walk or cycle to activities, while preparing for the big wide world of their gap year, university or the workplace.

OUR CHILDREN ARE NOT FRAGILE

There is a notion that our children are fragile and that, like Humpty Dumpty, they might break, won't be put back together again and, more importantly, need protecting from the 'bad' world out there. We may not consciously realise that our parenting approach is based on worry and concern. We may be anxious about things that are not life-threatening for our children but this will trigger the same fear response in us as life-threatening events. Our stress response will be the same whether our young adult drives their car too fast and we are worried that they will get killed or if they go out with their friends and are not back when they said they would be.

It may therefore be useful to pay closer attention to the reasons for your fear response and for parenting choices. Are they rooted in fear, or in love and trust? Where possible we need to avoid parenting through fear, and trust that we make our decisions and choices through love, while allowing our children to slowly separate from us and develop their independence and identity.

PARENTING STYLES

Another factor that affects our children, alongside the change to a more safety- and security-conscious approach to parenting, is parenting 'style'. Experts have described different parental styles and, as you might expect, these have a significant impact on how our children grow up *and* their well-being.

Four types of parenting style have been proposed and are generally accepted by researchers and experts:[83]

1. Authoritative
2. Authoritarian
3. Indulgent (permissive)
4. Neglectful (uninvolved)

However, we are likely to move between different styles along a spectrum depending on scenarios (and our mood!), and they don't occur in isolation but can be additional to health and safety parenting too (as we shall see).

Authoritative

Authoritative parents tend to raise happier children.[15,16] These parents are warm, emotionally responsive, create boundaries for their children and stick to them, and demand good standards of behaviour, while being prepared to be flexible and discuss challenging behaviours. Their children are more likely to become independent and self-determining in nature. This parenting style *actively reduces* the risk of self-harmful behaviour in their children and encourages well-being.

Anna Muller-Haas, a childminder and mother of three daughters aged four, ten and twelve, as well as having a stepson and stepdaughter aged twenty-four and twenty, gave us a good tip:

Take time to listen to your children. Sometimes they will want to talk to you when it is not a good time for you. As parents, we can't always be accessible (you might be cooking, on the phone or taking care of a younger sibling). Either way, it is important to stop what you are doing and simply say, 'I want to hear you right now, but I can't listen properly. I will make time for you later on. Is that okay with you?' If it is important, they will come back to you later. You may also want to ensure that you do follow this through, when you have a bit more time and can focus on them.

In this way you will show your child that you care, and you are responsive but in a realistic way. If they are being very difficult, talk about how you are feeling and how they are feeling. You might say: 'To me, it looks like you are sad/angry about this.' This gives them room to use words to label their emotions and feelings and to normalise this rather than to 'swallow it all and keep it inside'. When you are angry or annoyed with your children, let them know. Do not shout at them, if you can help it. Just leave the room to allow space to calm down and, before you leave, say 'I love you, I hear you' and hold them if you can. They will learn that emotions are normal, but that they can be controlled, and that they are still loved when things are difficult.

Authoritarian

The authoritarian parenting style ('my way or the highway'), which many parents employ in the belief that it will 'toughen' kids up for the future, actually creates a feeling of chronic emotional stress, and also has negative consequences for well-being. These parents are very demanding of their children, but without the empathy, positive feedback and discussion of the authoritative (warm) parents described above. They dole out punishment without rationale or explanation if standards are not met; are strict, harsh and aggressive; and are highly critical of their children. Unlike authoritative parents, authoritarian parents are not nurturing.

Multiple studies worldwide in different cultures have elicited evidence of the negative effects of authoritarian parenting on children's long-term emotional health, including:

- less socially adept
- more likely to be involved in bullying (victim or perpetrator)
- less self-reliant

Children of authoritarian parents also suffer more with low self-esteem, anxiety and depression. Interestingly, despite the probable authoritarian pressure to do well at school, evidence is mixed but tends to suggest that the children actually do *less* well academically, and in the longer term they are more likely to reject their parents.[86] This is not an effective way to create happy, successful young adults.

Indulgent

The indulgent (permissive) parent brings their own issues. These parents are nurturing, like the authoritative parents, but are also lenient, placing few boundaries or limits on their children. They see themselves more as friends than parents. They allow children to regulate themselves and prefer not to exert control, though they may use reason or manipulation to achieve desired results. Interestingly, this approach, which has been called 'peer-enting', leads to significantly worse teen drinking issues than the authoritarian (strict) approach (while the authoritative, warm but boundaried style has the fewest).[17]

In terms of longer term behavioural traits, children raised by indulgent parents tend towards more aggression, anxiety, lower self-control and poorer school conduct and academic achievement. However, the evidence against permissive parenting is mixed and seems to imply that depending on *what* the parents are permissive about, the child may also learn independence, self-reliance and autonomy. The risk, however, is that in being allowed to make, for example, all their own food choices or activity decisions, children may choose unhealthy foods and to watch TV or play on their screen unregulated for hours at a time.[18] It is a fairly 'hit-and-miss' approach to parenting, with mixed outcomes for children.

Neglectful

Neglectful parents are generally described as providing the basics such as food and shelter, but are emotionally uninvolved. They may be too concerned with their own problems (mental health issues, alcoholism or overwork) to engage with their children, they offer little warmth or affection, and may even avoid their children. They are unlikely to attend any school parent–teacher events, or similar occasions, and expect very little of their children. They neither respond to their children's needs, nor demand anything of them. Such emotional detachment and neglect have wholly negative effects on a child's development and are associated with a variety of detrimental future behaviours, including a heightened risk of suicidal behaviours.

HELICOPTER PARENTING

To these traditional parenting styles has been added a new style for the twenty-first century: 'helicopter parenting', which can transform into 'snowplough parenting' at its most extreme (where parents remove all obstacles from their off-spring's path).[19] Helicopter parenting is described by academics as 'a form of overparenting in which parents get overly involved and developmentally teach inappropriate tactics to their children who are otherwise able to assume adult responsibilities and autonomy'. According to the same researchers, these tactics far exceed the normal needs of adolescents and young adults. The issue with helicopter parenting is that it limits the requirements for young people to act in ways that would enable them to create change in their own lives. In real terms, this means that helicopter parents give excessive advice, problem-solve and provide unnecessary assistance, while being unwilling for their child to take risks. In other words, young people do not learn how to do things for themselves. Helicopter parents also become increasingly involved in their child's emotional well-being, trying to solve their emotional problems for them, such as falling out with friends, in a well-intentioned bid to reduce any potential distress. However, this may not allow their child to develop strategies to cope with the normal emotional ups and downs of life.

Helicopter parents also tend to over-organise all their children's time, fitting in activities around busy school days to maximise 'developmental and growth' opportunities, but unfortunately radically reducing the time young people have to just 'be', get bored and be creative with their spare time. One mother we spoke to, Heather, mentioned that she wished that she had pushed back against the pressure to 'do more' and create a full timetable of activities for her son, and had made home 'more of a sanctuary' for him. She wanted to share that, 'Getting the best grades and having the fullest CV doesn't actually lead to a happy, fulfilled and independent young adult.' She advises parents to let their children develop interests at their own pace, and that one hobby is enough.

The effects on our children's well-being

Parents 'overparent' because they care and have good intentions and want to make sure that their children get positive outcomes (and sometimes because they have invested a huge amount of time and other resources in their upbringing). It comes from a good place and is well-intentioned. However, recent findings consistently show that overparenting has negative effects on the well-being of children. Researchers argue that excessive problem-solving on a child's behalf could easily diminish their perceived sense of competence and perhaps 'self-efficacy' (our belief in our ability to do something or not).[20] If we problem-solve for our children, we will reduce their self-efficacy and their belief in themselves as capable of doing things independently. The self-efficacy theory explains what motivates some people to put a lot of effort into something and others to simply sit back and not even try.[21]

MILLIE'S STORY

Millie was a second-year university student about to embark on her year abroad. She had already made the choice to study rather than work during her time in France. However, Millie had just found out that there were issues with strikes in the city where she would be going and she needed to choose another university. She requested a meeting with her personal tutor. Her first words as she walked into the tutor's office were, 'I am so stressed, I don't think I can do this. I find it so difficult to make decisions for myself. In the past, I have always had advice and recommendations on what is the best thing for me to do. What do you think I should do?'

We can see here that Millie's self-efficacy (confidence) was low. The lower our self-efficacy, the less capable we believe ourselves to be. The higher our self-efficacy, the more we will believe that we are able to perform and accomplish a task. We will be less likely to attempt something with our full effort if our self-efficacy is lower for that task. This is because we tend to attempt and do things that we believe we will be successful in.

There is also increasing proof that overparenting might come from more critical, less supportive and accommodating family environments. Whatever the reasons for this parental behaviour, one study indicates that 'helicopter parenting' is negatively related to psychological well-being and positively related to prescription medication use for anxiety/depression and the recreational consumption of pain pills.[22] In other words, children of helicopter parents are less emotionally healthy and more likely to take medication. In another piece of work, students who reported having over-controlling parents reported significantly higher levels of depression and less satisfaction with life.[23] Another study also demonstrated that overparenting is more likely to lead to personality traits such as entitlement and narcissism.[24] Sometimes it manifests in students faced with difficult academic issues who approach their tutors with an 'I can't do it, do it for me' attitude. Such an approach is unhelpful both for the student, who needs to learn to manage challenges, and for the tutors who are teaching hundreds of young people and trying to treat them as adults. It will also disadvantage young people in the workplace, where such an attitude is even less likely to be tolerated.

PARENT POINTERS

- What is your preferred parenting style? Remember that we might take different approaches depending on our moods or the topic. Developing self-awareness of our own parenting styles can be beneficial because it also gives us an opportunity to choose a different approach, if we wish to.
- To help our children learn to problem-solve for themselves, it may help us as parents to lean towards a more authoritative parenting style, rather than helicopter style, wherever we can. This may also help our children develop a sense of security.

WHAT YOU CAN DO

According to motivational psychologists Edward Deci and Richard Ryan, autonomy, confidence and relatedness (a feeling that we belong) are essential for growth and integration, as well as for making friends, personal well-being and the feeling of happiness.[25] If this is the case, isn't it vital that we, as parents, encourage our young people to develop these? They need to take hold of the belief that they *can* do things that it is in their power and control.

Increase self-efficacy in your child

Talk to your young person about how successful they have been at a task in the past. Self-efficacy is about believing they can do something based on their past experience of success. It helps to see others, preferably peers, do something similar, so discuss positively other people's experiences. Remind them how they (or their friend) successfully read a challenging book, performed in a competitive sports event or concert, applied for a job, went for an interview, toured an open day of a university or work-place, or attended a social event with new people. The expectations of others are very effective in building confidence, so don't be afraid to give extremely positive encouragements. And finally, our physiological and emotional states determine to an extent our level of anxiety. In the case study above, because she felt so stressed, Millie was worried she would be making the 'wrong decision' and this lowered her self-efficacy. Had she associated the feelings with excitement or anticipation, which is often linked with achievement, that would have increased her sense of self-efficacy. Nicola, a business entrepre-neur and the mother of two children aged 16 and 20, summarised this very well with her use of the word 'terrixcited' – a mixture of being terrified and excited at the same time. Boost self-efficacy in your child by emphasising excitement, rather than fear of something new.

Find a 'trusted adult'

Many young people, especially as they move into their twenties, talk about the benefit of having a trusted adult (who is not their parent) to speak to. This may mimic the ancient tradition of having 'tribal elders', big brothers and sisters, aunties and uncles, or an older family friend, to turn to for advice and con-fidential support. Young people naturally worry about telling their parents everything, or certain things, and although some genuinely have a 'we can talk about anything' relationship with one or both of their parents, this is not the case for many. For them, a trusted adult, who may only be a few years older than them, can be a really positive influence.

Some university students have spoken of the support provided by older peers – students doing the same course or sport – who they look up to, and many of whom receive training these days to provide peer support to newer students. Other young people may turn to their best friend's mum or dad, who is considered more likely to be open and non-judgemental (even if their own mum or dad would actually be fine). In the workplace young adults can benefit from having older mentors, or well-being advisers, to talk through day-to-day issues with.

Ask about what peer support is provided in your child's school or university, or in their workplace, and ensure you are happy with the training provided for peer supporters (it can be variable). Having a 'trusted elder' as an alternative to their parent (think of them as your understudy or 'assistant parent') can be very important to a young person, and creating a network of support can prevent them from feeling isolated in times of need, even if you think they should be able to tell you anything. Talk to your child about who they might like to fulfil this role and work on it over time with them. Bring up the topic and explain that safely developing trust with another adult is helpful, that having a 'safety net of people' in life is better than just one supporter, but ensure that they understand what is appropriate and what is not in all relationships.

PARENT POINTERS

- Try to foster confidence (self-efficacy) in your child as it will stand them in good stead when they leave home.
- Think about who your young person might like to speak to if you are not available or if they are worried, and encourage a trusting relationship to build over time.

DEVELOPING SELF-IDENTITY

O ne of the most important stages in adolescence is developing an identity separate from our parents and families. In adolescence we start to curate the image that we want the world to see; we decide what we want to be known for, we may change our nicknames, or hairstyle, clothes or image, or we may develop new interests to make ourselves seem more adult, interesting or attractive. Taking a gap year, joining various causes and organisations and getting a job can all offer opportunities to reinvent ourselves.

Separating from the 'tribe'

There is a very strong and ancient evolutionary drive to separate from the family 'tribe' and become part of a new independent tribe, and it partly explains one of the quirkier aspects of the teenage years – why teenagers find their parents and families 'sooooo embarrassiiing'. This teenage embarrassment and self-consciousness is discussed sensitively and engagingly by Sarah-Jayne Blakemore in *Inventing Ourselves: The Secret Life of the Teenage Brain*. It is thought to be an evolutionary behaviour developed to allow the young person to pull away from one social group (their family) and join another, which is an essential part of becoming an independently functioning adult. They feel embarrassment much more physically and acutely, and teenage brains literally 'light up more' on scans when they are feeling self-conscious than those of adults or children.

It is about more than just worrying over the opinions of others, it ensures that as we leave the family tribe we are not left isolated and alone, but can identify with other teenagers. It is part of the separation process and is evolution in action. Adolescents are therefore biologically designed to gradually identify less with their parents and families and more with their chosen new 'tribe' (of friends and other people they identify with). So when your teen rolls their eyes at you, disagrees with you, even fights with you – remember, they are programmed to do just that. Your job is to see the bigger picture, continue to be their rock and not descend into petty arguments.

It may help to remember this, and keep telling yourself 'It's evolution, they can't control it, it's nature's way' and so on, when your teen won't look at you so much, or talk to you, or be seen with you. Remember that they will go through the process of separation, come out the other side and, hopefully, if you have been able to tolerate it, humoured them (not teased them excessively, as it can be tempting to do) and maintained open channels of communication, they will reappear as an independent, confident and separate young adult, ready to be seen in your presence again.

This need and drive to develop and create their self-identity is also worth bearing in mind when you are dropping your child off on day one of senior school, university or in any new environment. Such occasions are a key moment of 'image projection' for the young person, and they will be acutely aware of the need to immediately impress potential new friends with their appearance, views, opinions and likes and dislikes, to ensure that they can join a new friendship group (evolutionary 'tribe'). Parents interfering at this point can be viewed disastrously by the young person. They may not wish to be reminded of childhood nicknames or be subjected to public displays of affection. If, in a new flat at uni, they are telling their flatmates of their newfound vegetarianism, a parent pointing out that they had a bacon sarnie on the drive up will not be helpful!

These moments are pivotal for young adults. We all know that first impressions matter, and for young people and adolescents these moments matter perhaps more than we have previously realised; not just as superficial social interactions, but as deeply driven, human evolutionary touchpoints in their lives.

PARENT POINTERS

- Be aware of the evolutionary embarrassment factor and where it may stem from. You can then perhaps more easily let it slide, accept it as a temporary phase and keep talking when your teen wants to. Remind them, though, that remaining polite and respectful is still essential on both sides.
- Try to avoid the temptation to be deliberately embarrassing in front of their friends.
- At key moments of 'self-image projection' for your offspring, like parties or arrivals day at college or uni, take a step back, be sensitive and supportive, but let them get on with it as they gradually separate from you, establish their identity and find their new 'tribe'.
- Many families have found that getting a pet is helpful when children reach the teenage years, as the young person receives unconditional love and affection from another being, and can show affection unashamedly, as well as learning to be responsible for and look after the pet.

WHEN THEY FEEL LOST OR WITHOUT PURPOSE IN LIFE

It is very common, in our experience, for young people to have what might be described as an 'existential crisis': the feeling of having no clear meaning in their life, and the world seeming 'pointless' and life 'futile'.

The crucial thing here is not to dismiss such emotions; they can sometimes lead to suicidal thinking, so they are important to ask about, acknowledge, talk about and normalise (not dismiss). Use phrases such as, 'That's actually quite a common feeling, it must be very difficult for you. Let's think about how we can support you and maybe change how you're feeling.'

This questioning and potentially confusing time of life can be managed with professional counselling if helpful, encouraging them to talk to trusted adults around them, and by setting mini goals that will boost their morale, self-esteem and fuel their sense of purpose. Anything from walking the dog, going for a run, helping out a friend or neighbour, volunteering at a charity shop or cooking dinner for family or friends can help reconnect with daily life, but make the goals realistic and achievable, otherwise if they 'fail' it will reinforce the feeling of negativity and hopelessness. They should do things that are achievable and make them feel useful and build their confidence. This approach can even be helpful if they are depressed, though they might need support to start with.

THINKING POINTS

Parenting is hard, so remember to give yourself a break. Parenting is not the only influence on how our children grow up or develop. There are many different elements that impact our children, but it may be helpful to reflect on some of those that we can affect most directly, such as how we relate to our teenagers and young adults, and how we role-model behaviour.

Parenting has changed for many reasons but if you can try to take an authoritative approach, encourage your child to solve problems for themselves, and try to avoid helicoptering over them, or worse, snowploughing in front of them, they will learn how to negotiate life's challenges and relate to others success-fully. Use positive psychology to build their image of themselves as kind, compassionate, thoughtful or strong ('You are a resil-ient person!'), and motivate them to believe that they have the ability to achieve things, to relate to others and belong, and that they can be effective at what they choose to do.

It isn't easy, but these are all techniques and approaches that have been found to create resilient, happy, confident and inde-pendent adults.

Here are a few examples of helpful approaches you can take:

- Role-model the behaviour you want to see in your children.
- Don't spread your stress, nurture them instead.
- Practise self-compassion.
- Be interested in your children as individuals.
- Build independence into activities, and encourage self-efficacy (their belief in themselves).
- Try to parent through love and trust, not fear about their 'fragility'.
- Lean towards an 'authoritative' style of parenting.
- Love them where they are at, not where you would want them to be.
- Tolerate their embarrassment of you – it's evolution at work!
- Cultivate purpose: find them activities to try if they are feeling lost or need help, and talk about it.

CHAPTER 4

Education, Education, Education

'The top 10 in-demand jobs in the future don't exist today. We are currently preparing students for jobs that don't yet exist, using technologies that haven't been invented, to solve problems we don't even know are problems yet.' So stated former US Secretary of State, Richard Riley in 2004.[1]

When we use the word 'education', we need to consider what ideology we are referring to. Are we meaning training and moulding into shape, focusing on building on past experiences and knowledge and ensuring that knowledge is passed from parents to children, thus guaranteeing that it is preserved – 'walking on the shoulders of giants'? Or are we referring to education as preparing young people for their future and enabling them to deal in an effective way with the problems they will be faced with in the future (drawing out their abilities)? The second definition aims at developing a holistic child and at preparing them for future potential challenges. As parents, the way we view education ourselves will influence how our children view and approach it too.

The revised National Curriculum in England for Schools states that 'every state-funded school must offer a curriculum which is balanced and broadly based and which promotes the spiritual, moral, cultural, mental and physical development of pupils at the school and of society, and prepares pupils at the school for the opportunities, responsibilities and experiences of later life'.[2]

And yet currently the majority of state schools in the UK, but also many educational systems across the world, rely on standardised testing and creating A* students (or level '9' students with the new GCSE classification in the UK). They do not focus on questioning, creativity and independent thinking, which are all skills young people are expected to have on leaving school or to develop throughout their university life. There seems to be a contrast between what governments are *trying* to achieve and what is *happening*. Teachers thus have to focus on the act of teaching rather than on learning, but we need to encourage our young people to develop independence in their learning before they arrive at university or in the workplace. We need to empower young people to become independent learners in order to become lifelong learners.

The standardised testing implemented in schools influences what is being taught and how it is taught. When teachers' pay and continued employment are dependent on how students perform on standardised tests, teachers will teach in the way they think is most likely to produce satisfactory scores. As a result, the function of the educational system changes from providing students with a well-rounded education to preparing them to pass that all-important test.[3] The current education system encourages 'surface learning' and 'teaching to test' rather than 'deep learning'. Deep learning focuses on substance and the underlying meaning, personal commitment to understanding, reflection on relationships between pieces of information, and applying knowledge to 'real life'. Testing has its place in an educational system as a way of checking that learning is happening and as a way of supporting learning, but it should not be the main focus. Curiosity, adaptability and imaginative thinking will all be valued in the workplace of the future so we need to foster these.

A thought-provoking example of the impact of education on creative thinking is illustrated by George Land and Beth Jarman's study on 'divergent thinking' (which is the ability to look at a particular problem and propose multiple solutions).[4] In their book they explain how they gave a test to over 1600 children aged 4 and 5. If you scored at a certain level, you would be considered a genius at divergent (creative/innovative) thinking. Of these 1600 kids, 98 per cent scored at genius level. Excited by these incredible findings, the team decided to turn this test into a longitudinal study and give the same group of children the same test 5 years later. Once again, their findings were quite shocking, but this time for different reasons. These same children, now aged 9 or 10, had rapidly declined to just 30 per cent 'genius level'; a 68 per cent reduction! The same study was conducted again 5 years later on the same group of kids – by now in secondary school – and they had dropped all the way down to just 12 per cent. One of the reasons for this massive drop was the fact that the children were now in an education system which told them that 'there is only one answer and it is at the back of the book'.

We need to nurture creative and innovation skills, not stamp them out.

PARENT POINTERS

- Reflect on how you can encourage your child to develop deep learning, which will help them more at university or in their career. Can you encourage them to watch a documentary, or read some articles that analyse the topic

further? Maybe have a debate at the dinner table or they
could explain what they have been learning to a younger
sibling to engage more than just superficially with a topic,
beyond passing a test.

- Take a moment to consider how as a parent you can help
your child develop their creativity and innovative skills.
Challenge them to solve problems and puzzles, but also to
work out day-to-day issues for themselves.

WHY EDUCATION IS FALLING SHORT

In his TED Talk entitled 'Changing Education Paradigms', Sir
Ken Robinson, an international figure in the world of education, described how education is falling short.[5] Sir Ken points
out that education is modelled in the interests of industriali-
sation and in the image of it, and is therefore not fit for the
modern world. Some examples he uses to highlight his point
include: schools are still organised on factory lines with ringing
bells, separate facilities and separate subjects, we still educate
children by batches and we put them through the system by
age groups. Sir Ken argues that if you are interested in education, you don't start from a production-line mentality. He
also adds that many countries are unfortunately trying to 'meet
the future' by doing what they did in the past and on the way
'they are alienating millions of kids who don't see the point in
education'. (Sir Ken has another TED Talk 'Do Schools Kill
Creativity?', which is the most watched TED Talk of all time,
and well worth 20 minutes of your time if you can spare it.)

The issue is that the current educational system was designed
and conceived for a different age, in the intellectual culture of
the enlightenment and in the economic circumstances of the

Industrial Revolution. Before the middle of the nineteenth century there were no systems of public education. Public education (paid for by taxation, compulsory for everyone and free) was a completely radical and new idea. Running right through it was an intellectual model of the mind which was that there were really two types of people – academic and non-academic (smart people and non-smart people) – and the consequence is that many genuinely smart people think they are not because they are being judged through this particular lens. From a young age, children start to 'put themselves in a box' – clever/not clever – and, as parents, we encourage you to challenge this narrow view.

'Academic' versus 'non-academic'

When we start labelling our children as 'bright/clever' or 'intelligent' when they are simply achieving good results in current standardised testing at school, we are giving them an identity. We are buying into the 'clever/not clever' view. For children, when adults categorise them as 'clever/not clever' they internalise it and it becomes part of their identity. Children learn to believe that they are clever or intelligent if they do well academically and get good grades. They will also make the internal association that the opposite is true, and assume that if they don't get good grades, they are not clever. They will not understand that they are not succeeding at the *system* as it stands, but that in a different environment or with different tasks they might do very well.

They will view themselves as 'fixed' a certain way, unable to change. You may have previously heard of this in terms of having a 'fixed' or 'growth' mindset, a theory created by Stanford University Professor Carol Dweck.[6] Having a growth mindset means not believing that your intelligence is fixed (that innate talent alone defines you), but instead believing that you can develop and become 'smarter' by stretching yourself. The problem with labels and identities is that they can lead to a feeling that a trait is permanent and something that our children may be stuck with for the rest of their lives.

It is far more difficult to change who we are (our self-identity) than it is to change the way we behave or what we do (our behaviour). Our behaviours do not define who we are and it is a mistake to suggest that someone who is doing well in their tests is 'clever'. 'Clever' limits their efforts by leading them to believe that if they *can't* do something they are not 'clever enough'. They stop trying. They feel like a failure. This can be linked to perfectionist traits, which also lead people to stop trying if they cannot achieve what they view as 'perfection'.

Dweck recommends using the powerful 'yet' when children are struggling with something, so you might say, 'Don't worry, keep trying, you just can't do it … yet.' She also suggests avoiding using statements such as 'clever girl/clever boy' when they can do something well as these may lead to a more 'fixed mindset'.[7] It is better to encourage your child to do their best, not label them and avoid linking successful achievements with their level of intelligence.

As we saw in the last chapter, we now know that how we parent, and how we discipline or give guidance, will influence our children. We pass on many of our values and beliefs to our children, sometimes without any idea of how much impact they might later have.

There is a crucial difference between behaviour and identity: *what* we do and *who* we are. Our children are *not* their academic results. Grades and academic results simply indicate how well young people are doing in school or at university, that they were lucky with exam questions or how they were feeling on the day. It should not define who they are. We can infuse in our children positive beliefs about their own character and personality: 'You are a thoughtful, kind, helpful boy' or 'You are a generous person' and so on. You will imbue in them a sense of their own character, and possibly have a positive impact for years to come!

PARENT POINTERS

- Try to describe your children by their character traits (kind/ generous) rather than by their actions, and avoid putting them in a box as 'clever' or not, as they may then retain this narrow view of themselves, potentially for life.
- Explain to them that just because they don't do well at something that is not to say they are not 'smart'. They might do brilliantly at something else. Conversely, if labelled 'clever' they may assume they don't need to try hard or push themselves.
- Praise their character, not their behaviour, in order to build their belief in their strengths, and vice versa, criticise their behaviour but not their character.

Education and stress

Is the current approach and emphasis on testing really helping our children to become better equipped 'for the global race' or is it creating a lot of unnecessary stress and anxiety? A recent article by Sally Weale, education reporter for the *Guardian* newspaper, suggests the latter – that new exam structures are creating a rise in stress.[8] Maybe the issue is not so much with the stress experienced before the exam but more with the perception that these exams are vital, and will define who children are and what they will do next. It is not surprising that if we ask young people to sit more challenging exams, it is likely to put them into a 'stress position' which any human would find challenging. Some university final-year students reported that they saw exams as something 'they had to take and do well in because it showed how intelligent or bright they were' but that they saw their essays throughout the year 'as an opportunity to shine and to show their knowledge and expertise'. With such an emphasis on exams, is it surprising that our children are reporting feeling more stressed before and during examination periods? Martin, the father of two girls aged 16 and 19, summed it up well when he told us 'my daughters often tell me that they don't feel the pressure to conform or to fit in with their peers, but they do feel the pressure to perform'.

PREPARING YOUR CHILD FOR UNIVERSITY

As it stands, with its focus on grades rather than holistic learning, the education system is not preparing students well enough for university. On moving away from home they are experiencing what we call 'culture shock' (which normally applies to foreigners when they enter a new country that has different values and beliefs from theirs). Through better communication at each level (primary to secondary to further education or university), we need to encourage young people to develop the skills they require to be more 'culturally agile' (adaptable) and able to move from one culture to the next (by being open, curious, accepting and able to trust). By helping our children to deal with tension, frustration, confusion or embarrassment effectively, they will develop the coping strategies they need to transition to university (skills such as listening and the ability to observe and enquire). In order to understand the new system, make friends and feel that they belong to a community young people need not to feel helpless and fearful. If your child is the first in the family to go to university they may need extra preparation for potential culture shock.

Deep learning

Students can experience stress when they arrive at university because the system requires a lot of 'deep thinking' as well as 'independent research' and 'critical thinking', which are often foreign to them. Many students spend a lot of time with tutors during the first weeks of term trying to understand what a literature review is and what they need to do to write a good essay. Some tutors have noticed that they ask fewer questions, perhaps because they are given so much information at school level, and they are not used to delving deeper. This is also seen in the workplace where new young recruits are unprepared for some of the independent initiative-taking expected of them.

During their first term at university, students are told that the purpose of their studies is to become a critical, analytical thinker who will question the information provided to them and be able to work independently and reflect on specific topics. They are told that there might not be any 'right' answers and, in fact, there might be several 'possible answers' that they might wish to explore. They need to be creative and to go beyond the information given in the popular press – beyond the simple Google and Wikipedia search – to be able to move from the superficial to a much deeper level of analysis and to learn how to delve into the most subtle and specific aspects of the subjects they have chosen to study. This skill is also valuable for jobs such as journalism or project management, and for entrepreneurs, all of whom may enter the world of work straight from school.

Jay, a first-year university student, captured this need for analytical skills when he said:

Coming to university, I have seen a real change in the way I have started thinking. I now always presume that I know nothing, I'm more curious and work hard to learn enough and always accept that, as a result, some of my preconceived ideas or things I believe I know or believe to be true, might not be, and might suddenly be challenged to be replaced by a brand-new perspective.

While it is important to acknowledge that not all young people wish to go to university – and Chapter 9 will discuss alternative options – our principles about building independence and resilience apply to all young people. The truth is that university is supposed to prepare students for the world of work and, if institutions fail to do this, young people will have to learn these skills at a later date, when they start their first job. Employers expect graduates to have these abilities and it might be harder for them to progress if they don't; the transition into employment might be even more tricky and challenging, and the 'culture shock' even deeper. The sooner we help young people to develop the skills and competences they require to achieve this, the better.

From A-level thinking to degree-level thinking

The academic workload is clearly a major factor in the reported stress of students. This is mainly because the learning and studying that students are expected to carry out at university level is drastically different from what they need to do during their teenage years. For school, students are required to 'chunk down' their essays into 'bite-sized bits' that they 'digest' and 'regurgitate' to get the grades they need to secure a place at their university of choice. They are asked to practise for the exams by doing as many past papers as possible so that they understand the structure and format of the exam, and have 'prepared' answers. This couldn't be further away from what is expected of them at university, and is no doubt a contributing factor to their culture shock.

Students often ask what they need to 'do' to get a First or a 2:1. It is as if they believe that there are 'hoops' to jump through to pass their university examinations. More worryingly, a colleague whose specialism is in biomolecular research recently told us that a medical student had asked her if the content of her particular lecture would be included in the exam. Taken aback by the question, she asked the student why he wanted to know, to which he replied, 'Well, if it is not in the exam, I don't really need to know about this, do I? I mean what are the chances of me ever needing this when I am a family doctor?' This is both naive and scary!

When your teenager revises and prepares for their exams, encourage them to explore wider aspects of the topics they are studying, not just the ones they think they will need for their exams. Developing curiosity and interest for different aspects will prove useful when they start their degree course. This is not to say that they should add an even greater quantity of work to their timetable, but they could read around and know a little more about it, which can then also be useful to emphasise their understanding in exams, as well as broadening their knowledge.

WHAT DO EMPLOYERS WANT FROM GRADUATES?

A 2014 survey of 198 business leaders focused on the key competencies that companies are looking for during and after the recruitment stage.[9] Employers reported that they were looking for the very best candidates in graduates, with expectations that the 'right' graduate would not only have strong degree results but would also have excellent interpersonal skills. The top three skills they were looking for at the recruitment stage were: effective communication (73 per cent); numeracy (64 per cent); and being a team player (61 per cent). In fact, the general theme was that employers were recruiting for *attitude*, and then training to upskill (this survey had a higher percentage of finance professionals responding, hence numeracy ranked highly). Essentially employers are looking for graduates with strong communication skills and a positive attitude so they can be developed into professionals. It would not be unreasonable to assume that employers would look for these qualities in all employees, not just those who have a degree, of course.

Another skill is 'cultural agility'. Being culturally agile has been defined as: being able to tolerate ambiguity; being curious and trying to make sense of things around us; and believing that you can succeed in any given situation (this demands self-efficacy which is a part of being culturally agile – see pages 64–7).[10] Cultural agility means being adaptable in new circumstances. It also encompasses the desire to form relationships and an ability to see situations from multiple perspectives, and being able to change how we view the meaning of behaviours. Finally, it requires young people to use divergent thinking (finding multiple solutions to problems), creativity and receptivity to adopting diverse ideas, which we discussed at the beginning of this chapter.

These skills are ones that our educational system needs to teach young people and nurture, not only so that they can become 'global citizens' (they will be able to live or work with people anywhere) but also if they want to transition effectively from one 'learning culture' to the next (secondary school to university or university to the world of work) and to be the best professionals that companies are looking for.

PARENT POINTERS

- Be aware of your own cultural agility. How effective are you at dealing with cultures that are different from yours and how can you help your child to learn from your own skills and experience?
- Show them how to be curious, to observe and learn about new cultures and environments, and not to be scared of differences.

A VISION FOR THE FUTURE

We all play a part in the education system and we each have an influence, even if it is initially hidden from view. We can use our influence to challenge current systems, push back on constant exams and targets, and value creativity and deeper learning.

Many parents and teachers express their dislike of constant 'testing' and yet we contribute to its continued application in the following ways:

The government: imposes new policies and strategies on a regular basis, most of which tend to focus on attainment and obsessively measuring progress through standardised testing, thus putting pressure on schools (and teachers) to perform. League tables based on these results are produced. The aim is to raise standards or make sure that they remain good.

Schools and teachers: apply these policies and measures. They strive to be at the top of league tables (because their funding depends on it) and spend a lot of time preparing pupils for and testing pupils. At parents' evenings, teachers tell us where our children are in terms of attainment: 'working towards', 'on target' or 'working beyond target'. Of course, this is really important for mainstream state schools, particularly in England, because good exam results mean more students, which means more funding.[11]

Parents: consciously or unconsciously accept these policies by adopting this concept of attainment and of creating 'A* pupils', sometimes having to take drastic measures, such as moving to a new area to get into a 'better' school, or spending money to educate children privately, thus feeding the system of 'standardised testing' and 'attainment'. At parents' evenings we want to know how well our children are achieving.

Children: start to believe that their marks and results give them an identity, a label. They believe that they are 'clever' or 'intelligent' because they get straights As. Some stop being curious and interested in learning and some get bored because they spend a lot of time going through practice exam tests.

Universities: degree courses require most students to achieve a specific (very often high) set of grades at A level or International Baccalaureate (IB) to enter a university.

Employers: require a First or 2:1 for most of their graduate schemes.

The press and media: regularly publish articles that tell students which degrees they 'should' or 'shouldn't' be doing in order to get the best (and most well-paid) job when they graduate. They, too, play a role in how we view grades and tests, exam results and degree programmes. There is undoubtedly an impact on young people who have decided to follow a course that won't provide them with a high salary.[12]

PARENT POINTERS

- As parents, if we value education and trust teachers, and show our children that we do, they too will start trusting and having faith in their education.

- By encouraging our young people to slowly develop independent thinking and confidence over their teenage years, they will be empowered and ready for university, if they choose it as their next step.

- Each of us has an impact on the whole, and yet we tend to only consider fragments of the system. Change in education can therefore only happen if we take a more systemic approach and we *all* work together to be the change we want to see in the world. One conversation at a time, one person at a time.

- Talk to your children about flaws in the systems, and how creativity should not be lost in the drive to meet targets.

We are in no way suggesting that there is a simple answer to this but there is amazing work being carried out by other countries such as Finland that do not value academic attainment alone and do not test their pupils constantly but who value and trust their teachers.[13] We should, perhaps, approach the education of our young children in a more systemic way rather than the traditional approach, and, most importantly, from a perspective where 'teaching to the test' becomes an alien concept and where competition and league tables do not exist.

Years spent in this system may partly explain the academic stress young people report when they start university. It is time to look at other options so that we can implement a more holistic approach to education, be inspired by other countries and learn from their experience so that we can introduce relevant and meaningful change.

The education system is not all doom and gloom and there are ways to improve the situation. One might be to ensure that there is greater communication within the system. Secondary school pupils often visit universities to be exposed to some of the courses and see what it would be like to do a degree, but there is need for greater collaboration between secondary schools and universities so that we can make that transition easier. It may be useful to remind our children that university transition is one of the first of many periods where they will experience challenges in life that may require them to be flexible and adaptable. Starting university can be one of the first steps in a life of transitions and change. If we support and enable teens through this we are helping them to develop a crucial life skill for future transitions because, as we well know, change is the only constant.

THINKING POINTS

Many factors influence our children's education. We are all part of the system and all part of the solution. We need to consider what we as parents can influence and what we cannot. It would take a lot of time and effort to influence the educational policies drawn up by the government or the way schools are run, but there are things that are within our control. If we help our children to develop a passion for learning and thinking from a young age they will be prepared for life, as education is not simply about school years but also about lifelong learning.

If, while reading this chapter, you are wondering how you can influence your children, think of any opportunities you may have (especially in the holidays) to teach them to be curious, creative, innovative and flexible, ready for whatever the world has in store for them.

Here are a few examples of helpful approaches you can take:

- Encourage creative problem-solving.
- Try not to label your children as 'clever' or 'smart'; praise their character rather than their intelligence.
- Develop their growth mindset – they may not be able to do it ... yet!
- They are *not* their grades.
- Encourage deep learning rather than superficial learning.
- Develop 'cultural agility' – adaptability to new circumstances.
- Value education and teaching, and the benefits they can bring.
- Encourage independence and curiosity.

PART 2

TECH LIFE

CHAPTER 5

Technology: A 'Double-edged' Screen

A sk any parent these days what they worry about most with regards to their children and the likelihood is that one of the first things they will mention is technology such as social media and online gaming, or other negative aspects relating to the Internet. Conversely, if you ask young people what they love most about living in the current era they will cite 'Google Maps', 'Snapchat', 'learning things on YouTube' and being able to connect with their friends all over the world! Technology and the Internet have brought both advances and conflict into our homes, and managing that double-edged sword is a parenting skill few of us gave any thought to when we had children. Now, however, it is an unavoidable topic in the vast majority of households, from debates about how much screen time is too much and which social media accounts are deemed acceptable, and at what age, to which YouTube channels are 'safe' and how to deal with online bullying, trolls and other negative aspects. Schools are doing a lot of work around learning to be safe online from a young age, but there is also much for parents to be aware of, and for most parents it is a 'brave new world', far removed from their own experiences of childhood. We are learning as we go, and often more slowly than the teenagers we are trying to police and supervise.

Those born after 1995 have grown up with technology since they were babies and toddlers, and have never known a world without the Internet. They are tech-savvy and most handle technology better than their parents and educators do. Marc Prensky, the American author and educator who coined the term 'digital natives' in 2001, refers to them as 'native speakers' of the digital language of computers, video games and the Internet, and states that parents who have, at some later point in life, become fascinated by and adopted many aspects of the new technology are, and always will be, 'digital immigrants' compared to their children.[1] His simplistic categorisation has, however, been criticised as being too limited by age and background, and a more recent categorisation has been of people as either 'visitors' or 'residents' of the online world.[2]

'Visitors' will visit the online world, find the information they need and leave. They do not have a profile on most of the social media platforms and are worried about privacy and identity theft. On the other hand, 'residents' see the Web as a place where they have friends and colleagues they can get in touch with and share information about their life and work. They feel that they belong to a community online and will have social media profiles.

You may recognise yourself and your children in this description, which is a continuum, rather than based on age. Regardless of where we are on the continuum, it is important to also be aware of what behaviour we display in front of our children and which we want them to copy. If we spend a lot of time on the Web as 'residents', it will be much more difficult to ask our children to behave differently, should we wish them to do so. When it comes to technology use, you as parents set the tone. Children will also be influenced by friends and peers, so it is important to negotiate boundaries that feel appropriate and relevant to your family (see pages 103–05 for more on this).

ALWAYS CONNECTED

Technology enables us to do so many positive things; from the moment we wake up to the alarm on our phone, answering emails on the move throughout the day, ordering the weekly shop online and booking holidays or cinema tickets, we are efficient, connected and productive. We listen to music online, and stream and download podcasts or audiobooks that we will later listen to in the car or on the bus, on the way to school or work.

Our children as digital learners access information quickly and easily. They like to multitask with their Word document open for their essay as well as having several other tabs open (such as YouTube), and they go back and forth from one to the other. They are used to instant gratification and regular rewards and much prefer to learn through games. 'Gamification' of learning (and even psychological therapy) is now an accepted approach used to educate and appeal to young people.

In contrast, when most of us were growing up, we would come home from school to an often quiet, and possibly boring, house, with homework that required us to look things up in a book. We had access to a TV with only a few channels and with programmes airing only at specific hours of the day. We might also have looked forward to chatting with our best mates on the phone, sitting on the stairs whispering for hours.

Teenagers these days can have all their friends in their pocket and on their screens all of the time, with notifications and messages popping up several times a minute, including after lights out. There is a pressure to 'have a good feed', look great (#IWokeUpLikeThis), stay up to date, know the latest memes and be in on the chat. Young people are communicating even at 3am, and when they wake in the morning they immediately check what has been happening on their timelines and spend time getting Instagram-ready. Our children can bring their friends to our tables to have breakfast, lunch and dinner remotely with us through their favourite app. Lara, mum of a 13-year-old teenage girl, told us:

> Maddie walks around the house with her phone and video on and talks to her best friend. Sometimes, she will be on a video call with her, but she will be doing her homework and her friend will be doing the same thing, and they will only look up and ask each other questions when they need to. Once, I even saw my daughter in her bedroom, doing her own thing and then remembering that her friend was there on the side, by her bed, and she went over and spoke to her.

In the past, doing several things at once was seen as a great skill. Today, our devices actually encourage us to multitask – to read our emails, respond to a quick text, do our online banking and browse the Internet all at the same time. But research shows that multitasking actually stops productivity.[3] In one study, researchers identified that whenever participants switched between tasks, significant time costs were noted, which only grew when the tasks became more complex.[4]

While these 'switch costs' were small in isolation, when totalled up for repeated switching back and forth between tasks, they amounted to a significant length of time, that led researchers to conclude that multitasking *inhibits* overall efficiency.

PARENT POINTERS

- When you notice your child is doing three things at once, take a moment to talk them through how having their attention divided will affect their ability to do any one thing properly. If they just do one thing at a time they might also notice that they feel less overwhelmed as there is less going on.
- Some parents have reported that reducing the number of distractions might help children to become more focused, particularly if they struggle to self-regulate.

TECHNOLOGY AND EDUCATION

Teaching in secondary schools and universities has radically changed over the last 15 years to accommodate advances in technology, and many institutions are now using learning management systems (LMS) to provide all the materials and information students need in one convenient place, called a learning platform, a hub or intranet. Homework can be accessed online and students are expected to submit essays and do research online. These digital natives have a real hunger for new ways of learning which involve technology and, as a result, teachers and institutions are willing to adopt new ways of teaching and to offer innovative tools to help students learn better (for example, online recording of lectures and seminars made available to students after the event). The concept of 'flipped classrooms' has also been introduced where students are provided in advance with the PowerPoint presentation of the concept that will be discussed in class, and they are expected to come prepared and ready to engage in the discussion.

The downsides of instant access to information include a tendency to seek the easiest and quickest answers, preferring superficial learning to deep learning approaches (see pages 81–2), and the potential for inadvertent plagiarism as students gather information from the Web. Plagiarism is very heavily policed at university in particular, and poorly tolerated, so understanding the implications and importance of plagiarism is crucial for would-be students.[5] Young people need to learn new disciplines for managing this online learning world. 'Essay mills' (paid essay-writing companies) are now being investigated, and students are even at risk of being picked up for plagiarism if they accidentally forget to reference appropriately or take a sloppy approach to using online content.[6]

These educational tools are a great way to keep all the information in one place for students who then have a 'one-stop shop' where they can find details on university policies, marking criteria, lecture notes and recordings, to name but a few. The downside of such platforms is that we are not encouraging students to retain information. More than ever, tutors notice that their students do not take notes when they share information with them and report students contacting them to ask 'Where can I find a specific document?' or 'What do I need to do next?'

Although all the information is there, our young people might not automatically think about looking for it first before asking for help. All too often it seems quicker and faster to 'fire a quick email' to be given the exact location of a file rather than to spend 10 minutes locating it. Possibly as a result of our 'instant info' society, some of our young people seem to be losing the skills required to search for information, which is an important skill not just for studying – travel and holidays, preparing for interviews and most jobs require us to pull together disparate pieces of information and create a coherent plan, so it is vital to be able to search effectively and efficiently for relevant and useful material in a world of bottomless data.

> ### PARENT POINTER
>
> • Once in secondary school, encourage your child to find out information for themselves and to read important documents, taking notes to help with retaining knowledge. This will be extremely useful as they go through secondary school, university or into the workplace.

THE 'DANGERS' OF TECHNOLOGY

Parents often feel confused and unsure about how much they should let their kids use technology, when and which content is safe. Many feel out of their depth, and are aware that even their youngest children may know more than they do about tech. Parents are faced with a deluge of information (very often contradictory) about screen time or social media, and the media makes regular claims and counterclaims about the potential dangers of technology, for example with regards to online gaming or self-harm. It can feel overwhelming, but it is important to keep some context around this, and remember that we have seen such alarmist headlines before.

Young people we spoke to likened using social media to 'smoking in the fifties', when it was considered 'cool' but before there was evidence of its significant harm. They want to know if it will turn out to be the 'new smoking' and to be avoided, or if it will be more like alcohol, which generally tends to be in the 'acceptable in moderation' category. Our society has seen moral panics about rock 'n' roll, punk music, TV and swimsuits over the last half century or so, none of which have turned out to cause the damage they were feared to.[7] Is our anxiety about social media or screen time the latest moral panic, or will it justify our concerns?[8]

The evidence so far

In 2018 the UK Secretary of State for Health and Social Care, Matt Hancock, issued an urgent warning on the potential dangers of social media on children's mental health, stating that the threat of social media on mental health was similar to that of sugar on physical health. He asked the Chief Medical Officer (CMO) to come up with guidelines for the use of social media.[9] Was his comment based on evidence or was it yet another moral panic?

In 2019, *The Times* reported that a study carried out by researchers at the University of Oxford indicated that social media and watching TV had such a 'tiny' effect on teenagers' mental health that 'eating potatoes or wearing glasses' appeared to be just as risky.[10] Cannabis use and bullying were much bigger threats to young people's well-being than screen time, it found. The reporter added that the dangers of screens have been exaggerated by the cherry-picking of vague research that throws up dubious links. The research team added that the government should instead devote more effort to things that were known to have important health benefits, such as helping children eat breakfast or get a good night's sleep.

In the same month, Dr Max Davie, Officer for Health Promotion at the Royal College of Paediatrics and Child Health (RCPCH), said we needed to 'let parents be parents' and adjust the amount of time spent on screens by all members of the family. This new RCPCH guidance on screen time use looked at the evidence so far and concluded that an 'in moderation' approach was pragmatic and that this should have no negative impact on mental health and well-being.[11] This report did find negative effects, however. For example, children who used screens for longer periods of time seemed to have an unhealthier diet and were more likely to be obese. The negative effects were related not to the use of screens directly but to the activities screen use displaced, in other words exercise and sleep were losing out to screen time. This may be the real danger of screen use (see Chapter 11 for more on this).

It is also important not to conflate screen use and social media – they are *not* the same thing. Though they are often used interchangeably, it seems that the evidence for screen use is that in moderation it is probably fine, but that social media use, while being positive in many aspects, may have higher risks, and we will examine these more closely in the next chapter.

You could be forgiven for being confused, as the government advised urgent action, and yet the experts appeared to take a more practical and realistic approach advising moderation and the need for more research. Many guidelines have been criticised as not being fully evidence-based and being focused on risks, rather than recognising the potential benefits of digital screen use in education and industry. Just as you would probably not give your teenager unlimited access to your drinks cabinet or allow them to eat only sugary foods and drinks and not have their 'five a day', so too should screen time and access to social media be in moderation. No authoritative body has yet issued time-specific guidance on screen time and media use for children in the UK. We therefore need to take a reasonable approach based on the evidence we have so far.

Some screen time may actually be *good* for your child's health

Credible studies have shown that *some* screen time is better than none, but children who spend *more* than two hours per day on screens seem to develop more depressive symptoms. This research recommends two hours per day as being the maximum ideal length of time.[12] The reason for the 'some is better than none' observation may be that those who have no screen time may be more isolated and cut off from their friendship groups or peers, thus leading them to have poorer mental health. Or it may be that those who are depressed don't go online as much; we have yet to establish cause or effect.

Being connected *some* of the time seems to be associated with better well-being than being connected none or all of the time.

How much is too much?

The RCPCH has developed four key questions for families to use as a guide to review their screen time:[13]

1. Is screen time in your household controlled?
2. Does screen use interfere with what your family wants to do?
3. Does screen use interfere with sleep?
4. Are you able to control snacking during screen time?

If, as a family, you can ask yourselves these questions and are satisfied with the answers, you can be reassured that you are likely to be doing well in this brave new world. In the absence of unequivocal guidance to date, the most pragmatic approach to designing a family screen time guide may be as follows:

- A maximum of two hours of screen time a day.
- Reward the respect of boundaries and family rules.
- No eating when using a screen (or vice versa).
- No screens for an hour before bed (even if 'blue light emission block' is switched on).
- No screens in the bedroom at night – leave phones outside the bedroom when it is bedtime.
- Use screen time control apps or technology for tweenagers.

- Check age certification of games and apps to ensure they are age-appropriate.
- Talk about sharing photos and information online and how photos and words are sometimes manipulated. Parents and carers should never assume that children of any age are happy for their photos to be shared. For everyone – when in doubt, don't upload![14]
- Advise children to put their screens away while crossing the road or doing an activity that needs their full attention (including walking down the stairs).
- Consider agreeing 'binge days' and screen-free days (or tech-free family nights) for flexibility.
- Agree together what the sanctions might be for not following family guidelines – framing it as a loss of privilege rather than punishment.[15]

As with so many activities and behaviours, it is difficult to give strict guidelines because each family will be different and will want to set different boundaries – you may agree no phones when visiting and talking with older relatives, but they are fine on the journey or in the car. We also don't have the evidence base yet on which to set clear rules, like we do for alcohol or smoking. As a rule of thumb, as long as technology is not interfering with your family life, then you need not worry. If it is, and you notice new mood changes, deteriorating school or work standards, or increasing isolation from friends and family, it may be time to set up some clear boundaries for all of you to live by.

Setting boundaries

It is not always easy or possible to monitor or control teenagers' screen time, particularly if we are 'visitors' of technology and they are 'residents' (see page 94). When you first buy your child a mobile phone (for many it is at around the age of 11, to start secondary school), it might be worth exploring specific apps that allow you to set usage limits or see where your children are. Basic security and privacy settings are crucial at this time.

Carla, the mother of 12-year-old Joseph, told us:

We had a discussion with Joseph about what was reasonable. His phone does not go on until 8am so he can listen to music on his way to school. He has it after school until 6pm. At school they have a 'power down' rule. If a phone is seen or heard inside the school gates, it is confiscated and parents have to come in to collect it. So essentially, he has his phone for 45 minutes in the morning and about 2½ hours in the evening … when he's not at after-school activities. I have found the key is to be rigid. *I will not lift the restriction.* It stops any discussion/argument. I think my job is to enforce healthy habits. If I didn't do this, he would absolutely use it well after 6pm.

In this way Carla has negotiated the agreement with her son, and the plan allows Joseph to use his phone in a way that is practical, and connects him to his friends, but does not encroach on sleep time or other physical activities.

Another approach for younger tweenagers starting out on their social media 'careers' is to initially only allow them to have accounts if you as their parent can be a 'follower' or 'friend' too. As they get older they will likely want to have some privacy, so may set up new accounts that you are not linked to. This should be fine if you have discussed security and online safety with them. One dad we spoke to advocates having a conversation with your tweenager that would cultivate a trusting approach by saying to them: 'You don't need to be secretive, I trust you to use the Internet in the way we have agreed, with me being involved to start with. When you are older, once I know that you understand how to be safe online, you will be allowed to have some privacy.'

Online safety

As parents, it is vital that we check *what* our children are doing online. We need to build their understanding of what they might see, that some of it might be distressing and that they can say 'no', switch over (or off), and that they can control their content viewing. Young people have always been exposed to things they shouldn't or might not like to see, so parents need to talk about this and discuss strategies to cope with such tricky situations. In our own teenage years we might have gone to a sleepover where horror films were on the VCR, and we had to learn that it was okay to say 'no' if we didn't want to watch them. There might have been fewer celebs but they influenced us nonetheless, and porn was harder to find accidentally, but it happened.

Clear boundaries within a trusting context make life easier for everyone. For older teenagers it is reasonable for them to have their screen in their room for privacy, but engage them in discussion about what they look at, the risks and your concerns. Ask them if they are happy that they are making good choices and have conversations about what content will bring most rewards, for example TED Talks or podcasts.[16]

Entry to senior school is a good time to ensure that your child is briefed and ready, but you may wish to bring it up (gently) earlier than that. Much of this will have been discussed with younger children at primary school, so you may find that they have a good basic understanding of online safety already.

PARENT POINTERS

- Talking about online content and the potential risks in an open manner is helpful, and encouraging your child to talk to you if they see something that upsets them, to work through it, will help too.

- Your child needs to learn to say 'no', turn away, moderate or turn any upsetting content off for themselves, much as we did when we were young with cigarettes or alcohol. Learning to say no is a lifelong skill – they will need to say no in a variety of situations, from needy friendships, to sexual consent, to unreasonable requests from overly demanding student supervisors or bosses.

- Simply trying to stop your child using technology won't work, as teenagers will just customise whatever tech they do have access to and make it work for them. Even Google Docs (considered dry by most adolescents) has now been 'repurposed' as a social messaging app in the classroom![17]

As always, remaining calm, and not overreacting, while listening to your child's concerns about difficult content, is vital to keep the lines of communication open. If you get cross or shout at them for looking at stuff you disapprove of you can be sure that they will never tell you again! As one very experienced teacher and school pastoral lead told us:

> If your child gets things wrong and shares their mistake with you and then you take their favourite app away (like Snapchat) they won't tell you anything again. If you need a sanction, better to say that you will be randomly checking their feed or accounts for a couple of weeks. That is much more manageable and keeps the relationship open.

Online gaming

Whether teenagers and young adults game alone or in multi-player games (some with players online anywhere in the world), and with or without the ability to chat on screen or via a headset, there are basic principles which can help to keep them safe and minimise the risk of addiction. Gaming can bring a sense of community to young people, it can give them a release and they may have a lot of fun and enjoy it, but it can have its downsides.

Parents often believe that online gaming can encourage violence and crime, but researchers at the University of Huddersfield have also found the opposite can happen, depending on the nature of the game.[18] They state that: 'The research is clear: when children play aggressive computer games they behave more violently; but when they play more socially conscientious games their behaviour correspondingly improves.'

Online gaming is therefore not a 'bad' thing as such, but as with so many activities and behaviours, moderation and care is sensible. The main points for young people to remember are:[19]

- behave in a manner that is considerate
- be aware of the potential for grooming
- know that some content may be upsetting
- be aware of the addictive potential of gaming

We spoke to Cam Adair, the Canadian world expert on online gaming addiction, whose advice to parents is this:

> Setting limits from an early age is important. Move devices to a central area in your home to reduce isolation. Focus on building a positive and healthy family relationship by having dinners together without screens, and doing activities together on the

weekend. Have frequent open conversations about technology use and how it intersects with your family values.

He added that time limits of a couple of hours a day were important, as was limiting the opportunity to spend money or gamble 'in-game'. And never try to negotiate any of this while your child is actually gaming!

If gaming is interfering with your child's school or uni work, sleep, friendships and relationships, it is important to seek professional advice or counselling, as they may be addicted, but the key question to ask is *why* they are gaming so much. Is it to escape other issues, to stay 'in' with a friendship group or for money, or other reasons? Addressing these other issues is as important as addressing the gaming itself, as people often use gaming to manage low self-esteem, anxiety and poor social skills.[20] Parents can help by being aware of this 'coping strategy' angle to gaming, and by talking to their children about it, and seeking support if necessary. Taking an 'authoritarian' or dictatorial approach (see pages 59–60) will be actively unhelpful, and may lead to deterioration of family relationships, running away and other negative reactions.[21] Discussion and negotiation is the most successful approach, and can include asking your young person what they think the boundaries for gaming should be and what sanctions should be agreed if these are not respected.

Online gambling

Gambling has been made increasingly accessible and easy for teenagers and young adults to engage in, and most of them will be unaware of the old saying that 'the House always wins'.[22] They may be reeled in with free plays and games, or via in-app purchases on other games, initially winning and then lured further into the risk-taking and 'reward' cycle. 'Loot boxes' (random rewards that can then be used to make in-game purchases of players/weapons) which exist in more than 60 per cent of mainstream games, such as *FIFA*, *Overwatch* and *Star Wars*, are essentially ways to teach young people to gamble, and Belgium has been the first country to ban them.[23] Studies have shown that people who spend more money on loot boxes are less likely to be able to keep their gambling in check.[24]

For young people, whose brains are still developing, the 'reward centre' lights up powerfully with the risk-taking 'hit' of gambling, but the dampening down 'handbrake of the brain' (in the prefrontal cortex, which is the last area to develop) is not yet available to counterbalance the pleasure of the reward. They enjoy, and to a certain extent, find it difficult to control, the impulsivity they feel, and have little inbuilt restraint mechanism. It's a double whammy – and high-risk for addiction.

Help and advice is increasingly available as the problem is growing, and there are useful resources online for concerned parents, such as GamCare (see page 312), that may offer a self-assessment tool or a phone helpline, which may be a starting point for a conversation with your teenager if you are worried. As with gaming, gambling can be a way for young people to deal with other difficulties in their lives, such as depression, anxiety, ADHD or social skills issues, so starting with the 'why' can be a pragmatic approach here too.[25] Seeking help for any underlying problems, learning skills to make new friends or joining a support group can all be effective ways to deal with gambling problems. Finding alternative healthier activities that give young people a 'high', such as go-karting, climbing or mountain biking, can be valuable in 'weaning' them off gambling too. It may take time but it will be a worthwhile undertaking.

Sexting

The sharing of intimate images or videos may seem difficult to understand in a world where such things can subsequently be so easily spread online to be viewed forever, and by anyone. However, a 2018 study of 110,000 young people under 18 found that: 1 in 4 had been sexted; 1 in 7 had sent them; the split between boys and girls sexting was roughly equal; and children as young as 11 were sexting, though the average age was 15.[26] This is all despite the fact that it is illegal in the UK to possess a sexual image or video of a young person under 18, even of themselves.[27]

Parents may not be surprised that teenagers choose to 'sext' (they have the 'interest' and the resources to do it, so why wouldn't they?), but it can seem incredibly naive to share images that make them highly vulnerable longer term, when they generally understand the way the Internet works better than their parents do. Of course, it may be that they feel pressured or even blackmailed ('sextortion') into sharing such images. Or it may be done as a test of trust, with young girls sharing such images with a boy they like and, if he doesn't share it with his friends, this 'proves' that he is trustworthy and they could date him (though sadly they give little thought to what he might do if they split up). We need to be open to having conversations about these topics, without judgement and without blame. Sexting is an issue at school, at university and in the workplace and can create an expectation of 'hooking up' (having sex) on the part of the recipient, increasing the pressure to have sex.

We need to teach our teenagers not to share other people's images either, because it seems 'funny' at the time or in revenge. They may be asked to send such messages as 'proof' of feelings for someone, or may receive them without consent.

Sharing intimate photos with partners is not new in itself, but as studies show that 88 per cent of self-taken sexually explicit images have been shared on other sites, believing that they will remain private is optimistic, to say the least.[28] Discussing all of these topics may be tricky ('Have you heard of sexting?' is a good opening question), but talking through the consequences of sexting can help your young person avoid future difficulties. There are good resources available to support parents and teenagers or young adults in learning more, which cover what to do if you feel your privacy has been violated or you need to manage a particular scenario.[29]

THINKING POINTS

Technology provides young people with tools that can be extremely useful and can improve their lives in many ways, through social support and connectivity. Unfortunately, it can also be associated with many negative influences and poorer mental health, so until longer term research becomes available, a pragmatic and 'in moderation' approach may be best for screen time use and social media engagement. It is important to remain balanced when parenting, as technology itself is not bad or good, it is what young people choose to use it for that matters. Technology will play a significant part in our children's professional and future lives and therefore it is best to encourage them to become tech-savvy and to use technology to their advantage (rather than it using them).

Here are a few things to consider:

- You set the tone for how technology is used in your family.
- Make a family plan of how to use tech, and how much screen time is healthy. Agree boundaries and sanctions together.

- Balance screen time with healthy exercise and activities, and watch snacking.
- Check the content of screen use, rather than focusing on time spent.
- Build responsible screen and tech use through trust and education, rather than over-invasive monitoring.
- Encourage young people to slowly learn how to self-regulate (and say 'no').

CHAPTER 6

Social Media

Ninety per cent of 18- to 29-year-olds are on social media and they can spend many hours surfing those platforms.[1] Understanding the challenges of social media use is therefore vital, as well as enjoying the positives it brings. It may be more important for parents to focus on what their children are looking at than for how long they are online. The challenge of *content* may be the biggest issue.

In her TEDx Talk 'Is Social Media Hurting Your Mental Health?' the founder and CEO of SkillsCamp (an organisation that teaches young people 'soft skills' for future employment), Bailey Parnell, may provide some answers.[2] She tells us that numerous studies in the US, Canada and the UK have linked high social media use with high levels of anxiety and depression in students.

She identifies four stressors created by social media:

1. The highlight reel
2. Social currency
3. Fear Of Missing Out (FOMO)
4. Online harassment

This may be a helpful framework for discussing these topics with your teenager.

The highlight reel

The highlight reel is a collection of our best photos and moments; a showcase of our 'best self' and our 'best life'. Teenagers we spoke to when researching this book told us that they were well aware of this tendency we all have to airbrush our lives. They are not naive and oblivious. They realise that people don't post photos of themselves doing their washing or slumped on the sofa, tired and grumpy, but they still feel the pressure to maintain the illusion of a constantly fun and fabulous life. This pressure can be relentless, and across multiple platforms, such as Facebook, Instagram, Twitter, Snapchat and others. They talk of 'airbrushing their emotions', posting a picture and a caption instead of talking to people and feeling the pressure to have perfect conversations, which are easier to perfect of course, if they are written rather than spoken.

Social currency

A currency is something we use to attribute value to a good or service. The likes, shares and comments of social media have become a new social currency by which we attribute value to something. We have become the 'products' of social media, and if pictures or posts don't get enough likes, young people may take them down – they 'remove their products from the shelves'. This tallies with what Joseph, a final-year student, told us. He had to delete Facebook because he felt addicted to the newsfeed and compelled to check it frequently. He often felt very insecure and regularly texted his friends to request that they like or comment on his pictures when he didn't feel he had received enough.

This constant grading or commentary on their activities is another form of competition and pressure for our young people to live with, even if they don't always realise that they are immersed in it, and requesting more. Older students told us that although Facebook was bad, they found LinkedIn to be 'like Facebook on steroids', taking the competitiveness into the world of work and career achievements, which was terrifying to them.

FOMO

Fear of missing out is a social anxiety stemming from the fear that you are missing out on a potential connection, event or opportunity. One young adult told us: 'You might post that you have done five things, then someone else will always have done seven or eight! It's endless. One girl last year posted that she had been to twenty-six countries! How can I compete with that?'

A collection of Canadian universities found that 7 out of 10 students would actually get rid of their social networking accounts were it not for the fear of being 'left out of the loop'.[3] The students were asked if they had thought about deactivating, or had deactivated, their own account and almost everyone responded in the affirmative. They also all said that it was the fear of not knowing about an event or a party that prevented them from doing it. This is a strong theme we also encountered when talking to UK sixth formers who seemed conflicted, both wanting to be connected to friends and know what is happening, but also disliking the constant pressure from the 'social currency' demands of their feeds. Many had tried deleting certain accounts, but reconnected when they felt left out, though sometimes only reconnecting as observers, rather than engaging fully. This seemed to allow for a happy medium – being in the loop but not posting stuff that demanded 'ratings'. Others only had their social media accounts on their laptops, not phones, so as to reduce the time spent looking at them.

PARENT POINTERS

- When discussing social media with your young person try to encourage them to follow positive feeds like well-being accounts or National Geographic for its beautiful scenes of nature and wilderness, and others that they may find uplifting, in order to balance some of the competitiveness they are exposed to elsewhere. Reading positive affirmations or seeing peaceful, beautiful places may subconsciously support them or make them feel more grounded and connected to the wider world.
- Talk to them about how they feel about themselves and their lives after they have been on social media, and get them to reflect on the effect it has on them. In time they may then be better able to moderate their use.
- If they see lots of people at a party they didn't go to, for example, try to get them to think about something good that they did at another time, to understand that everyone's lives have differing highs and lows.
- Remind them that everything posted on social media is essentially there forever, and to ask themselves before they post if they would be happy for a grandparent to see it, or to explain it at a job interview one day. Nothing stays private.

Online harassment

Bullying and harassment are sadly all too common, with UK studies showing that about half of 11- to 18-year-old girls and 40 per cent of the same aged boys have experienced it online.[4] In Australia the figures show 1 in 4 pupils has.[5] The problems range from being regularly contacted by a person who is bothering them, to critical personal comments and occasionally threats. Many have changed their online behaviour to protect themselves or avoid the negativity. Many others don't recognise the issue, tolerate it or don't know what to do about it.

Talking to your teenager or young adult about these issues and letting them know that they can speak to you openly, and that you will be supportive, can be hugely helpful and can avoid the situation building up into a crisis.[6] Many organisations have excellent resources to help parents know how to discuss it or manage it should it happen. Young people need to understand that they should treat others as well online as they would in real life and they need to be 'share aware' before they share images or information about themselves. It's so important, too, that they know what to do if they see something that upsets them.[7] Many websites, such as Net Aware (see page 313), can help parents to better understand the different social media platforms and learn about the world their kids inhabit in order to keep them safe. There is also information online about how to report concerning content.

PARENT POINTERS

- Watch for changes in mood and behaviour in your young person that may indicate they are being harassed.
- Remind them that they can talk to you about anything: 'There is nothing that you could say or do, or tell me, that I wouldn't want to hear about or try to help you with' is

a useful comment throughout their life, when they may stress about worrying you or letting you down.

- Ask them to let you know if they are asked to share pics they are not comfortable with, or if others share personal images of them without consent, or make unpleasant comments online.
- Mention that blackmail is a possibility if they share explicit images – it may never have crossed their mind.
- They will likely be aware of this, but it's worth emphasising that they should never share any private information online, such as real names/school name/phone numbers, or put such info in usernames.

GROUP CHATS

Some group chats are genuinely fun and are great for making plans and socialising, but several parents interviewed for this book mentioned the fact that some can become really toxic. One mother told us: 'My daughter does have WhatsApp but I have now banned her from being on big groups as they are toxic and kids say things they wouldn't say to her face', while another added:

Yes, that's the word – 'toxic'. Lots of the group chats are just people having a go at anyone and everything. As a teenager, the emotional effect of this is extremely negative. I've seen perfectly normal chats quickly turn into arguments, name-calling and swearing. Luckily our son doesn't read most of them. He said it's just spam and won't get sucked into an argument.

PARENT POINTERS

- Encourage your children to speak to you if they see upsetting comments, so that they feel they can come and share anything they are not happy about, or are worried or concerned about. Starting these conversations from an early age is helpful.
- This may also be an opportunity for your child to try to use social media to counter negativity, and use it as a *force for good*, by posting positive messages and comments, or using it for socially positive reasons such as campaigning, but not for personal sharing.
- Remember that chats can be muted if your young person wants to stay involved but not be updated constantly.

SOCIAL MEDIA AND MENTAL HEALTH ISSUES

It seems likely from studies done so far that more than two hours of social media a day is associated with poor mental health, but this could be because those who are unwell spend more time online, as well as the social media causing the ill health.[8] In terms of which platforms appear to have the most positive or negative effects, a 2017 Royal Society for Public Health report found that YouTube was the only one of the five examined to have a net positive effect, with Twitter, Facebook and Snapchat all being negative (in that order), and Instagram the most negative, for young people's mental health.[9]

There is a lot written in the press about social media and the potential for harm in our children's (and potentially our own!)

lives, so it is very helpful that in 2018 the Centre for Mental Health (a very widely respected UK institution) published a summary of the evidence so far, to allow us all to get some perspective on this contentious and emotive subject.[10] The main negative impacts identified may allow for an informed discussion with your teenager:

- Addiction to social media (about 5 per cent of users), which interferes with normal life and makes it harder to relax.
- Interference with sleep, which has multiple negative effects.
- Unhelpful comparisons between their lives and those of others (self-esteem and self-worth were affected).
- Jealousy and FOMO, which can lead to anxiety, inadequacy and distress.
- Cyberbullying (less common than traditional bullying, but linked to self-harm and suicide).
- Loneliness increasing, as those with social anxiety (shyness) avoid social contact, so the online world becomes a substitute for social interaction and learning of social skills.

Habituation

We have evolved in a way that enables us to quickly get used to and adapt to situations that give us pleasure – habituation – but, as a result, we may get used to these positive experiences and over time they stop having the same lovely effect.[11] This is why when we get a promotion at work we are very happy and then we get used to the amount of extra money we are earning and we start wanting more money (to buy more things).

With the prevalence of social media in our young people's lives and its 'highlight reel', habituation is an important behaviour to be aware of. Young people compare themselves constantly in terms of personal attractiveness, wealth, social status, academic and athletic achievement, and their level of happiness is influenced by how they rate themselves against others, as well as how others rate them.[12] This process of social comparison was useful for our ancestors because it encouraged them to strive to be the best and have the best resources. But nowadays, if we start measuring ourselves against the successes on social media, we can't keep up and this can negatively affect our happiness and well-being.

Luckily for us our level of satisfaction is not just determined by comparisons we make between people who are better or worse off than ourselves, but also by comparisons to our past circumstances, our future aspirations and our needs and personal goals.[13] This means that we have a choice about improving our happiness or low self-esteem when comparing ourselves negatively with the positive images we see on social media, in magazines or on TV. Instead we can value the relationships, positive strengths and achievements that *we* have. We can compare ourselves with *ourselves yesterday* instead of with others, and see how well we have done. We can also judge ourselves against our immediate local reference group, and not the fake images or displays we see on social media or on TV.

PARENT POINTER

- Encourage your children to do this from a young age and, most importantly, to question the validity of what they see on their social media newsfeed or what they read online. This will help them to improve their own well-being by comparing themselves more realistically.

Addiction to social media

Sean Parker, the 38-year-old founding president of Facebook, is said to have admitted that the social network was founded not to unite us, but to distract us.[14] He also added that whenever someone likes or comments on a post or photograph, 'we ... give you a little dopamine hit'. In a 2017 article the *New York Times* columnist David Brooks wrote: 'the tech industry is such that it is causing this addiction on purpose, to make money. Tech companies understand what causes dopamine surges in the brain and they lace their products with "hijacking techniques" that lure us in and create "compulsion loops".'[15]

Snapchat has Snapstreaks, which rewards friends who snap each other every single day, thus encouraging addictive behaviour. Teenagers can get very upset if they cannot continue a streak because a parent has tried to separate them from their device, and they fear that the friends involved will criticise them for essentially 'turning their back on them'.

Newsfeeds are structured as 'bottomless bowls' so that one page view leads down to another and another and so on forever. Most social media sites create irregularly timed rewards; you have to check your device compulsively because you never know when a burst of social affirmation from a Facebook like may come. Young people recognise this behaviour in themselves – the drive to check and refresh feeds that they looked at not five minutes before – but while it frustrates them, they are not always able to stop themselves. Talking to your child about the inbuilt addictive devices of social media may give them back some insight and control over their behaviours, or allow them to choose which feeds to follow and which to delete.

Secondary schools are currently doing a lot of work around this and educating children, who are seemingly very aware. As parents, you can help by having these conversations too, once your young people engage with social media, and you can work with your child's school to ensure consistent messaging or by attending workshops offered by the school.

Screens at night

As parents you may want to be aware of a recent report that calls for support for young people to help them find a balance between social media and a good night's rest, particularly on school nights.[16] Although the study does not blame social media directly for sleep deprivation in teenagers, it shows that those who are 'very high users' are more likely to fall asleep after 11pm on school nights than their peers who use social media less. Those who hardly used social media were least likely to fall asleep late or oversleep in the morning, suggesting that minimal use was best for a good night's rest.

Expert advice is to turn off *all* screens one hour before sleep and to block the 'blue light' emitted from our screens once evening comes by using filters, apps or the settings in our smartphones. Blue light prevents us getting good-quality sleep so this is one small hack that can help us all sleep better.[17]

A really important point is that it is not how long our children spend online but what they get access to that matters; *content* is far more important than length of time. We need to have conversations and discuss all of the potential sources of stress or influence with our children. Of course, there will also be positive content, so it is important not to assume that everything your child is looking at is negative.

Self-harm online

It is understandable that young people may seek support from their peers if they have mental distress, for example if they self-harm or have disordered eating. The unfortunate irony in this is that using social media sites for support for self-harm actually leads to poorer mental health, and raises the risks of self-harm and suicidal thinking in these same young people.[18] Looking at these sites or images can in fact *trigger* distressing thoughts, or promote self-harm as an option for relieving emotional pain, especially in younger adolescents.

If young people wish to seek support online it is important that they use supportive sites that are monitored or facilitated by professionals with appropriate credentials, and which have clear boundaries for all users.[19] Good support will come in the form of professional organisations, while bad 'support' will involve multiple distressing images and encouragement to self-harm more. There are some excellent apps available via the NHS App Library. One mum, Cathy, said: 'As a parent you may feel helpless and not know what to do when dealing with self-harm, but it's important to know you are not alone in feeling like that, and to talk to professionals. Your child needs help, and you need support.'

PARENT POINTERS

- If your child is looking for support for a friend who is self-harming, discuss with your child why the self-harm might be happening to establish the urgency of your response (child sexual abuse, parental conflict or eating issues are all triggers).
- Share with your child that it is a coping strategy, so kindness and listening are needed, with encouragement to speak to a trusted adult (teacher, lecturer, healthcare professional or school counsellor).

In terms of eating disorders, young people have used online 'thinspiration' sites for years. Groups which often claim to be supportive for those with anorexia sadly have underlying themes of competitive weight loss and comparative thinness, and actually promote the anorexia ('pro-ANA').[20] Websites also exist that promote bulimia ('pro-MIA') and both approaches encourage the 'integration' of unhealthy eating behaviours into sufferers' lives. They may promote the idea that eating disorders are in fact a lifestyle choice, demonised and stigmatised by healthcare professionals, but to be protected as a personal 'right'. They will talk about 'thigh gaps' and promote protruding hip- or collarbones as laudable aims.

For young men the emphasis may be slightly different, with more priority given to body shape, and even brief exposure to media images of muscular men can lead to muscle dysmorphia, where young men think that they are less muscly than they are.[21] This is comparable to people with anorexia thinking that they are less thin than they are, and is similarly detrimental to well-being.

PARENT POINTER

- Challenging these views and raising the topics above is important, so a gentle and compassionate tone and being in 'listening mode' are key. We will talk more about eating disorders and self-harm in Chapter 14.

Loneliness

Over the last few years, young people have learnt to communicate things that are difficult via their social media platforms rather than directly to a friend. They tell us that they are more likely to tweet how they feel than to say it. This is because they have fewer close friends on Twitter and so they feel safer to state publicly how they feel, as not many of their close friends will be aware. They might post a sad message on Facebook, but when they see their 'friends' 30 minutes later they seem fine – they are experts at building an 'I'm fine' facade and projecting that they are okay. It is much easier to post a picture and a caption, or an emoji, than to say how you are feeling; much easier than sitting and chatting to friends. As a result, it would also seem that they do not always know how to make friends and build relationships with people. They also comment that they worry they may be getting worse at reading each other's emotions as a result.

PARENT POINTERS

- Learning to read each other's human emotions is a life (and survival) skill. Emojis dumb down our ability to do this. Engage with your children and talk to them about picking up on people's emotions, expressions and language tone.
- Encourage them to speak to people, even if they feel awkward. Those tricky conversations with their older relatives or parents' friends are actually great ways to build social skills. Maybe those family parties and gatherings can actually be a covert learning experience! Every opportunity to communicate counts.

Our children are more likely to be on social media platforms when they feel isolated or bored. The issue with loneliness is that, just like happiness, it may mean different things for different people. The students we interviewed for this book were clear that for them loneliness is more about social and emotional loneliness rather than physical loneliness (such as an older person might experience sitting at home alone). They tend to focus on the photos that they were *not* part of, and it links to FOMO. Sophie said, 'I see how much fun my friends had without me at an event, and it makes me feel like I don't belong, that they can be without me, that I am not needed.' Another student added, 'If I can't go out much, I spend more time on social media, then I feel worse, and this exacerbates my mental health issues.'

Social media has made it easier for our young people not to have the deeper conversations we might have had with our friends over the phone or in person. As a generation, they feel they are not having deep conversations on a personal level. They have moved away from writing a letter or meeting someone, and so relationships are becoming much more super-ficial. The other interesting aspect linked to loneliness is that our children tend to feel less happy to spend time by themselves; they are less okay with being alone and as a result they feel 'lonely' more. Cynthia, a second-year student, told us: 'I would rather stay at the library or at university longer if I know that my flatmates are not going to be back. I don't like being on my own much. In fact, I hate it.'

We have found that while students who are flourishing report being able to surround themselves with supportive people and possess the ability to develop satisfying interpersonal rela-tionships with others, others that we will call 'languishing', or failing to flourish, don't always know how to make friends with people and they say that they prefer to message someone on social media rather than call someone or make a coffee date. Online banter or conversation can be perfected and rewritten, allowing it to create the perfect image of a relationship, but it is also less messy and less deep. These young people are scared to engage in face-to-face friendships where they would have to see people's facial expressions, which might be pitying if they are told something sad, but also more supportive.

THINKING POINTS

WhatsApp, Facebook messenger, Twitter and Snapchat are great platforms that enable young people to stay connected with friends and family wherever they are in the world. This level of connectivity is one of the things that young people love most about their lives. They love making friends with people all over the world; they can 'meet' people who share their interests and views, or, later on, politics and ideals, and feel genuinely united with these people, as we do with our own good friends. 'My daughter loves surfing the Web and looking at a specific blog and sharing her recipes with others', one mum told us.

Communities of support are created on various online platforms, not least of all for those with mental health difficulties or in need of specific support. Those who have been bullied, or those with social anxiety or who feel unable to leave the house, can link up with others who empathise and can support them from their own sofa. While technology has allowed people to form these online supportive communities, and can ensure access to reliable health information or self-help resources, as well as facilitating self-expression and self-identity and is therefore absolutely a tool for good, it needs to be used carefully while so little is still understood about its long-term impact.[22]

Here are a few things to consider:

- Social media use for more than two hours a day is associated with poorer well-being, so try to moderate this, but remember that what they are looking at is more important than how long they are online.

- Be alert to mood or behaviour changes that might indicate bullying or other upset online.
- Suggest they use social media as a force for good where possible.
- Encourage the use of uplifting feeds and well-being accounts to support a positive mindset.
- Remind them that nothing online is really private, and it *will* last forever.
- Remind them to stay respectful – if they wouldn't say it face-to-face or do it in the street outside their house, then they shouldn't put it online.
- They should talk to a trusted adult if they see things that upset them.
- They should never do anything online (like send intimate images) if they feel uncomfortable. If they hesitate, that is a sign that they should stop and think about it a little longer, or talk to an older person they can be open with.
- Reassure them that there is *nothing* you wouldn't want to hear about and support them with, especially difficult things that are upsetting them. You are always here for them.

PART 3

SOCIAL LIFE

CHAPTER 7

Relationships and Romance in the Twenty-first Century

Developing close and supportive relationships with family, friends and other social networks leads to greater well-being, adjustment and may even help you live longer. 'Social health' comes from the positive effects of having a very good social network and community.[1] This comes from belonging and having something in common with our community, believing in the goodness of others and believing that we add value to society. People who are socially integrated and close to other members of their community feel good and safe in their community. Most importantly, they trust others and know that they can talk to them about their challenges, or difficult times, and this feeling of belonging helps them. This was confirmed by a recent Australian study that found that 'social connectedness' may act as a protective buffer against the negative mental health effects of cyberbullying.[2]

In fact, when giving talks to school and university students our number one 'top tip' for resilience and well-being is to 'build and maintain your social networks'. We emphasise to young people how important it is for their mental health to have a network of support, in real life or online. They don't need to have hundreds of friends – just one or two that they trust, can spend face-to-face time with and who can be relied on in times of need is enough.

The opposite scenario – social isolation – is the breakdown of personal relationships that provide meaning and support, and this can have damaging effects on our health and well-being.

Why connectedness is vital

We are social animals and we are hardwired to seek happiness through our network of friends, family and acquaintances.[3] Psychologist and *Wall Street Journal* writer, Susan Pinker, explains that in villages in Sardinia, 10 times as many men live past 100 than the average and a key reason is that they are not lonely.[4] Social interaction or the feeling of being part of a community fosters resilience. American social neuroscientist John Cacioppo says that its opposite, loneliness, 'is like an iceberg and it goes deeper than we can see' and that feeling accepted and supported make us less likely to develop a disease, while feeling isolated 'leaves a loneliness imprint' on every human cell.[5,6]

It's clear how important social support is for our well-being, and yet the students we interviewed told us how they tend to emphasise quantity rather than quality of friends as they feel a pressure to have as many friends as possible (rather than a few good friends) to define their popularity.

PARENT POINTERS

- Encourage your child to develop healthy and close relationships with you, other members of the family and friends over the years.

- Teach them how to be a good friend, how to develop trust, to be reliable and to have supportive conversations.
- Encourage them to treat others as they would wish to be treated.
- Building relationships for social support is essential for well-being.

BUILD A 'MENTORING' RELATIONSHIP WITH YOUR YOUNG ADULT

You may not think you would be able to influence your young adult that much, but what may differ from your own teenage years is that today's generation is likely to view their parents as 'trusted mentors' or role models.[7] In other words, for the youngest generation of adults their *parents* are their heroes alongside pop stars, celebrities or well-known figures. Of Generation X (those born between 1965 and 1980) only 29 per cent named their parents as heroes, but of Generation Z a whopping 69 per cent view them as their number one role models.[8] This relationship – of parents as mentors – means that parents are emerging as the person young people turn to for advice, to talk things through with and to guide them, but not instruct them. The authors of *Generation Z Goes to College* surveyed 1100 college students and found that it was likely to be the honesty, trust and openness that their parents had displayed early in their lives that had fostered such a relationship.[9]

Give your teenager hugs even if they seem awkward. One 16-year-old girl told us how every night as she lay in bed she would hear her mum walk past her bedroom door to go to bed, and she would hope her mum would pop in to say goodnight or hug her, but she never did. The mum was just trying to give her daughter privacy and space, but neither felt able to say anything to the other, so it is vital to offer your teenager a hug and see how they react, even if they're not always in the mood. Sometimes they will reluctantly accept it, sometimes they will push you away, but they will always know that you are there. Build closeness and intimacy where you can.

The young people we spoke to for this book craved relationships with their parents where they could talk openly, but in some cases had found it difficult to be honest in their relationships because of what they viewed as harsh, unfair or hypocritical boundaries. They were absolutely in favour of boundaries, but hoped for a more negotiated approach to agreeing them, with compromise, not immediate 'shutting down' of discussions. Sixth formers in particular felt that they needed to learn how to be able to go out safely at night, ready for university or the workplace, and that if their parents said 'no' to all their requests to go out with friends, they might not have the skills to self-manage once they left home. Other young people told us that because they felt their parents were 'too strict', they always halved the amount they told them they had drunk on a night out, rather than feeling able to be honest. This could, in turn, reduce the likelihood of them asking for help if they needed it when out.

PARENT POINTER

- Honesty, trust and openness certainly seem to be a good way for both sides to build and create mentoring relationships, though knowing how challenging communicating with teenagers can be, parents may need to add patience to the list! Keeping the communication channel open is vital even in difficult times.

This chimes with what Ros, the mother of an independent and happy 18-year-old daughter, told us:

> I think the best advice you can give parents is to encourage them to have open conversations with their kids (be non-judgemental) and show that you trust your kids from an early age. Let them see that if they are open and honest with you, you'll give them more freedom. This builds a virtuous circle of trust. I saw many examples with teens where the kids lied about being out, about being in the park and so on, and where the parents showed no trust in the kids (for example, walking into their bedrooms without knocking). This is something to be avoided if at all possible.
>
> I have an open and enjoyable relationship with my daughter. I don't know everything about her life and I wouldn't want to, but I know enough. I trust her and we enjoy being together.

Below are some suggestions – from students, pupils, parents and teachers – for bonding activities:

- going out for a family walk or mountain bike ride
- playing board games
- birdwatching
- following a sports team together
- going on a road trip to visit something fun (like a theme park) or to the seaside
- retail therapy (a dad told us how much he enjoyed going shopping with his teenage daughter, especially if she eventually bought something that he had picked out!)
- doing courses together, such as cooking or textiles: these could be really good fun, not just for your young people but for the whole family

THE ROLE OF THE FAMILY

Family plays a key role is supporting young people and, as before, we will use the terms 'parent' here to also mean 'carer' or 'supporter', though pupils and students without a family can be disadvantaged and need extra support. Ninety per cent of students describe themselves as 'close to their families', and it is well recognised that close family attachments set children up for positive relationships in the future as well as helping them to manage their own emotions better.[10,11]

Teenagers and students generally welcome parent involvement and support in many ways, especially around academic stress points, such as exams or deadlines, and families can dispense positive motivation in person or at the end of the phone, boosting their self-belief or reminding them of their aspirations and of the bigger picture, when needed. Ellie, a confident and bubbly third-year university student in Leeds, was clear about loving her new-found independence while also appreciating her mum's support at the end of the phone when she was unwell. She said:

> If you're not feeling great, it can be so reassuring to hear your mum tell you that it is okay to take a day off, or for her to be sympathetic and advise me if I need to go to the health centre, but not to get too involved. That sort of support is brilliant.

Families are also brilliant at providing perspective if young people are unsure about school-related decisions or thinking of dropping out of uni, not by telling them what to do or by being 'preachy', but by listening, exploring what is happening for them at the time and discussing options and where to get reliable advice.

Young people say they want someone to care about them, to share their frustrations with, to rant to, and occasionally to pick up the pieces, but the secret to doing this successfully as a parent, of course, is knowing when to step in, when to coach from the sidelines and when to step back.

Australian counselling psychologist Annie Andrews advises:

The parent's challenge is to become a 'guide on the side' who practises respectful and compassionate listening. When the parent can hear the words, read the behaviour and search to understand the underlying emotion before responding from their parent perspective, they can step into the role of the wise guide. Young people will trust and accept a guide who respects and understands their challenges and knows that maturity grows over time. They need their guide to respond compassionately to the sharp retorts, the errors of judgement and the emotional outbursts.

PARENT POINTER

- It may feel difficult to imagine having a positive mentoring relationship with your teenager if they are at the uncommunicative or irritable stage right now, but with time and patience, your unconditional love, your consistent availability to listen to them if they need it, your non-judgemental approach, your compassion when they need support and your advice given *when asked for* will evolve into a supportive and trusting relationship longer term.

Some parents also take a positive 'coaching' approach to motivate their young adult, setting goals with them or helping them to problem-solve. This can involve asking them questions to help them reflect on what they should do, such as 'What do you think might work?' or 'What would happen if you didn't do this?' The key is to try approaches that suit you and your child and find what works for you both, over time. One student, Georgiana, told us, 'One of the best questions parents can ask is "Are you okay?" and really mean it. Really listening for the answer. It's less helpful if they say "Are you having a great time?" which assumes that you should be, and can be hard to say "no" to.' If in doubt, ask open questions, listen and offer what support you can. (And perhaps ask if they would like to hear it, *before* offering an opinion or viewpoint!)

THE BENEFITS OF SOLITUDE

We have previously mentioned the negative impacts of loneliness on our health, but what about solitude? Is *being* alone the same as *feeling* alone? Solitude is the state of being alone and it might in fact have really positive benefits, which our young people have yet to understand and recognise.

To recharge our batteries, we need to unplug both from people and work. It is not only necessary for our brain to have time away from pressure, but it's also essential for our wellbeing (emotional, mental, physical, social and spiritual).

Many articles in the press have already told us about the benefits of solitude: time to reboot our brain and unwind.[12] Unfortunately, our children rarely seek to be in alone or in silence to unwind. The minute they are on their own, they pull their phones out to listen to music or to check their newsfeeds on social media.

It is not that they don't understand that time in nature, sitting looking at squirrels or walking in a wood is not helpful.

They simply feel they have constant distractions and don't connect with nature as much as in the past. Solitude is a frequently cited motive for visiting parks, forests and wilderness areas. Solitude can bring freedom, creativity, intimacy and spirituality.[13]

Work on American adolescents' experience of solitude confirms that being alone is an essential contribution to development and mental health.[14] And although the teenagers in the study didn't describe their time alone as a positive experience, the majority did admit to feeling better afterwards. Furthermore, the same study showed that 'kids who spent between a quarter and a half of their non-class time alone tended to have more positive emotions over the course of the study than their more socially active peers, were more successful in school and were less likely to self-report depression'. Time spent alone actually made them feel better, and do better at school.

PARENT POINTERS

- We should encourage our children to learn to spend time on their own (from secondary school age). Teaching our children that it is beneficial to be bored or to spend time alone in their thoughts and reflecting (not the same as 'in isolation'), is vital.
- Let's familiarise ourselves with the benefits of boredom: increased creativity and productivity; motivation to change goals or tasks; more future planning; and more altruistic behaviours and increased happiness.[15] Might this be enough to embrace boredom?
- We need to role-model taking time to stop and be with others, or sometimes be alone.

DATING

Relationships are not only limited to family and friends of course, but also to dating.

And, with the introduction of matchmaking and Internet online services and apps, our approach to dating changed. In 1995 Match.com appeared and things slowly evolved, so that now we have multiple dating apps available.[16] Online dating is now the second most common way for couples to meet, though meeting through friends is still number one.[17] But do these apps make dating easier for our children? Not necessarily. Some students tell of countless meaningless 'hook-ups', while others, like 24-year-old Ben, told us that it was much easier and simpler when he was younger. If he liked someone, he told them and, if they felt the same way, they got together. Now, things are much more complicated (and frustrating).

The new approach to dating

It would appear that many young people have a different approach to the one Ben described, which might be more familiar to older adults. Forget about telling someone you like them face-to-face or on the phone, our children are the kings and queens of instant messaging. Except that instant messaging is not very 'instant' as they report spending a lot of time working and reworking their messages.

Young people have become very strategic about their responses and feel that responding straightaway comes across as 'desperate' and too available. They will therefore wait before they respond to show that they are busy or unattached. Much as their parents' generation would have played 'hard to get' so they do even with instant messaging. There is a casual culture of hook-ups and 'friends with benefits', which means that serious dating is not as valued as it was (and this may partly explain why there is a rise of sexually transmitted diseases being reported).[18] It would seem that young people are focused on sex and it is now more easily available than ever. This is referred to as the 'Tinder effect' – the huge increase in dating apps has made casual encounters and dating easier, but it is not necessarily leading to long-term relationship success. Interestingly, even teenagers who told us that they were not yet sexually active still used the same language, such as 'hooking up'. Most of the time sex doesn't lead to a relationship, but simply leads to more one-night stands because 'going steady', or as they would say 'being exclusive', is not really the norm for the younger generation.

If the relationship is not working out and they want to end it, young people 'ghost' each other. They don't bother telling the other person; they simply stop responding to texts or instant messages. This means that the 'It's not you, it's me' conversation that we might have had just doesn't happen anymore. As Lucy said to us, 'If the other person is upset, well, it's not really my problem – it is the other person's issue and it is for them to solve.'

PARENT POINTERS

- Be aware of this approach to dating and try to have informed conversations with your young person about what it is like from their perspective. From a young age it can be useful to discuss romantic relationships.
- Emphasise how important it is to respect others' feelings and the need to be considerate.

- If you want your child to share with you, try not to overreact to things emotionally. Try not to get angry and, most importantly, don't bring things up too often (even if you are worried). Having a calm discussion will be much more productive.

The language of dating

In order to understand modern dating and flirting, it may be helpful to learn some of the words young adults might use in their daily lives:[19]

Catfish: originally a term used when someone adopts a totally fake online persona, traditionally to take advantage or manipulate someone (for online fraud), it is now meant in a more informal sense. A 'catfish' is someone who uses flattering photos of themselves on dating apps to reel people in, before meeting up with them in real life.

Chirpsing: the same as flirting, and the 'chirpse' is the person they are flirting with.

Cracking on: means deciding to seriously flirt with someone.

Cuffing season: refers to the cold winter months when young people might start looking for a relationship and someone to cuddle up to during those cold dark nights.

Exclusive: commitment, security and long-term relationships are not necessarily the Tinder generation's favourite activity. 'Exclusive' means that they agree not to see anyone else (but they are not 'officially' in a relationship).

Feels or catching feels: meant as a negative and means that someone might start liking a friend with benefits or might have feelings for a friend, which was not 'part of the deal'.

Gaslighting: when someone emotionally manipulates the other person and makes them doubt their own understanding of events, making them feel bad for their actions.

Ghosting: involves 'dropping' someone completely online; when, even after a couple of dates, without any warning they stop replying and provide no explanation.

Grafting: the agonising and elongated process of trying to attract the chirpse's attention.

Online flirting: not so much a word but a concept. Online flirting, or 'social media chirpsing' as it is sometimes known, is when you 'have a thing' for someone, so you consistently 'like' their recent Instagram posts/Tweets/Facebook updates.

Proofing: sending a copy of a message to a group of friends (usually via group chat) so that they can help you to respond. Just as the name suggests, they help draft, edit and proofread the response to a text.

Sliding into the DMs: refers to messaging someone on social media but with flirtatious motivations. DMs – or 'direct message' – is the messaging system on Twitter.

The 'Ick': they go out on a few dates with someone and it is going well and then suddenly, for no real reason, they start getting annoyed with the person, not liking anything they do or say.

A final word of advice: don't try to use these words (it will be *painful* for your young adult to hear!). Just bear them in mind and consider the shift in dating etiquette to a shorter term, less personal (online) and shared (with *many* friends) experience of starting relationships.

Dealing with the first breakup

This may be something you are dreading, or you may already have supported (or survived!) the first heartbreak, but our advice here would be similar to that for dealing with other difficult events or behaviours: listen, believe and give hope.

Really listen to what your child is feeling, and resist the urge to dismiss it or make it all better straightaway. Believe how they feel (if it felt momentous to them, then it was momentous, even if you didn't like the ex) and gently encourage them to have hope that things will get better slowly and with time. It can help to recommend a 'tech break' from social media for a while and to distract them with other activities, or give them time alone to recover.[20] Be guided by them, and be available if they need to talk.

SEXUALITY, GENDER AND IDENTITY

The youngest generation seems to be the most tolerant and accepting of people who choose not to ascribe themselves a gender, who are non-binary (not exclusively male or female) or who are transitioning from one gender to another, and in our day-to-day lives we will witness this tolerance as we use unisex public toilets or tick bureaucratic forms asking us to choose 'male/female/prefer not to specify'. Similarly, many cultures and societies, though there are notable exceptions, are moving towards much greater inclusion and support for LGBT+ communities and couples, as 'gay marriage' becomes just 'marriage' and equality is driven forwards in schools, in the workplace and in higher education.

Discovering and declaring one's sexual or gender identity can be a huge milestone in many people's lives, and many factors will determine how early or late in life (if ever) people will feel able to be themselves and reveal that to those they love.

Many well-intentioned and loving parents struggle with their child's sexuality. Plenty will, of course, barely bat an eyelid when their young person comes out, but it may be helpful to bear a few things in mind if this topic feels relevant for you. It is important for parents not to make assumptions, for example by asking your son 'Have you got a girlfriend yet?' Dom Smithies from the charity Student Minds shared some very helpful insights with us, which may prove useful to you:

When a parent asks, 'I think my child is gay; what should I do?' it implies that there is something that needs to *be* done, but actually the young person may not be ready to discuss their sexuality, they may not have insight themselves or they might find it awkward. After all, you don't need to 'do' anything when you discover a child is not gay. Initially try to be guided by them, and if you would like to do something then be supportive indirectly, perhaps by making positive comments about openly gay celebrities or by watching TV programmes or films with gay storylines together, and making *subtle* positive comments.

Dom adds that once they have come out, it is really important to be supportive and say reassuring things such as, 'Nothing will change for me; I love you just as you are.' Try to avoid comments like 'I just feel sad for you' because you worry about potential LGBT+-related challenges in their life, as they may in fact feel much happier 'being themselves', so would love you to be happy for them too. And find a balance between being happy for them and being 'too inclusive', in other words you might offer to go to Pride with them, but don't insist – it may be 'their space' and they may wish to keep it private.

Finally, a word about the first holiday at home after they come out, which can be tricky if they have come out at uni but not at home. They may decide to hide their sexuality again, or they make go to the other extreme and be very ostentatious about their sexuality, but it is worth being aware that this is a challenging time for them, and being supportive and tolerant will be appreciated as they find their way. Support from loved ones is also one of the greatest protective factors for LGBT+ young people against self-harm and suicide.[21] Family acceptance can make all the difference.

PARENT POINTER

- It is important to ask if your child wishes you to share their news with others or if they wish it to remain confidential until they are ready. This may be particularly important for certain communities or cultures, where added understanding may be needed.

SEX AND RELATIONSHIP ISSUES

The influence of pornography

Surveys show that only a small percentage of kids seek out pornography on purpose, and most respond appropriately by quickly leaving the site, though few report such incidents to parents.[22] For example, a survey carried out in 2014 with 500

18-year-old participants found that 8 out of 10 said that it was 'too easy for them to accidentally see pornography online'.[23] Therefore, as with so many difficult teenage behaviours, it is important to ask 'Why?' if you discover that your child has been viewing sexually explicit online material. Why have they looked for it? Try and assess whether this is simply out of curiosity because they are trying to find out more about sex and their own sexuality, or if it has become a problem and is an ongoing issue. Your approach will depend on what you find, but remaining calm is important whatever the reason.

Dr Lynn Margolies is a psychologist looking after students at Harvard Medical School. She recommends trying to have an open and sensitive discussion about what they are looking at.[24] She adds that if curiosity is the main reason then we should simply accept that this is what teenagers or preteens do and know that the impact is likely to be low and no long-term issues are likely to follow. If, however, our children are looking at pornographic sites on a regular basis, this may have potentially detrimental effects and she believes that it may be motivated or perpetuated by loneliness, isolation and compulsion. While it can be difficult to know for sure what your teenager is looking at, having a conversation that mentions the risks of repeated or compulsive viewing may offer an opportunity to educate them.

Dr Margolies writes that in the absence of any context, and without having learnt about or known healthy sexuality, young people may find some of the sexual scenes they watch confusing and take the images they see to be representative of 'real' adult behaviour. The issue with this is that they are introduced to sex before they are ready, through images they do not understand, which often involve sex detached from relationships or meaning, responsibility and intimacy.

This is again confirmed by the survey mentioned above where 7 out of 10 respondents said that 'pornography led to unrealistic attitudes to sex' and that it 'can have a damaging impact on young people's views of sex or relationships'.[25] Almost 8 out of 10 young women said 'pornography has led to pressure on girls or young women to *look* a certain way', while almost as many said that 'pornography has led to pressure on girls and young women to *act* a certain way'. This is a comment that has been echoed by many of the students we interviewed. It would seem that young people wish it wasn't as easy to have access to pornography, with two-thirds of young women and almost half of young men surveyed agreeing that 'it would be easier growing up if pornography was less easy to access for young people'.

Young people are most at risk when they see pictures which are overstimulating and potentially addictive. Dr Margolies warns that: 'If viewed compulsively and accompanied by sexual release through masturbating, Internet pornography can have a desensitizing effect, requiring greater intensity and frequency [of access]', which could potentially lead to cybersex (online) addiction.

Another danger teens are exposed to online is unwanted sexual solicitation.[26] Teens are the most vulnerable of any age group to such unwanted sexual advances. An estimated 1 in 7 American youths aged between 10 and 17 received at least one unwanted sexual solicitation or approach over the Internet in a one-year period. This can be from unwanted male or female 'admirers'. And it doesn't just happen at school age, but at university too.

To protect your teen, it will be most effective to work with them and discuss potential risks and scenarios, taking opportunities that arise from TV or in the press, and consider practical ways for them to stay safe, rather than trying to impose rules or tech boundaries which they might be able to work around, and which will not prepare them for the wider world. Building trust and remaining calm are the two essential instruments for navigating this particular deep water with your young adult.

> ## PARENT POINTERS
>
> - Talk to your young adult and give them comfort, reassurance and support so that they know that it is safe to talk to you and to share.
> - If you want to be aware of what is going on, make your home a 'safe place' that encourages sharing and communication. Just because your child has looked at pornographic material a few times does not mean that they will become sex addicts. Most young people and teenagers don't develop an addiction. There is no need to panic or to chastise them. Anger will not make them more likely to bring their worries to you.

Consent

Sexual consent is a tricky topic and, unsurprisingly, parents worry about their child staying safe. It may help to bring the idea of consent up with your child in snippets, over time, dropping it into conversation if it feels appropriate, for example when watching a film or TV programme, or when you hear a story on the radio or in the news about sexual assault or relationship difficulties. According to the NSPCC website, sexual consent means 'being able to say yes and agreeing to have sex or do sexual things'.[27]

Young women interviewed for this book told us of regularly being 'groped in nightclubs' and of being harassed when out, so they felt very strongly that parents should be prepared to have these difficult conversations with their children. Young people are now much clearer on what is and is not acceptable behaviour, and if they are not sure then they are probably more likely to challenge or ask about it.

The key messages to give to your child will always be about respect, building trust and only doing what feels comfortable, and not being pressured into any behaviours that they are unhappy about. For older teenagers there is the brilliant 'cup of tea' video on YouTube which you could send or mention to them (be aware – it does use the F word briefly).[28]

A 2016 report by Universities UK acknowledged that universities are a 'microcosm of society' and that, as approximately half of all young people now go to university, and the most common age to be sexually assaulted is between 16 and 19 for women, there was a need for universities to raise awareness and have policies and processes in place to ensure that students felt safe on campus.[29] Schools and universities themselves offer a lot of education and support around this topic, but it may help to share with them the information and facts in different formats and use analogies such as the 'cup of tea', that use humour to smooth over the awkwardness. Some students who have been at single-sex schools find themselves feeling less prepared for the consent conversations and for the occasional sexual harassment they encounter at uni, so it's important not to make assumptions about their 'consent education' and ensure that you bring up the subject yourself as a parent too.

Young people should also know what to do if they witness an assault ('bystander training') or if they experience it (how to report/get help).[30] Consent and bystander training and advice on sexual assault is now standard in most universities and in some workplaces.

PARENT POINTERS

- Practical tips for young adults may include telling them not only that they can say 'no', but they should not be afraid to say 'no' because they might hurt someone's feelings. It can be done firmly but kindly, and consent can be withdrawn at any time, so they can say 'stop' anytime they want to.
- Just because they may have had a relationship or sexual contact with someone in the past does not imply consent again in the future.
- If they are out and partying then they may wish to have a 'safe word' that they say or text with friends to indicate that they need support or help. Some students use personal safety apps, others complete online modules to learn about sexual consent and most young people are pleased to have had the 'consent' conversation even if it feels awkward at the time.[190]
- Sharing by email or text some of the resources that you've found may avoid some of the awkwardness, if you prefer.

THINKING POINTS

The importance of strong friendships and social networks are undeniable. There is no doubt that social health (or social ill health) is one of the most powerful factors for the well-being of human beings. We have seen that there are specific things that young people can do to enhance the benefits of these relationships on their levels of happiness. There has also been a shift in attitude to dating and intimate relationships, so parents need to be prepared to talk to their young people about this, teaching them to value other people's feelings, and helping children to build the skills needed for creating and maintaining a whole variety of personal relationships throughout life. They need to learn what it means to be a good friend: to show loyalty, to be trustworthy and to take an interest in another person's life, as well as having fun with them and sharing interests or passions.

Here are a few things to consider:

- Remember to disconnect from work and stress regularly (and encourage your children to do the same).
- Do stuff as a family. Find activities you can enjoy together – be creative.
- Use self-compassion.
- Encourage your children to enjoy solitude, and be bored sometimes.
- Try to help them learn to communicate with a variety of people and to read emotions.
- Teach your children about being thoughtful in their relationships with their friends, or boy/girlfriends and to be kind online too.
- Don't be afraid to talk to them about sex and relationships, when it feels acceptable or appropriate, to emphasise that porn is not like real life, and that they should only ever do things (with regards to sex) that they are comfortable and happy to do.
- Have difficult conversations about sexual consent.
- Accept them for who they are, whatever their sexuality or gender.

CHAPTER 8

Alcohol, Illicit and Study Drugs

lcohol and drugs will always feature in the teen and young adult landscape, but behaviours are changing, and parents may need to challenge their own assumptions and approaches to dealing with these milestone topics.

In Australia 55 per cent of high school teenagers are teetotal, compared with 30 per cent 15 years ago.[1] A quarter of the UK's younger generation drinks no alcohol at all.[2] In fact, this age group is less likely to drink alcohol than any other age group. However, though Generation Z may drink less overall, when they do, they really go for it and tend to binge drink. The young adults we spoke to told us they 'drink to get drunk'. Trying to find out *why* they are drinking too much (or using drugs), if they are, will be the first step in any recovery process.

There is a particular stereotype of students as big drinkers, and there is indeed a drinking culture at university, but it is also true that nowadays 1 in 5 students is teetotal, mirroring the decrease in drinking occurring in 16–24-year-olds in the general UK population.[3] Luckily, it has become a lot easier to say 'no thanks' or drink less as a student, and some universities now have alcohol-free ('party-free') halls of residence, as well as there being multiple alcohol-free social events on offer.

GETTING WASTED: THE RISKS

If your young adult *is* going to drink then they need to understand the potential risks, in particular of binge drinking. Drinking alcohol will make your liver, heart and kidneys less healthy, but these factors may not interest a young person who thinks they are indestructible. They may also point out that *you* drink, so 'why does it matter' if they drink. A more effective and pragmatic approach may be to have an open and honest conversation, accepting that it is likely that they will drink, but pointing out some things that may catch their attention, such as how much money they might spend on alcohol, the weight gain that comes with drinking (the Americans call it 'Freshman Fifteen' as students who drink typically gain 15lbs in their first term at uni) or that their studying and learning will be adversely affected. It can also play out badly in the workplace when they are trying to impress senior colleagues, and arriving with a hangover will not help performance or reputation. And we all know how wrong the office Christmas party can go, though participating in other work social events also needs to be done judiciously. This may be something they will take to heart as they are trying to prove themselves and achieve something.

Alcohol also affects self-control and memory, brain development (and the brain *is* still developing significantly until their mid-twenties), especially their motivation and reasoning, and also leads to poor-quality sleep, so they will be at risk of underperforming academically or in the workplace, when they really need to be hitting the ground running.

When talking about risks, it is worth stressing (without scaremongering) that alcohol is associated with many negative, and some more serious, long-term, outcomes, including:

- being a victim of a crime or assault
- sustaining injury

- experiencing an unplanned pregnancy or contracting a sexually transmitted infection
- poor mental health
- self-harm
- suicide

It's important to try not to come across as attempting to scare them, but an open and frank discussion of these risks may allow young adults to make better informed decisions about when and if they choose to drink.

Alcohol and mental health

Unfortunately, there can be no doubt that alcohol negatively affects mental well-being. It is a depressant, makes anxiety worse in the long run and increases the risk of self-harm and suicide.[4] While we may think of young people using alcohol for relaxation, socialising and fun, it is common for them to also use it for 'self-medication' of anxiety, low mood, social anxiety (shyness) and poor sleep. It seems cruelly ironic, therefore, that it will make all of these situations worse. Although alcohol is a sedative and will numb them, it has also been shown to cause depression via biochemical effects it has on the brain and metabolism, and although it may initially briefly alleviate anxiety it will then lead to a rebound higher level of anxiety soon after.[5,6] This is now colloquially known as 'hangxiety' (that increased anxiety that comes with a hangover).

Alcohol and sleep

The enormous effect of alcohol on sleep (particularly critical because of the importance of sleep for so many functions, not least of all study and learning) is eye-opening. If you are struggling to get a cautionary message about excessive alcohol across to your young person, then discussing sleep and sleep quality may prove a useful way in, as the evidence is black and white and young adults traditionally love their sleep.

In his fascinating book *Why We Sleep*, Matthew Walker explains how alcohol is falsely believed to be helpful in inducing sleep, whereas alcohol in fact sedates us but does not lead to natural sleep. It leads to a fragmented night of repeated (mainly unnoticed) awakenings, which leads to exhaustion the following day. It also prevents dream (REM) sleep, which is essential for memory processing and thus learning. It basically leads to partial amnesia, even when people are only a little drunk before sleep. Pupils and students will forget between 40 and 50 per cent of what they have learnt in a day when alcohol is drunk that night, or even three nights, *after* studying.[7] So the young person who has a really great revision session and then goes out that evening to relax and drinks a few pints will actually be wiping out about 50 per cent of what they have just learnt, which is a sobering(!) thought. Similarly, in the workplace a young adult who has learnt about a new topic (in law, accountancy, medicine, and so on) and who then drinks over any of the next three nights will also be at risk of significant memory loss, negatively impacting their ability to do their job well and impress their boss.

PARENT POINTERS

- A conversation about binge drinking, self-care and safety is important: 'Spread your drinking over the week; don't drink all your recommended allowance in one night.'
- Talking about drinking in terms of cost, weight gain or academic impact might be more effective than talking about liver damage when discussing alcohol.

- If a young person is feeling low then a relatively easy first step can be to stop alcohol for a few weeks (as long as they are not dependent on it, in which case stopping should only be done with medical support), to see if their mood brightens or the anxiety fades away.

- Your young adult may argue that alcohol is helping them by numbing their feelings, lessening anxiety or helping them sleep, but the reality is that it is actually making things worse. Understanding *why* they are using it will help address the issue.

- A sleep diary or app can prove useful for monitoring sleep, alcohol and energy levels or anxiety, and reflecting on performance.

- And it may be boring advice, but abstinence from alcohol really will help them to learn and remember better when studying. So even if they don't abstain all year round, they might like to consider doing so at revision and exam time. This might also be helpful for high-pressure times at work, for optimum performance.

DRUG USE

While drug use in the young is reducing dramatically within the UK population, as well as in many other countries, some doctors have told us that they are seeing certain types of drug use being 'normalised'. One doctor said she had recently had a consultation with a bright, engaged student, who, when asked if he used any street drugs, replied, 'Oh no, just a bit of MDMA [ecstasy], cocaine and ketamine. Nothing bad.' Other young people have mentioned the casual use of Xanax (a sedative benzodiazepine, similar to Valium) to zone out for hours at a time. It seems that this relaxed point of view may be increasingly common among students.

The attitude taken by many, from teenagers through to 20-somethings, is that drugs are everywhere, that they need to know about them, not be told 'just say no' and that it is better to be informed, with many believing that alcohol is a bigger danger. They feel very strongly that parents and teachers take too negative a view – 'Don't do drugs – you'll end up homeless/ an addict/dead' – whereas most of them just want to know the facts in a balanced way. Taking too apocalyptic a standpoint prevents a helpful conversation, which might allow them to feel more informed and in control. Many choose to say no to drugs because they *know* that they are not regulated, that they won't know what they are taking or they are worried about the effects, but they want to know what the effects might be and how to help their friends if they are taken unwell when taking drugs.

If, as parents, we are to convey the dangers of drug-taking, such as the significantly higher risk of certain long-term mental health disorders, we need to know our facts and whether such facts relate to regular or occasional use, and which drugs cause specific problems.[8] The evidence to date clearly shows that using cannabis under the age of 18 leads to a higher likelihood of depression and psychosis in adulthood, but we have little evidence about the risk for individuals who only occasionally smoke compared with those who use regularly, and the impact of high-grade cannabis ('skunk') compared with 'weed' for example. Starting a conversation with open questions (that don't lead to a yes or no answer only) such as, 'What do your friends think about drugs?' may allow for a non-judgemental and balanced discussion. And try to remember that trying drugs is not the same as regular drug use, so don't panic or overreact in either situation, and certainly not if they are just experimenting.

PARENT POINTERS

- Looking at expert websites (such as Frank – see page 312) together may be helpful for young teenagers, and signposting older ones to them may be a reasonable approach, but we need to avoid an overly negative tone, without trying to be too 'cool' and permissive.
- Realism mixed with credible facts is the key to successful drug education.
- Get professional help from your doctor if drug or alcohol use is interfering with family or daily life.
- Ask for help yourself from experts, if you feel worried or need support too.

Jo Mallinson, a young people's drug and alcohol specialist and founder of the BE Project which works with schools on drug education, told us: 'Parents may not realise how much influence they have over their teenage children, even if their teenager stops talking to them. They are still listening, and parents should maintain the relationship and the boundaries. Don't assume you have no influence, especially on important topics like drug misuse.'

She also warned against taking a 'cool' parent approach to cannabis, for example allowing your teenager to smoke it at home 'because at least then you know where they are'. She believes that putting up 'barriers' and making it harder for them makes it easier for them to stop or say no. Well-intentioned attempts to 'keep them safe' may instead *facilitate* an unhealthy behaviour. It will be a personal decision, and depend on family circumstances, but not making it easy may actually be something your child will be grateful for in the longer term.

TEENAGE PARTIES

It's not a great idea to host teenage parties at home, but here are some ideas for keeping teens safe, whether or not you are the host:

- Avoid open invitations via social media – stick to a known guest list.
- Have a calm conversation with your teen about party rules and agree them in advance, advise them to avoid alcohol and drugs and why, so that they understand your concerns, and also how to stay safe/to call you for help or a lift immediately if they are worried.
- Be present in the house if you are hosting and they are under 18, or ensure adults will be present where they are going, though keep a low profile.
- Provide lots of soft drinks and water and carb-heavy snacks, and be aware that alcohol will be snuck in, so keep an eye out for anyone becoming unwell or vulnerable. Don't leave them unattended and do call for help or their parent – it is not illegal in the UK for children (over five) to drink alcohol in private premises, but it can lead to dangerous situations.[9]
- Lock away prescription medications and your own alcohol supply.
- Have a zero tolerance approach to drug use.
- Patrol the bedrooms and watch out for non-consensual activity.
- Warn the neighbours and be ready for the clean-up operation.[10]

Which drugs and why?

A few students have told us that they now use cocaine before exams in a bid to stay alert, and many use study ('smart') drugs regularly for academic work, but the commonest drug used by students is cannabis.[11] MDMA (ecstasy) comes in second and is followed by cocaine and nitrous oxide ('Nos'/laughing gas), according to the National Union of Students 2017/18 survey.[12] They also found that students were most likely to take drugs at home or in accommodation, or at house parties on 'special occasions'. Drugs were generally taken for recreational purposes, though most students said they did not feel pressured to take them. About 4 out of 10 respondents in the survey took them to ease their social interactions and, worryingly, around a third to 'self-medicate' anxiety or mental health issues. In schoolchildren, cannabis is also the commonest drug used, and Class A drug use (cocaine, heroin) is extremely rare. They also sometimes use Nos or new psychoactive substances, also known as 'legal highs'.[13]

One dad we spoke to mentioned his son Dan's use of cannabis, and how he had used it to self-medicate for anxiety, but that unfortunately the anxiety became worse with the drug use. Dan was also then more likely to binge drink when he was stoned. This made him vulnerable, so his dad sat down with him and worked out a 'plan of action' for what to do if he was ever in trouble or difficulty: who to call, where to get help and useful resources, all programmed into his phone for easy access. A 'disaster action plan' may be an approach you wish to talk through with your child.

On the whole, when we spoke to young people they knew where to get help if they need it, tending to go online for information. Disturbingly, they were not all aware of the potential criminal, or university disciplinary, consequences of drug use, especially when they are used on university premises. This might be something to discuss with your young person, as they may never have considered it. Each university has its own drugs policy so it is worth them being aware of their own institution's regulations. School pupils may also not be aware of just how hard a school might come down on them if they are found to be using or involved with drugs, so this might be another conversation to have.

Students and senior school pupils we spoke to advised against parents assuming, 'Oh my child wouldn't do drugs, they're too sensible,' as actually drugs are present at most parties, so realistic and balanced advice is more effective. In university cities, drug dealers will target student houses and accommodation by putting cards and leaflets through their doors marked 'dentist' or 'lawnmower repairs' with a phone number, which are clearly not genuine professional businesses. Students recognise the cards and can work their way through them if the first dealer doesn't answer. Other students meet dealers in dark alleys or get into the back of local dealers' cars to buy. The risks they take can be significant. Parental awareness and realism is therefore essential.

PARENT POINTERS

- Suggest your young adult watches the short YouTube film called *No Smoking in the Booth* about Grime artist Jammer, if they use cannabis, or if you think it might help them to recognise the dangers of high-grade cannabis (skunk), although it probably isn't suitable for younger viewers, and the message is not 'don't do drugs' but 'if you're going to smoke weed, don't smoke skunk'.[14]

- It's about knowing what they are getting into and understanding the dangers to their mental health. It may help you to start a conversation without asking them to stop completely if they aren't ready for that. Brief discussions, if opportunities arise, may be one way to bring the topic up, such as when a news article mentions drugs.
- Spotting the signs of drug misuse can be tricky in teenagers, but key things to look out for include: isolation and withdrawing, mood swings, erratic behaviour, petty crime and friends who use drugs.
- If your teen is already involved in drugs and you need more active help, the NHS, schools, universities and the voluntary sector are all set up to help you, so do reach out and ask for advice, guidance and support through what can be a very difficult and emotional time.

STUDY ('SMART') DRUGS

Using medication for performance enhancement is hardly new, and the use of prescription drugs for non-medical reasons, to boost mental performance or to stay awake, was a habit of historical figures as varied as JFK and Hitler (and apparently James Bond in *Casino Royale*).[15,16,17] In the UK, students tend to use medications that are usually prescribed for Attention Deficit Disorder (ADD) such as Ritalin (related to amphetamines) or those prescribed to help people with narcolepsy (which leads people to fall asleep suddenly despite being active), such as Provigil. Students may also buy medications such as Adderall online, which is licensed for ADD in the USA but not in the UK, and which is a combination of two stimulants: amphetamine and dextroamphetamine. The list of side effects of all study drugs is long and the risks of using them when they have not been prescribed for you are significant.[18] One of the main risks is that what you order online and think you are taking may not be what you're actually taking.[19] Many drugs bought online are not pure, have been tampered with or are counterfeit (fake).

This is true, of course, for many illicit or street drugs and, in Bristol, a not-for-profit charity The Loop has become the first in the UK to offer an anonymous test to check the actual chemical content of your stash.[20] They will analyse it and tell you what's in it, and then destroy the sample or give it to the police for their information, but not for investigation. Counselling and support is offered alongside and, so far, one in five samples has been found to be contaminated, and nearly half of users in the pilot said they would stop or reduce their drug use as a consequence. It is proving an effective way to reduce harm and educate users.

Many students will say that study drugs 'work' for them and are therefore not keen to quit, so it is worth finding out what they mean by 'work'. Medications created to keep people awake (Provigil) will definitely keep you awake, which is, in itself, completely counterproductive to good learning and effective memory (see Chapter 11)! The drugs that they take for 'memory, concentration and focus enhancement' have been shown in studies to have minimal, if any, (clinically significant) benefits, so it may be that if a student is finding that ADD meds help them, they may in fact have undiagnosed ADD![21] It's definitely worth your student having an assessment with an educational psychologist or at their university Disability Service if this is the case. Importantly, study drugs have not been shown to be effective and they don't make you smarter.

PARENT POINTERS

- If you think your student could be using study drugs, or is tempted to use them, it may be helpful to discuss any pressure they are feeling that is leading them to consider or use them. They may feel exceptional academic pressure; they may struggle with time management and be using them to stay up all night to meet work deadlines; or they may feel that the playing field is uneven and this is the only way to keep up with their peers.

- Having a calm, balanced conversation about the potential risks and side effects, and about ways to manage the pressure (or time-management skills), may be helpful to them.

Young people may have no idea that such medications could be dangerous because they know that lots of young people take them for ADD. They may not be aware that they are linked to anxiety, heart palpitations, high blood pressure and headaches, among other side effects.[22] Rarely, Ritalin can also be associated with seizures, hallucinations and heart attacks.[23] It may feel less worthwhile taking the risk when they realise this. They may also wish to bear in mind that universities will have policies about the use of study drugs and may consider them to be cheating.

When experts are asked by students what they can do to optimise their studying capabilities, be effective and efficient and perform as well as they can, *instead* of taking study drugs, the answer is remarkably simple ... get at least eight hours of sleep a night (see Chapter 11)! The benefits of sleep on learning are proven beyond a doubt and there are no side effects. The benefits of study drugs are debatable and they can be dangerous. Sleep is definitely the better and safer bet!

THINKING POINTS

Alcohol and drugs are ever present in young people's lives and, even if they avoid them, their friends might not, so being aware and informed in a balanced way is vital. Any conversation about alcohol or drugs should be calm and realistic, and young people need to be able to make their own decisions. Online resources are plentiful if you are keen to know more about individual drugs or how they might interact, but it is an ever-changing body of knowledge with new drugs appearing on the scene all the time, so principles may be more helpful than specifics for keeping safe.

Study drugs are used frequently, but at what cost? Success by any means necessary may not be the way your young person really wants to go, so reflecting this back to them may help them reconsider. Young people's brains are remarkably 'plastic' and resilient, so the good news is that if they stop overusing alcohol and drugs they are likely to recover well and get back on track reasonably easily. The key to sustained success will be addressing the underlying reason for the overuse in the first place and asking for help early if you think it is needed.

Here are a few things to consider:

- Honesty and openness – and avoiding apocalyptic warnings – are key to success in discussing these topics with young people.
- Sleep is more effective than study drugs for academic performance (but alcohol will ruin any benefit, so avoid it at revision and exam times).

- Young people use drugs and alcohol for many reasons but mainly for fun or to relieve distress or anxiety. Talk to them about their own reasons and understand their 'why'.
- Don't be permissive and allow them to use drugs at home (or get drunk at home).
- Young people are highly influenced by 'social norms'. If they believe that everyone else is drinking they will likely wish to too, but if they realise that one in five students is now teetotal, for example, this might reduce their keenness to drink. Ground them in reality. Fewer young people are drinking these days and it's okay to say no too.

PART 4

FLYING THE NEST

CHAPTER 9

Learning to Adult: Life and Independence Skills

W e would argue that the first two decades of parenting are about guiding your children's development to allow them to function successfully and independently of you. This chapter will help you to navigate one of the biggest life changes for them (and for you!): when they leave home to start living and working independently, or for university.

Leaving home for university or a new job can be a wonderful opportunity, full of excitement and new experiences, but it can also be stressful, sometimes even resulting in psychological issues, such as anxiety, depression, sleep disturbance, reduction in self-esteem and isolation. Parents hope that their child will be eager for new friends, the chance to learn or follow their passion and enthusiastic about their new-found freedoms, and, for most, this is indeed what happens. However, for a few, the struggle to balance the competing demands of study or work and personal commitments (as well as financial pressures) can lead to significant declines in their overall health and well-being.

Experienced welfare professionals describe how, on the surface, a young person may have a veneer of maturity that can be misleading. It can lead us to think that our child is ready for independent life away from the home environment, without 24/7 support, but the reality sometimes is that at the first sign of pressure the veneer cracks, or even breaks, and they feel exposed and vulnerable as their dependence on parents and home support becomes all too visible. Building a deeper level of independence and genuine ability to manage bumps in the road will ensure the maturity is authentic.

Alan Percy, the well-respected Head of Student Counselling at the University of Oxford, who has 30 years of experience in caring for young people, describes students in transition, moving from home to university, as being 'like hermit crabs without a shell'. They have outgrown their 'home' shell but have yet to find their new 'university' shell and can feel vulnerable and defenceless in their unfamiliar environment, until they settle in and adapt with time. Preparing them as best we can for this sense of vulnerability may help them deal with it better. This is likely to be the case for young people leaving home for work too.

ANDREA'S STORY

Andrea's well-meaning parents had driven her to and from school until the very last day, in an attempt to keep her stress to a minimum and to allow her to 'focus on her studies', as well as to ensure timely attendance and to get her to all the school activities she enjoyed. When she started going out in the evenings with friends, in her teens, they collected her late at night, so that she would feel safe and be protected, and so that they wouldn't worry. It all made perfect sense, but, unfortunately, as a consequence Andrea did not develop her own travel independence, so when her gap-year trip arrived, the

first public bus she ever took was into central Bangkok.
It was quite an experience!

Andrea's may be an extreme case, but she is by no means alone. Her parents were doing what they thought was best for her – smoothing her path and removing obstacles – but they were also inadvertently removing opportunities for her to develop independence in terms of transport and travel skills. When students go to university, they not only very often move to a new city, but they also leave behind their support networks of family and friends and need to be independent very quickly. They need to have life skills.

LIFE SKILLS FOR INDEPENDENT LIVING

There are many life skills, of course, and learning to use public transport might be considered quite a minor or 'soft' life skill, whereas swimming is a life-saving life skill, but learning to shop for food, cook a few basic meals, do laundry, drive, manage money, earn a wage (Saturday or summer job) and make a doctor's or dentist appointment (and attend it alone) are all skills, somewhere between swimming and using public transport, that are needed for surviving life without your parents. Yet quite a few young adults have not achieved these by the time they arrive at college, university or the workplace. An Irish university nurse told us of a mother who flew out to Germany to unpack her son's luggage for him when he went on his senior school exchange placement abroad, which does seem extreme. More commonly, parents travel hundreds of miles across the UK each year to do their children's laundry at university, taking it to the laundrette or taking it home, but also taking with them a potential opportunity for their child to develop independence.

Parents with adult children in work have been known to make them a daily packed lunch or iron their shirts for them each week. This is all well-intentioned and kind, but ultimately undermines the young person's independence.

PARENT POINTER

- Think about which skills your young adult has already acquired, and which ones they need to master before leaving home. If they have already left home, are there some you could encourage them to learn? Below are some ideas about what you might try.

Learning to be a domestic god or goddess

Whether you run a tutorial on kitchen appliances for your teenager (to ensure they don't put a metal can of beans in a microwave and blow up the kitchen – true story!) or involve them in your rota for household chores, the important thing for them is to know how to avoid starvation or self-poisoning from poor food hygiene. Both professionals and parents emphasised to us how important basic domestic skills were for a less stressful independent life. Learning to do laundry, iron a shirt, sew on a button and keep things vaguely clean (especially shoes and toilets) will ensure they are not hated by flatmates, and can look presentable for interviews and important occasions like meeting their future 'out-laws'. Learning how to use a washing machine, hang out clothes and wash up are all basic skills for modern living.

When they are eight or nine years old you might start them off making their own breakfast, then sandwiches, then beans on toast and, as they get older, they might progress to making a meal for the family once a week. Advice from a counsellor on this topic was pragmatic:

> Don't be a family where every meal is 'on the table', so that they never know when they are hungry or what to do if they need food. Once they are older teenagers let them sometimes find their own pattern, and fend for themselves occasionally, then sometimes have family meals to catch up on news.

School cookery lessons are great, but not available everywhere, although some sixth forms have introduced 'cookery for uni or independence' lessons which focus on basic, tasty and reasonably healthy recipes that they can choose from (although some parents still prepare all the ingredients the night before – try to resist this!). Keep it simple and practical, and focus on three or four recipes they really like to eat, such as Bolognese, veggie pasta, cottage pie or curry.

Learning life skills should be useful, not just to tick a box on a Duke of Edinburgh Award checklist! Bear in mind that if your teen is applying for a gap-year job that requires culinary or baking skills, such as being a holiday or ski rep, and, for example, it requires them to take a cake to the interview to show off their skills, it is not helpful to bake it for them the night before 'because they are busy'!

Booking their own appointments

Booking appointments is another skill to master. A very experienced counsellor summed it up well when she said:

> If you walk with a crutch, muscles can weaken. Young people may not believe that they can do things for themselves, because

they have never had to. As parents we must avoid trying to be their 'crutch' and let them 'walk' independently.

Remind them of what they have done before. Remind them of strategies that have worked for them. Support them, but don't do it for them.

Many health appointments can now be booked via 24/7 online systems from smartphones or laptops, so there is little need for parents to get involved in phoning up on their young adult's behalf (for example, because their offspring is in meetings and unable to phone). Parents phoning receptionists to book a doctor's appointment can actually cause problems and frustration for both sides, as practices are bound by confidentiality, so unless a young person has given explicit consent for a named parent to be involved in their care, the reception teams are not even allowed to acknowledge if they are registered there. Parents then become frustrated with what can be perceived as 'obstructive behaviour' but is actually designed to protect the best interests of the patient. The same goes for phoning for results or accessing copies of medical documents (for example vaccination records) of course.

PARENT POINTER

- Teach your young person to book their own appointments, even if they are busy (we all have to learn to multitask) and to attend them confidently on their own, or with support if needed (but they should lead the discussion). They need to build their confidence speaking on the phone, even if they don't like it, as it will be a useful skill in later life.

Registering with a doctor and a dentist should be a priority for all young people arriving at university or moving to a new town for work. It can be really helpful if families support and encourage them to start attending such appointments on their own at home, from about the age of 16 wherever possible, even if Mum/Dad sits in the waiting room initially. Building the confidence and ability to discuss one's own health issues and obtain medication, such as contraception or treatment for minor illness, allows them to feel more able to seek help if they ever have more serious problems, such as mental health symptoms. They will be familiar with the system and potentially less put off booking an appointment and discussing personal matters. Anything that could potentially make it easier for them to seek help when things get difficult, and before crises occur, is to be encouraged.

TRANSITION OF HEALTHCARE (MOVING SPECIALISTS AND CLINICS)

We have covered the need for all young people to be able to book and attend appointments alone, but for those who have been in the care of local health services beyond their family doctor, such as in a hospital or clinic, leaving home can mean a 'double whammy' of also leaving well-known specialist teams and healthcare professionals and moving to new services. This geographical move is usually twinned with the transition from child and adolescent health services to adult services, and the shift in culture that this entails. Suddenly young people are expected to access and use services independently and confidentially, and that can feel challenging. Discharge from child health services is sometimes abrupt and unceremonious, due to pressures on appointments and poor communication, and attachment to doctors or nurses is broken off as the care comes to an end and transferred elsewhere. The entire experience has been likened to 'falling off a cliff', as young people are ejected from one service and the system fails to connect them appropriately to the new service somewhere halfway across the country. Even within cities the transition is rarely smooth, and sadly child and adult services do not always 'talk' to each other.

Below is a checklist for transferring healthcare as smoothly as possible which can apply for young people travelling to study abroad too. This can be useful for all young people leaving home, not just those with known health issues.

- Get a summary printout from the primary care doctor of the young person's health record (if they have had significant issues) to take with them.
- Register with a new doctor as soon as possible.
- Make a routine appointment to set up care and prescriptions.
- Ask specialist hospital teams to refer them directly to a new specialist team before discharge, rather than asking the young person to start the process on arrival via the new primary care doctor (which is additionally tricky if they don't have a local address yet).
- Take a two-month supply of any medication to the new location, to allow time for registering and obtaining a new prescription/getting referred for specialist prescriptions.
- If young people over 18 wish their parents to be involved in their healthcare, they need to give specific named written consent, and have it documented clearly.
- If going overseas, check to see if the same medication is available in that country and, if not, switch to one that is before travel, or take enough to cover the visit.

Learning where to get help

'I just didn't really get that mental health was a Thing,' said Zoe when she eventually sought help for her eating issues, 'or that help was available in the university, or that it was free.'

It is a very common finding of multiple surveys that, despite widespread advertising by university support and health services, young people regularly say that their biggest challenge in seeking support is not knowing *where* to go for help. For young people not at university it can be equally difficult to know where to get help. Sometimes there are too many choices, so they don't know which service to approach first, or they don't realise that family doctors deal with mental health, not just physical health. They may have heard about long waiting times, which puts them off, but are unaware that if they tell the receptionist the nature of their concerns, they may be triaged to a more urgent appointment if possible. Young people tend to turn to their friends and phones first for support, so it is important that reliable information is available online, and that families make them aware that mental health issues can affect anyone, and are very common, but that they are treatable and such treatment is free in the UK (although they may have to pay for prescriptions).

Learning to make decisions

Young people frequently say how much pressure they feel under to know what they want to do from a young age. Which GCSEs to pick, which A levels or IB to study, whether to take a gap year or not, whether to go to college or uni, or start an apprenticeship, are just some of the decisions they are expected to make, each of which feels momentous at the time. They feel that if they put a step wrong, if they don't make the 'right' decision, then everything will collapse, all their options will concertina down and they will be left stranded and a 'failure'. The young people we spoke to aged between 16 and 25 all mentioned this pressure: 'every decision you take might have a huge impact, and picking GCSEs at 14 feels overwhelming'. Young people give up subjects too early, fearful that they won't be the 'right one' and feel pressured to 'have a passion' from a young age.

As parents you can support, guide and, most importantly perhaps, remind your child at each stage that life choices are *not* set in stone or irrevocable. They can choose subjects they enjoy and are good at, or delay going to uni, or take more than one gap year, or even change course (and uni) if they do choose that path. Remember you are not planning your own life here; you are facilitating your young adult to think through their own options and minimise the anxiety around making a choice.

PARENT POINTER

- You could encourage your young adult to draw up lists of pros and cons, or prompt them to consider the impacts of various choices (a bit like a 'careers' or life version of those Dungeons and Dragons books or games they play, where you can test out what might happen if you choose this fork in the road).

IS UNIVERSITY RIGHT FOR EVERYONE?

There is little doubt that there are significant benefits to a university education: higher average salaries through life, lower unemployment, healthier lifestyles, more likely to vote and volunteer within the community, and graduates' offspring are in turn more likely to engage in educational activities with family members.[1] Such benefits may go some way to explaining why around 50 per cent of UK school leavers now attend a higher education institution by the time they are 30, with 1 in 3 UK 18–24-year-olds in full-time education.[2]

But university is clearly not right for everyone. For many reasons, including financial, health or personal circumstance, half of young people choose to go straight into the workplace, volunteer, travel, move abroad, do an apprenticeship, intern or find a vocational training course instead. The important thing is that they do something that they are interested in and find a purpose. We discussed the importance of purpose on page 70.

PARENT POINTER

- There is a very helpful section on apprenticeships, internships and travel in the 'Alternatives to University' section of the UCAS website, to consider options for 'earning as you learn' or gaining experience before making big decisions.[3]

Which uni?

When looking at universities (which can feel overwhelming), offer to make a list together of factors to consider, such as distance from home, students' union events, course reputation, welfare support and cost of accommodation, and try to remain objective and unemotional about their views and opinions (yes, they might go far away, but it might be the best course for them; no, they might not want to go where you would prefer). They may find it challenging enough without your emotions clouding their thinking. They may, of course, want to do this on their own, so try to respect their space and just ask to check in with them at intervals to hear their ideas and progress so far.

Young people's tendency to black-and-white thinking may frustrate you (but is a feature of all adolescent development) or they may delay and avoid the process because they are so worried (or laid back), so you may need to coach them by gently probing their thinking, or setting specific times aside to sit down and deal with the issue. If they have specific needs or disabilities then consider doing a bit of research to help and share with them, but let them make the decisions and take ownership of the process.

Don't be tempted to write their personal statement for them. The statement is a key way for your child to crystallise their thoughts about why they want to study a particular course and where they might see life after university, and they will be asked about it in interviews. If you have written it for them they will be at a disadvantage both in terms of knowing what they want to do and why, as well as not being able to discuss it in depth with future tutors. They should avoid using clichés ('I am passionate about ...') and quotes from historical figures or celebrities, which really wind up the academics who have to wade through hundreds of such statements, and who are also adept at spotting the parental touch! They don't want to read sweeping generalisations and list of achievements; they do want to read a genuinely personal essay from a student who is interested in studying with them.[4]

Taking time out

The gap year has been parodied mercilessly (it is now known as the 'gap yah' in some sections of the media), but there remains a very useful purpose to taking time off between school and university or the workplace. For many people school will have been an intense experience, with fairly unrelenting pressure or expectations, and the year off can allow them time to relax, rediscover their hobbies, see new places, develop and broaden their perspective on life, earn some money, give back to the community, do something useful for their CV or even decide what they want to do next. One inspirational teacher we interviewed tells his pupils that he 'took six gap years' while he tried out new opportunities, to illustrate that it is better to take your time and *then* do something you find satisfying and interesting, rather than rush into another long-term commitment, such as a university course. A year out is not a luxury.

PARENT POINTERS

- Try to let your young adult make their decisions, including not going to university, and take ownership of the consequences. If in future they decide to try higher education, they will do so at a time that feels right for them, and will be fully engaged with the process.
- Think about internships, which have benefits in terms of finding out if they actually like the field of work they are exploring, as well as being valuable fodder for the CV and interview, but they are unpaid and this may be a significant hurdle for some young people. If they feel exploited then it is time to move on.
- Let them choose their own path in life – it is *their* life after all.

The workplace

Gen Z consider themselves to be hard-working, and they look forward to getting a job that they will love. They understand that, in the current economic climate, money-making opportunities may be less frequent and that they will need to work long hours, but they will aim for flexible working, some control over their own timetable, multiple jobs (likely freelance), their own businesses (or maybe a main job and a 'side hustle' of their own business on the side), and will use technology (some of which doesn't yet exist) to make it possible. They will be looking for a decent wage and a way to climb the career ladder. There will be less evidence of the Millennial 'work/life balance' mantra, as their lives will have been lived in a harsher economic climate. They may job-hop as needs dictate.

Technology is having an increasing effect on the business world, though currently nobody really knows what the impact of technology will be in the future. Many of the parents and young people we talked to feel that technology, and in particular automation, machine learning and artificial intelligence, will have a significant impact on the twenty-first-century workplace (and they fear that many jobs might disappear). But there is also hope that this technology, which has evolved so quickly in the last 15 years, will actually help create new job opportunities. Either way, what we can be fairly sure of is that our children's professional lives will look little like ours. Our children may upload video CVs for job applications, video conference from anywhere at any time, and work remotely to support their own mental well-being or family commitments. Many organisations will lack specific 'offices' or geographical locations, and even email might dis-appear (what joy!), replaced by employee apps and in-house communications.

CVs of the future will probably be interactive, with embed-ded links, videos and visual timelines, as well as headings that cover the skills employers are searching for, rather than just a list of qualifications and dates. You might like to encourage your young person to start thinking in these terms, researching ways to make their application and CV stand out in an online world.

Having said that, many Gen Z still love face-to-face interaction, and lots of feedback. Whether it's in their future workplace or talking to a counsellor about their worries, they often prefer discussions in person, over online, text or phone, so it is important to offer the option, and not assume that because they are young they will prefer online/phone options. Some things will always be better said human to human.

And where we older employees might have been perfectly happy with an annual review at work, this generation needs almost constant, frequent, personal, customised feedback, broken down by task and from a variety of sources.[5] Bear this in mind when communicating with your young adult, or if you work with any. They are not necessarily looking for constant rewards either, but guidance and advice. They don't need quantity – they want it short, quick and straight to the point too! They like their feedback instant, in person and two-way.[6]

There are many factors to consider when deciding between university and the world of work, but for most young people the decision will be driven by immediate requirements (such as the need to start earning money) and long-term aims (such as career options with a degree versus options following an apprenticeship, or from gaining experience as an employee). Apprenticeships are generally described as 'earn while you learn', as the young person spends part of the week being a typical employee and the rest of the time learning or being supported to gain qualifications.

Other considerations when deciding between paths is the need for entry qualifications to start further studies and living costs, types of learning such as independent or more structured studies, or full- or part-time. It may help your young person to do work experience or volunteer in order to know which path will best suit them, and there are multiple online resources to help the decision-making process and offering careers advice, as well as talking to the school or university careers departments. It can feel overwhelming for a teenager to consider all these possibilities, so it is important to be supportive, talk little and often about the choices and what they might enjoy or find rewarding, and take time out if needed, such as a gap year to gain experience in the workplace, learn a language, earn money or see the world.

Employers look for certain skills in most of their employees, whatever path they take, so any opportunity to gain such skills will be time well spent: communication and negotiation skills, teamwork, problem-solving, confidence and presentation skills, and the ability to work under pressure are all highly valued. Asking your young person how they might best gain these skills is a practical way to help them decide next steps.

INTERVIEWS

And so to a word about interviews. We have mentioned the increase in parental involvement in university open days, and there has been a similar rising involvement in the university application process (often characterised by the parent who says 'We are applying to ...' or who writes the personal statement). The USA, which is often a few years ahead of the UK in trends in young people's behaviour, has now documented a rise in parents attending job interviews with their offspring. In extreme cases (as if their mere presence at interview wasn't bad enough) they have even stepped in to take the interview when their child was unable to attend! Unsurprisingly, most employers do not take kindly to this over-involvement of parents in the workplace, so building your young person's independence and confidence is vital. Nor should young employees be asking their employers to speak to their parents about their well-being, which is now starting to happen in the UK.

DEALING WITH THE 'EMPTY NEST'

When your young adult leaves home and family dynamics shift there are several things that may happen. You may feel very 'empty nest' and sad about the changes. Or you may see this as an opportunity for a 'new you', either as a family/couple or single (that may be what's new!). It can help to make sure you keep busy but also make time for yourself to do things you enjoy. You may even feel very practical and decide to sell the house, downsize, rent out your child's room on Airbnb or sell the results of your 'decluttering' on eBay.

Whatever happens now try to remember that it will potentially have an effect on your young adult who has just moved out, as well as on any other offspring. It is very common for young people to be quite thrown and shaken by such changes in their home environment. One of the doctors we spoke with commented that more young people now seem to have very complex social and family situations. She told us with concern how 'The home they viewed as their "place of safety" sometimes disappears when they come to university, and they can be left feeling like they have nowhere to go, nowhere to fall back on.' They then rely on their university to provide more support when they need it.

It may also be worth bearing in mind *before* selling up that, while 20 years ago only 1 in 5 young people aged 20–34 lived at home with their parents, the figure has now risen to 1 in 4 and is expected to rise again, to 1 in 2 living at home, if the current housing crisis is not addressed.[7] This is despite the fact that the number of 20–34-year-olds has stayed the same. So your young adult may need your spare room again in the future!

PARENT POINTERS

- Talking through any likely changes with your child in advance may help to soften the blow or prepare them for the new status quo.
- Getting them to suggest solutions or ideas (even if they are not realistic or practical) will allow them to feel part of the family 'team', and engaged with the process, especially if it is a difficult one.
- However, it is not helpful to over-involve your child in divorce proceedings, for example, when there can be a temptation to use them to communicate between warring parents. Young people unsurprisingly find this especially distressing, and it can have a significantly negative impact on their morale and mental health.

'Commuting' offspring

Many young adults now choose to stay at home and attend uni as a commuter student or start work while still living at home, often for financial reasons, but sometimes for carer or cultural reasons. As a parent it will be helpful to still treat this as a transition to a new era, towards new-found freedoms and independence for your young person, and to facilitate them becoming an adult in their own right, living their own life but sharing your living space.

It will help to discuss expectations from both sides and clarify financial arrangements, such as contributions towards food or rent if necessary, participation in household activities from cleaning through to family meals, and any assumptions you or they might make around socialising, such as bringing friends home, having partners over to stay the night (or not) and having get-togethers. Commuter students in particular can sometimes feel more isolated, less like they belong to the university community, and are at risk of missing out both on lectures when their bus is late and fun stuff if the last train leaves too early. Being aware of these challenges as parents may help you to support your student's success academically, but also in keeping them happy and healthy.

PARENT POINTER

- Encourage your student to consider the above factors when choosing a uni, and also ask the uni for support once they are there. Universities are becoming more sensitive to the needs of this ever-growing group but not all will be clued up yet.

For those who are working and living with their parents there may be different challenges, such as not wanting to talk about work after a long day, with a parent who is naturally curious, or needing to be on the phone during family mealtimes, which may irritate you. Tolerance and understanding may be required on both sides!

FINDING THEIR TRIBE

Our hyper-connected kids are sometimes very lonely. We may think of our 16–24-year-olds as having hundreds of friends, both real and virtual, and being incredibly sociable and busy, but repeated surveys have shown that this is in fact the loneliest age.[8] Could the feeling of being disconnected be an evolutionary consequence of their searching for their new 'tribe' as they move from adolescence to adulthood? Are they discovering themselves and creating a new self-image, maybe finding that they have less in common with their current friends and searching for new people with whom they have more in common? It's also, of course, the time when many young people leave home to travel, study or work, and thus may become isolated from old friends.

The great thing about leaving home for university or the workplace is that it can lead to meeting a host of new people, a few of whom will share their interests or politics, even if they don't meet that crowd immediately. By being open to people who may be different from them or their previous friends, by talking to a wide range of people, trying new activities or studying modules that take them outside their comfort zone, they are much more likely to connect with others, a few of whom they can then get to know on a deeper level. At university, opportunities for socialising will be created by the residences, the sports teams, the academic departments and the various social clubs via the Students' Union, as well as through a whole range of external or other organisations. Some will be alcohol-free, some will involve helping the local community, some will be for charity, but there will be something for everyone. In the new workplace young people will be invited for after-work drinks, client dinners, team-building activities and on courses which might involve socialising to a greater or lesser extent.

There will be multiple opportunities to meet new people and curate their new identity.

PARENT POINTER

- Remind your young adult that finding their tribe can take time, and it may be more challenging if they have trouble with social skills, such as having social anxiety or Asperger's. However, it is possible for everyone to make new friends. The key is for them to keep trying, and not forget to smile – it really breaks down barriers.

THINKING POINTS

To enable young people to be resilient and independent as they reach adulthood parents can ensure they have learnt a broad range of life skills. These can include cooking, travel, healthcare and domestic skills. For young people to thrive on leaving home, but still be able to ask for help when they need it and before it becomes a crisis, they need to know that they can have open conversations with their parents, but they also need to be able to choose their own life path and make their own choices (and mistakes) about where to go and what to try in life.

Here are a few things to consider:

- Transition can be a stressful time, but building independence and resilience will help.
- Transferring healthcare should be planned well in advance.
- Think about which life skills they might need and which they have, and support them to address the gaps.
- Remind them that decisions are not set in stone and that life can take many different paths.

- Some young people bloom in the workplace in a way that they wouldn't in the pressure-cooker environment of university, and earning their own way in the world can give them an identity and feel rewarding in a way that studying for three or four more years would not.
- Uni isn't for everyone; what matters is having a sense of purpose and enjoyment.
- Which university they choose should be their decision if they are to have a chance at making it work.
- A year off is not a 'luxury' but can bring many benefits and life skills.
- Build trust and openness in your relationship.
- Finding their new tribe can take time. Saying 'yes' to new opportunities will help them meet lots of new people.

CHAPTER 10

University in the Twenty-first Century

The university experience has dramatically evolved in the last few decades, and the life our children will have in higher education will be (in many ways) unrecognisable from uni days even 20 years ago. If you went to uni in the seventies you were one of the elite 1 in 7 that made it, with many 16-year-olds not even continuing to sixth form as there was little guarantee that after another two years of hard work they would find a place at university. As the eighties arrived there was a huge expansion in higher education, allowing 1 in 5 to attend university. The numbers slowly climbed through the nineties and, by 2002, those numbers had more than doubled, seeing 43 per cent go on to higher education.[1] In Australia, the number of university places offered has increased 50 per cent in 10 years and numbers attending college in the USA by 42 per cent in 30 years.[2,3] As we reach the end of the twenty-first century's second decade, the UK has achieved the impressive milestone of enabling every other child to go into tertiary education.

This is a wonderful success story for the UK, particularly where we have widened the participation in university life for many who would not traditionally have studied for a degree. By improving career prospects, creating the opportunity to earn more throughout their life and developing in people a wide variety of skills through new experiences, both society and individuals will benefit hugely.[4] However, by increasing the number of young people competing for university places (and subsequently graduating) we have also created a *much more competitive* school, university and workplace environment. Getting into university, studying and graduating into the world of work is now a hugely competitive process. It is helpful to be aware of this when you see how stressed your child is and you think 'but it wasn't that stressful in my day'. You are absolutely right – it wasn't.

BE PREPARED

Sixth form (senior school) teachers have an essential role to play in preparing pupils for university, yet many of them believe that the young people in their care are unable to visualise the future or prioritise their preparation and planning for it, as they are so obsessed with current short-term goals, such as next week's essay or project deadline. Pupils have not therefore developed the skills necessary to plan ahead, or those that might be required to succeed at university, such as being strategic, assessing what needs to be done in the longer term, taking a long-term view and planning or organising themselves to achieve it. This seems to be borne out by the fact that fewer than 1 in 10 students say that their higher education experience matches their prior expectations.[5] It is very hard to prepare for something if you have no idea what it will be like.

PARENT POINTERS

- Parents (and teachers) need to help young people to prepare by thinking ahead, visualising what they might need to know and prepare for it.
- Very importantly, young people need to visualise and prepare for the new way of *learning* that universities expect of them – deeper rather than superficial learning (as discussed on page 81–2).

Uni open days

Consider letting your teenager go alone or with a friend to one of the hundreds of open days universities hold each year. Only 10 or 15 years ago it was unheard of to attend this first taste of freedom and student life with your parents. Students piled on to buses and took tours around their chosen campuses, meeting other prospective applicants and hearing from current students about the realities of life at uni. Fast forward to the present day and universities are swarming with parents, exploring and deciding together about the soon-to-be student's future. This may seem charming, and a way for parents to engage in their child's life, but there is also a strong possibility that they may overly influence the decision of which uni to attend ('But Mum/Dad went to [insert name of uni] ... you really should at least consider it'), when in fact the young person has discovered through their own research and open day experience that another university is currently the best for engineering/dentistry/creative arts or student life. It is normal for many young people to want to please their parents (or to rebel!) or to feel the pressure of expectation or of financial support ('Well, we are funding your studies, so we should have a say …'), when in fact this would be a perfect opportunity for them to discover and research the universities that interest them, and decide which they will be fully personally invested in and committed to.

PARENT POINTERS

- Encourage your teenager to consider going alone or with a friend to open days. If you do accompany them, let them to do the tours alone and lead the visit. You will be helping them to visualise what university is like, while avoiding influencing their decision-making.
- For students who may be sensitive to large crowds or noise, or have disabilities, there are always the university's virtual tours online to use as a starting point, before a visit in person.

A different way of learning

When asked, second- and third-year university students explained that they had had to learn to study and work in much more independent ways. Having expected to arrive and study just one subject, they were taken aback when, because there are so many aspects to a course, it felt like they were studying several subjects. Many students have no idea what they will be studying on their course at uni, or how they will be taught it, which creates uncertainty. And they particularly worry about presentations in front of others, essay writing and time management.

PARENT POINTERS

- Parents should resist helping their children with their essays or other work, if they are to be successful independent learners.
- Encourage them not just to listen and absorb information but to challenge it and ask questions (develop critical analysis skills).
- Ask them to practise debating both sides of an argument so that they get used to thinking about and evaluating tricky topics.
- Many universities release reading lists in advance of starting the course so that new students can prepare if they wish to, and these are often discussed on newly formed Facebook groups, prior to joining a course.
- Practising presentations and speaking in front of others will be a life skill worth having, both for university and the workplace, so it is well worth finding fun ways to do this, for example by challenging each other to speak for one minute on random topics over dinner!
- If they are disproportionately worried, they should speak to their tutor about presentation options or additional support.

Money matters

Let's talk about money! Most of the following information applies to England, but the UCAS website has great information for the whole of the UK. The rising costs of living (of accommodation costs, in particular) and the introduction of tuition fees (paying for education) in 1998, along with the removal of grants in 1997 (now replaced by a system of means tested 'maintenance loans'), have led to layer upon layer of money worries for students, but also for their families, who are expected (by the government) to contribute financially as a default part of the equation. Students are expected to take out two loans: one for tuition fees and one for maintenance (living) costs. Extra financial support is available in certain situations, such as if your child has a disability, so it is worth investigating all the options, and there is lots more practical information about this online.

THE BANK OF MUM AND DAD

Time will tell if the UK loan system will be overhauled significantly but if in the meantime you are interested to know what parents should be contributing (i.e. what the UK government expects you to contribute) the Save The Student website has a handy calculator to allow you to do just that: https://www. savethestudent.org/parentcontribution/.

If you are planning to contribute to your child's living costs financially, it is worth considering how you will do that in practical terms. Will you allocate them their total amount then let them get on with managing it and budgeting, learning to be independent in the process, or will you dole it out in weekly or monthly allowances? Unsurprisingly, we would err on the side of allowing them to learn to manage their money independently, though if they have a serious reason (such as a gambling or other addiction) for being unable to manage money, then of course you will need to follow the latter path.

Ellie, a current student, had a suggestion:

Students need to learn to manage money and, if they run out, they will have to learn from their mistakes and take responsibility, and earn more. If a parent can allow the student to take control of the full student maintenance loan, and ask the student to contribute from that any costs they (the parents) have to pay, such as accommodation fees, it will create a healthier balance of control between parents and student, and teach the student an important skill.

This certainly seems like a positive step towards developing financial know-how in your kids.

STUDENTS WITH DISABILITIES

The number of university students with a disability (physical or mental health) in the UK has dramatically increased, with 40,000 students (with a declared disability) taking up a place in 2016.[6] There are now great websites and sources of information for applying or preparing for uni (such as AccessAble – see page 315), to ensure that disabled students get the most out of their experience.[7] If your student has a disability or you think they might need additional support, they can apply for additional funding (Disabled Students' Allowance) once at uni, and access the university's dedicated services, whether they have a physical issue, mental health difficulties or autism spectrum disorder. It will be important to consider accommodation, mobility and transport options, accessibility to academic studies and social occasions, and whether the university provides a short summer school for students with specific needs such as autism, prior to arrival. Planning for the transition and good preparation should prove very beneficial for when your young adult arrives on campus.

Setting up healthcare

One of the most important things to set up when arriving at a new university is healthcare. As more people with complex health needs now go on to higher education, institutions are getting better at providing for their health and care needs, and you can check these out for any university under 'Student Support Services' on their website. Reading these web pages well before arrival at the new institution is very helpful to ensure young people know which services are available to support them, who can help them with different problems and that help is free of charge.

Many people wonder about staying registered with their home doctor, rather than registering with a university doctor. It is strongly recommended that they are registered with a practice close to university in case they become unwell and need acute or ongoing care. Most practices working with universities have clinical staff with a special interest and expertise in young people's health, including sexual health, mental health and sports or travel medicine. Taking a letter with you from the 'home' specialist is extremely helpful to the new doctor in case medical records take time to transfer. It's also a great idea to teach young people where to get over-the-counter medicines and prescriptions, and to encourage them to take a small kit containing essentials such as plasters, bandage/dressings, paper stitches and painkillers (make sure they know how to take them!).

THE BIGGEST WORRIES

When we turn to what parents expect their child to struggle with, compared to what students think might challenge them, a study by Unite Students found that, while parents thought that domestic skills such as cooking, washing their sheets and budgeting might be most difficult, the 16–19-years-olds questioned worried most about getting advice on mental health, sex and relationships, alcohol and drugs, as well as where to get practical help on these issues if they needed it.[8] Mental health is a worry for many young people and universities specifically ask them to 'declare' (make the university aware of) any issues so that they can provide the appropriate and expert support needed, from day one. Worryingly, 63 per cent of those who had a mental health problem in the Unite survey, were *not* planning on disclosing it to the university, meaning that they would miss out on specialist professional support and possibly financial aid.

Addressing this as parents and encouraging your child to disclose (confidentially) any concerns to the support services when asked before arrival or at registration could ensure appropriate support is provided, as and when it is needed. It will not be disclosed to future employers and allows the university to be as helpful as possible.

'I wish I had never come'

Some of the most difficult consultations for those working in university communities are around supporting young people who wish they had never come, feel trapped or whose families insisted that they attend. Sometimes it is the university that is wrong for them (too rural, too urban, too far away from home, too arty); sometimes the course is not for them (Medicine instead of English or Law instead of Sports Science), because it's what their parents insisted they should study or that's what clearing had to offer; and sometimes it is just 'university' itself that is wrong – they should never have come, they blame themselves or others, and they can be angry or resigned. The most worrying are those who seem withdrawn, genuinely unable to see a way out that keeps their family happy while meeting their own needs, and these are sadly the most likely to try to harm themselves in desperation.

Feeling trapped is very much a warning sign to welfare teams in universities. As parents, this 'trapped feeling' is something to watch out for and gently enquire about, so that you can start a conversation about alternative options if necessary. Your child may talk about feeling like they can't go on or 'can't do this anymore'. They may feel overwhelmed or exhausted, or talk about being a failure and letting you down. Reassure them that there is nothing that you don't want to hear about or help them to sort out. Whether changes need to be made to the location or the course, or whether to study at university at all, the important thing is that options are available and there is *always* hope and the possibility of trying something new. Many students fail to realise that there are myriad ways to change their path, for example changing accommodation if it is isolating, or changing modules or supervisors if they are proving too stressful. It may not always be straightforward, but there are options. The important thing is that nothing is set in stone; they just need to find the right person to talk to. The key parenting skill required here is to support them to speak to the right person, rather than do it for them.

Di, a very practical and supportive mum of a student, told us of the day her daughter called her in distress after a piece of work went badly wrong. She listened and then gently encouraged her daughter to go home, have a cup of tea and speak to the tutor the next day. Defusing the situation, listening and giving sensible advice were all that were required, and her daughter would know what to do next time. We strongly suggest getting help *early* if students are struggling, and not waiting until things reach crisis point. All is not lost!

While four out of five soon-to-be-students are excited about going away to uni, three out of five are also anxious.[9] Going to uni is a heady experience, and not always a fun or uncomplicated one, so talking about this well in advance, and in bite-sized amounts, may allow your young adult to be more resilient when the going gets tough.

PARENT POINTER

- If you want to chat through your child's concerns with them, you could say something like this: 'It's okay to be a bit worried – lots of people are. Shall we make a list, then work through those worries and address them together?' It may help to put the different worries into categories, such as 'money' or 'living away from home', and then make an action plan for each one.[10] Your child should also take every opportunity offered to chat with their academic tutor (too many students fail to turn up for these sessions).

ARRIVALS DAY ('THE DROP-OFF')

Think back to that first day of primary school. You, nervous and excited, your small child hanging on to your legs as you try to ease them into school for the first time. University arrivals day shares much of the anticipation and emotions with that earlier experience, but this time it is the child trying to make the break for freedom! This is a day that looms large for families, students and university staff alike. It is a much-anticipated day, and universities prepare for it as much as students, if not more, ensuring that a warm welcome greets the new arrivals, along with a cup of tea and a biscuit for families and supporters who have often driven or travelled for hours to deliver the brand-new student. It's a great day, so enjoy it, but a couple of things are worth remembering to make sure that expectations are realistic and that the 'handover' of the student goes smoothly.

Try to step back

First of all, try to let your young adult go up to check-in on arrival and collect their keys alone, or at least hang back if you can. Try not to speak for them or be 'helpful' by saying you'll do it for them, in your excitement to get involved. Accommodation teams are all too familiar with asking a new arrival their name, only for Mum, clutching a folder with all her documents arranged in alphabetical order, to lean across and say, 'This is Billy Smith', as the student stands by silent and awkward. Some colleagues have told us of students whispering in their parent's ear for the parent to relay the comment!

Most university accommodation providers lay on activities or talks for the parents, so take advantage of these – hear about what is planned for your child, meet other families and try to relax. You can always check with your young person later to see if they have got their key, found their room and discovered the laundry area. Another tip is to help them by carrying stuff to their room, unloading it, and possibly even helping to unpack a little, but try not to decorate the room and set out their belongings, as a wonderful aspect of coming to uni is that it is another opportunity for your young person to reinvent themselves and 'curate' their identity. They might enjoy taking the time later to unpack their things and arrange their room to their own taste. They may wish to bring some well-loved items from home, such as a duvet cover or photos, but just as many will want to start afresh and create a whole new image. Perhaps make sure they actually know how to put a duvet cover on though, as we have heard entertaining stories of students fully inserting themselves into the duvet cover, in an attempt to put it on the duvet and ending up in a tangled mess on the floor!

PARENT POINTERS

- It may be impossible to resist, but try not to do any food shopping for your student when they arrive, beyond basics such as milk and bread, as they will need to learn to do this for themselves.
- If you do go with them to a supermarket, perhaps try not to make all the decisions. Let them shop and work out their budget, while you hang back and carry the bags.
- Guide them to the bargain bin and show them bulk-buying options, for example rice, if that is helpful.

It may sound really difficult to have driven them all the way there and then be expected to hold back, but it will be appreciated by your young person as you allow them their space and independence. Not hanging around for too long after drop-off can be appreciated by new students, some of whom have told us that it was lovely to be accompanied and hard to say goodbye, but a relief not to have to worry about their family once they had gone home or to their hotel. Others, like Preeti, a third-year student, recalled her first day and that she enjoyed having her parents around until the evening, as she wasn't going to see them for a while, and after they left for their hotel, she phoned her best friend from home to share the weirdness of suddenly being alone in a new place. She explained how it took time for her to settle in, and she later regretted going home after a couple of weeks (for a pre-arranged event), as it left her feeling more disconnected from her new surroundings. She strongly recommends that new students do not go home in the first four weeks if they can avoid it. Accommodation staff also recommend against arriving to check in, going home for a day or two, then coming back to start term, as this is very disruptive. Conversely, we don't recommend necessarily going the whole term without going home – there's a balance to be struck.

Students have told us that they are keen to meet new people and blend in, and they don't like worrying about family, feeling that they have to look after their parents in their new 'home'. One student told of how his mum was concerned about him, as he had been very stressed in the last year at school, so she had booked to stay close by for the first three days after drop-off. She checked on him regularly, which he understood, but his feeling when she finally headed home was 'Thank goodness, now I can relax!'

Suggest that your young adult can send you a photo of their room or of new friends later, so that you can still feel involved, without being fully immersed. Try to find a happy medium between getting a sense of where they will be living and meeting a few new faces, and letting them get on with it, start their new independent life and blend in. Remember that first day of primary school and try not to be the parent hanging on to your child's legs as they try to (metaphorically or literally!) pull away from you.

Tempting as it may be to stay involved over the weeks that follow, it is important to let your student sort out issues for themselves, while providing a supportive ear. Don't be the one asking staff if your child has 'eaten well that day', if they are 'drinking too much' or if they are getting up for lectures. These examples and many others were shared with us by accommodation staff, who love working with young people but are not nannies or a hotel concierge!

PARENT POINTERS

- It may be helpful to plan for arrivals day, not just in terms of travel and packing but to discuss what your child will need to do alone on arrival, and how long you might stay. They will not want to upset you by asking you to leave, and if you ask them 'Shall I stay and sort out your room/go shopping with you?' it may be hard for them to say 'No, I'll be okay, you don't need to stay too long.' If *you* suggest that you won't hang around too long, you can see how they respond. Better that it comes from you, and then they can invite you to stay longer on the day if it feels right.
- If you have had a long journey to drop off your student, why not take yourself out for dinner locally or stay over in a hotel to recover? But try to let your young adult get on with their new life as quickly as possible.
- Be the parent who encourages their child to be independent, to make their own decisions or mistakes, and ask questions.

Keeping in touch

It is practical to plan how often and by what means you will have contact with your child over the coming term – phone, WhatsApp, Messenger or text? Many a misunderstanding has occurred because the family expect daily updates and calls, and the student is out of contact at lectures, socialising or staying with another student. Knowing how often to expect to communicate will massively reduce concern and the likelihood of the accommodation staff (or even the police) being called because a student didn't check in as often as expected.

Realistically it may be best to suggest that you speak on the phone once or twice a week (video calls can be too emotional, so check first) and have a family WhatsApp group (for random updates, photos or just queries about house or maintenance stuff) that is less structured and keeps it fun (rather than feeling like a 'duty'). Find out what works for you all, but consider boundaries in a positive way and discuss and plan your 'comms' well in advance.

The university perspective on parents

Universities are slowly shifting towards viewing parents as 'partners' in their objective to educate the next generation, but not all are at that stage yet, and many individual staff members may still view parents as, at best, tolerable and, at worst, incidental, as the student is an adult. The current legal position is that universities have a Duty of Care but are not 'in loco parentis'.[11] Students who are over 18 are 'autonomous adults and have a right to be in control of their own information and choices'.[12] This can be hard to accept if you are all too aware of the reality of your young adult's (historically) poorer life choices or emotional state on occasion, but universities cannot ignore the law and so must work with it and families to ensure that the students in their care are looked after but are allowed their freedom and autonomy.

Universities routinely ask students for an emergency contact's (next of kin) details on joining so the institution can contact that named individual should the need arise. This would be used only in an emergency and not all students choose parents to be that contact (some choose an older sibling or aunt/uncle). Either way, universities *cannot* talk to parents without the express consent and written agreement of the student, whichever system is in place. Most universities have a positive and pragmatic approach to working with parents, as do many accommodation providers. Open days, arrival day and other occasions now routinely feature events for parents, such as talks, information sharing and websites, as well as a few introducing termly parent newsletters for updates and blogs relevant to families. There is slow recognition of the fact that parenting has changed, and that parents can be allies and more involved, to ensure that a consistent message about independent learning and living is given to the student, and there is also acknowledgment that many parents are now financially as well as emotionally invested in their student's education.

Welfare and counselling services have perhaps been ahead of the curve in terms of appreciating what parents can offer, and although they too are absolutely bound by confidentiality, they are able to listen if a parent has a concern. While they cannot necessarily share information back with the parent, or even tell them if the student is seeing them or registered with them (this is also true for healthcare teams), they can take note and make a record of the concerns and will usually act on them. Welfare teams usually try to encourage the student to talk to their parents after such a call, to share with them updates and so on, if the parent is happy for the student to know that they have called. Parental 'gut feelings' are respected and treated seriously, although there may be limits to what actions can follow the sharing of such concerns.

FRESHER PRESSURE

So you've dropped them off, and their room, duvet and comms plan are all sorted. Now the fun (and hard work) really starts. The university years are rarely the 'best years' of anyone's life when viewed with some life perspective, but there is huge pressure on new students for them to be *amazing*.

Having a realistic expectation of what to expect and knowing that there *will* be ups and downs, can really improve the likelihood that your young person will have a good experience. Expectations that Freshers' Week will be awesome can be particularly unrealistic. Welcome Week (as Freshers' Week is now commonly known) can be pretty full-on, and students are hit with a whole load of new information. They will be keen to fit in, make friends, make a good impression and take full advantage of all the social opportunities that will come their way (and there will be many!). They can completely exhaust themselves or get really run down if they are not careful.

Some of these top tips for surviving Welcome Week (which are recommended by unis) may therefore be worth suggesting to your student if they need ideas or advice:

Welcome Week survival guide[13]

- Don't sign up for everything at Freshers' Fair (it gets expensive!). Just pick one or two societies or clubs that you will definitely go to (maybe because you've done that activity before) and maybe one new one that sounds fun (like the uni radio station or CheeseSoc – yes really!). Don't just sign up for things that are 'good for the CV'. You can always join others later on.
- Register with a doctor, have any immunisations you have missed (such as to protect against meningitis) and find out where the well-being services are, even if you might never need them.
- Know not only where the laundry room is, but where to report any maintenance issues or security concerns. Get familiar with the campus, bus routes and cycle paths.
- Go to welcome meetings and roadshows, where lots of useful info may be provided in one go, and put important contact details into your phone.

- Take time out if it all feels a bit much or if you are sensitive to noise or busy environments.
- Make new friends of course, but know that they might not be 'best friends for life' and try to avoid getting pulled into intense relationships early on (don't make 'panic friends'), and know that you might even 'fall in fresher love', high on life and all the excitement, but that it *might* not last forever. (It's worth reminding them about contraception at this point, as consultations for unplanned pregnancies peak in uni doctor practices about halfway through the first term!)
- Try to avoid initiation ceremonies completely – they rarely end well and have, sadly, but mercifully rarely, even had fatal outcomes.[14] (Your young adult may feel confident to just say no or they can duck out early with a 'migraine' or say they are unwell, if they are worried about how to say 'no' without drawing attention to themselves.)
- Clubbing, which is a big part of Welcome Week, and student life generally of course, is not for everyone, so it's fine to decline sometimes and have a quieter evening with new friends, just chatting and getting to know people in your accommodation.

This is a lovely quote from a student that may be helpful to share with your soon-to-be-student:

> Be patient with finding your 'place' at uni and with finding friends. It's better to wait for those genuine and good friendships rather than panicking and forming and holding on to friendships that shouldn't be there. There are so many people at university and you don't have to change anything about yourself to fit in with people who aren't really a good fit, wait for those you just click with.[15]

ACCOMMODATION PROBLEMS AND CONFLICT WITH FLATMATES

In an ideal world, your student will settle into their accommodation, get on with most of their new flatmates or corridor friends and enjoy discovering what uni life is like, but occasionally problems arise with the accommodation itself or with new housemates.

If the university accommodation (which may be provided by a private company) is unsatisfactory, it is essential to discuss this as soon as possible with the relevant manager or a member of staff in the accommodation block. It is much easier for them to sort out these issues early on than when term has got going and empty rooms have been filled. A few students leave uni after a couple of weeks when they discover it is not for them, so a few rooms become available every academic year at about this time too. If the problem is with housing provided by private landlords, the Shelter 'Health and Safety Standards for Rented Homes' guidelines are really practical and useful.[16]

The following pragmatic bit of advice on the subject of changing accommodation is from Rebecca O'Hare of Campus Living Villages:

> If for any reason your son or daughter is experiencing any issues within their accommodation, they should alert their reception team as soon as possible. Often, we hear stories about students being unhappy throughout the academic year and not letting our teams know earlier. If rooms are available, it's often possible to swap to another flat. Our residents spend so much of their time in their flats and rooms that it's just as important to our teams as it is to our residents that their experience is a positive and happy one.

If the issue is more of an interpersonal conflict, with your student finding certain new flatmates impossible to live with, this may be harder to fix quickly and may need some intervention by accommodation staff, if the challenging behaviour is illegal (selling drugs on the premises) or socially unacceptable (very poor food hygiene or extremely loud music, for example).

If your student wishes to try sorting things out themselves, and they think that the other person will at least try to engage in conversation, below are some practical tips to bear in mind when having 'difficult conversations'. Such skills will stand them in good stead for later life, whether at home or at work, so even if the accommodation situation doesn't work out, they will have learnt something useful!

Basic principles for difficult conversations[17]

- People want to be understood and listened to.
- People may feel threatened or they may become very emotional, so tread gently.
- There may be stuff going on for them that you are not aware of.
- There are always two sides to every story.
- Pick a good time. Mention that you'd like to talk and agree a time that suits you both.
- Try to avoid aggressive language/swearing, as it really raises the temperature and rarely achieves anything helpful.
- Plan three key points you want to make in advance.
- Be prepared to compromise, to allow the situation to be resolved.
- You may need to agree to disagree, to move on with your lives.
- We all occasionally have to get comfortable with being uncomfortable, in this case, living with a non-ideal situation.

If your student needs advice, encourage them to speak to the university student support service, the accommodation or careers team, a pastoral tutor or the Student Union advice team, and get the ball rolling.

EATING ISSUES

We will talk more about eating *disorders* (conditions such as anorexia nervosa, orthorexia and bulimia) in Chapter 14, but here we want to mention the more everyday eating and food-related stresses that can occur at university.

Students may not give much thought to their eating habits when at home as much of the time meals are simply provided for them. If you can encourage your young adult to consider which essentials should be in the food cupboard, how to make a shopping list, go shopping and meal plan, then you will go some way to preparing them for the next few years. Arriving at uni they may be in catered accommodation or self-catered, and therefore will need to think ahead about either making sure they turn up at planned mealtimes or, conversely, shop for food on a regular basis. It's fair to say that shopping and eating can all pass by the wayside in the frantic busy-ness of a university term – meals are missed, takeaways are bought and fits of the munchies are given in to – with the result being that they can either lose or gain a significant amount of weight (without having a clinical eating disorder).

PARENT POINTERS

- Reminding your student of the importance of regular meals, with a balanced nutrient content, an occasional vitamin, and having at least two meals a week that 'don't have any labels' (are cooked from fresh ingredients) may go some way to counteracting potential weight fluctuations and scurvy!

- They may also long for 'family' meals, so planning to eat with others once or twice a week can be nice.

New food fads

It's common for young people to suddenly develop new food habits, highly influenced as they are by their new friends and being keen to fit in. They may become vegan, try extreme diets or be influenced to avoid gluten. Many of these habits will be short-lived, but some will stick, and if it seems to be affecting their health or weight significantly it may be worth having a gentle conversation with them, or encouraging them to talk about it to a doctor. University doctors see a remarkable number of students with tummy problems, ranging from constipation (from poor diet), to new diagnoses of colitis (an inflammation of the lining of the colon), so it is absolutely worth them booking a consultation if they aren't feeling great.

THE YEAR OUT

Many students have the opportunity to spend time overseas or away from university on placements as part of their course. Some spend time perfecting their language skills, as well as being immersed in the culture of their chosen country, others spend time in industry or in clinical settings, or have an overseas module for a term, studying their own subject (such as Medicine) but in a foreign location. It can be a transformative experience for most and great for personal development, but it is important that support is available to them should they need it as homesickness, isolation, culture shock and anxiety can be potential issues. Placement students who continue to live with students who are embracing traditional uni life can become stressed by the noise and differing lifestyles of their flatmates, so it may be worth considering living with *other* placement students during such years.

It is worth asking about support while abroad when deciding which uni to attend, if that is likely to be a part of the course. It can be highly variable and asking past students on the open days can be helpful.

One refreshing approach taken by some language students, who were tired of seeing posts on Instagram about other students' seemingly perfect year abroad moments, was to create a website called 'All Abroad' on which they posted only the things that went wrong overseas! By sharing their own minor misfortunes in a humorous and heart-warming manner they wanted to reassure their peers about the normality of having a bad day and demonstrate that they could all get through it together.

Dr Ian Barkataki is a senior university clinical psychologist, who brings to his decade of front-line experience a thoughtful and considered approach to caring for students with mental health difficulties. He suggests that for parents whose child is going overseas it is vital to ensure that the student knows where to go for help if they need it, and to have agreed times to make contact, to reassure both parents and student. He adds that living away from your family and culture of origin can be taxing and is often an additional pressure to that of leaving home for uni, so it is important to put in place in advance any resources the student might need for their well-being, whether they be medical, spiritual or cultural.

> ### PARENT POINTER
>
> - Sending 'care packages' containing favourite foods, tea, funny postcards, special ingredients or herbs for cooking, magazine or books, and toiletries, can really boost morale, as can reminding them of 'lights at the end of the tunnel', such as holiday plans, Christmas or, in the longer term, why they are doing their degree. This goes for students staying closer to home too of course!

SAFETY AND SECURITY

Security is often not something students want to think about too deeply, associated as it is with the idea that things might go wrong or be frightening, but it is a crucial aspect of living a safe life away from the family home. The advent of personal safety apps that allow their friends to know where they are, or enable a young person to press a panic button on their phone if necessary, are great tech developments but should not replace old-fashioned common sense and the basic mantra of 'leave no man behind'. Looking after themselves and others should hopefully be something that is second nature to most people, but that sadly gets forgotten all too often when alcohol, drugs or a new potential 'hook-up' become part of the equation. Personal safety awareness is equally valid for male and female students, as crime statistics for England and Wales show that men are much more likely to be the victim of a violent crime than women (except in sexual assault and domestic violence incidents).[18,19] It is also worrying to read from the same crime survey that those aged 16–24 years are twice as likely to be victims of crime as older adults. Being aware may help protect your student.

Innovation is also fighting back in the battle with drink spiking (when alcohol or drugs are added to a drink without the person knowing). Students can now buy (and unis often provide free) plastic stoppers for their drink, through which they can poke a straw, to reduce the risk of anyone tampering with it. They should (at a minimum) never leave their drink unattended in public places, stick their thumb over the top of the bottle if they walk around with it and, if they start to feel woozy when they don't expect to, tell a friend immediately and go home safely (in a licensed taxi).

HOME FOR THE HOLIDAYS

They're back! Maybe you've missed them, maybe not as much as you thought, but here they are, back home for a break and to catch up with friends and family. Holidays are a great opportunity for students to rest and recover from the stress of uni, but they may also be an opportunity to get a job, earn some much-needed cash, do an internship or even get in some volunteering, possibly to spruce up their CV or just for fun.

The returning student may clear your well-stocked fridge like a plague of locusts or you may notice that their weight has changed dramatically (up or down), or that they are missing meals or taking food secretly. They may sleep for the first four days, or they may be feeling chatty and have loads to tell you. As one student told us, sometimes when you get home you can go from one extreme feeling to the other, wanting to be left alone or wanting to tell your family everything you have been doing:

> It's great if your mum or dad can be okay with that for a bit, and let you find your place again, let you talk when you want, and have alone time when you need it, and not ask you loads of questions or expect you to chat when you don't feel like it.

(And apparently, they *hate* being asked what they plan to do after uni!)

Coming home can be emotional for both parties it seems. For parents, the student they may not have seen for weeks or months can have changed in appearance (think haircut or colour, piercings, tattoos), opinions, politics, food choices (they may expect you to fully embrace their choice to be vegan *and* cater for it) or relationship status. It may help to think of this as 'they have changed shape but the hole they left behind has stayed the same', which is why they no longer quite fit where they were before.

PARENT POINTER

- A radiant smile over your gritted teeth will do wonders for family relations, until you can talk about their life choices in a 'sideways' conversation (side by side, doing another activity, rather than eyeball-to-eyeball over a table). This is all part of their self-identity development process and tolerating 'evolution in progress' in your home may help you to manage the changes.

Bringing up tricky topics

If your suspicion is that your returning child may have mental health problems please see Chapter 14, but the signs to look out for might include:

- how much time they are sleeping (a few days' recovery is one thing, but weeks at a time is not normal) and other sleep disturbances
- anger and irritability, which can signal depression
- marked changes in weight

- pronounced sadness or tearfulness
- secretive behaviour that might mask eating issues or drug and alcohol misuse
- deteriorating skin and hair, which are general signs of poor health

In all these cases, try to be tactful – 'You seem a bit run down/ tired/sad …' rather than a more dramatic 'Goodness, look how skinny you are!' When they do chat with you, listen, resist the urge to interrupt, let them tell you their story in their own way and try not to jump to conclusions.

Do not overreact! Overreacting is like kryptonite to teenagers and young adults. Try to stay calm, listen and believe them. Refrain from being dismissive ('There's no point in worrying about that') and don't 'over normalise' ('Oh, that happens to everyone'). Try instead: 'I think that happens quite often, but it sounds really difficult.' They need to feel that you take them seriously and validate their feelings. Help them to get help and see a professional or check a website for more information if that's what they would like, but don't do it all for them unless they are really incapacitated. Think of yourself as a guide, *not* their personal assistant.

TWO SIDES TO EVERY STORY

Be aware that you may not have heard the whole story, and that there are two sides to every story. They may say that they have received 'no help' from university services, but what they may mean is that they have been to see various teams, been offered support, advice, even medication, but have declined them and don't feel better, or that they have gone to therapy and they don't feel better. The point is that while feeling awful is dreadful, young people often expect instant results and can feel very frustrated and upset when things take time to heal or improve.

If they *have* had no help despite asking, then they should raise this issue with a different team.

> ### PARENT POINTERS
>
> - Gather what information you can, and perhaps take a break and come back to the conversation when you and they have had time to process it.
> - We advise against phoning the relevant university services to complain or ask what is happening, as it will not only undermine the student's independence but may create additional conflict that is unhelpful, when actually the services may be involved and doing their best. See pages 295–7 for advice on how and when to contact university services in a helpful and constructive way.

THINKING POINTS

At university, students will face social, financial, domestic and time pressures, but most importantly they will be under great academic pressure, and as parents you have a significant opportunity to reduce any excess weight of expectation they may feel, by talking about how *they* are not their studies or degree, and reminding them of how much you love them, whatever happens. University is often not the 'best' time of anyone's life, but it can be fun, challenging and life-transforming, and so your student will need your support and patience throughout.

Here are a few things to consider:

- Prepare them for a new way of living: independent learning, healthcare, financial, flatmates and daily living skills will all develop. Safety skills are also vital.

- Let them lead the way: on arrivals day, in help-seeking, and in talking about difficult topics.
- Encourage them to be themselves and make friends slowly – they will find their tribe eventually.
- Understand that university services' confidentiality is 'non-negotiable', so ensure your student consents for you to liaise with services if necessary.
- Tolerate their new identity and self-discovery, although if you have significant concerns, raise them tactfully.

PART 5

MENTAL HEALTH AND WELL-BEING

CHAPTER 11

The Importance of Sleep

We underestimate the value and importance of sleep at our teenagers' (and our own!) peril, and if there is one thing we can do to really help their mental health and well-being on multiple levels, it is to explain to young people the importance of sleep and encourage them to get their nine (yes nine!) hours a night.

WHY SLEEP MATTERS

Teenagers. Known for being up at night and asleep in the day, and irritable with it ... How and why does this happen, and why does sleep, and getting enough of it, matter? Understanding this might help us as parents better understand what's happening for them, why it matters that they get their 'beauty' sleep and how we can support them in a way that is pragmatic and tolerant.

Sleep is not neutral; it is a daily opportunity for the body and brain to process and repair after the day's labours. During sleep our brains have been shown to light up with activity as these processes get to work. Missing this opportunity can have significant negative consequences on physical and mental health. Dr Kirstie Anderson, a UK neurologist and sleep doctor, tells her teenage patients that, 'You are "revising" all your new learning when you're asleep.' She told us, 'When young people get fewer than eight to ten hours' sleep a night, they risk negatively impacting on the three Ms: mood, memory and metabolism, for example food cravings go up and weight gain can follow.'

It won't cheer you either to discover that 'catching up' on sleep is a myth – once it's missed, it's missed, and there is no way to regain that lost opportunity to repair and recuperate. Matthew Walker, a world-renowned sleep doctor, states that this is one of the primary messages we should take from his book *Why We Sleep*.[1]

One of the most fascinating phenomena linked to adolescent sleep is the shift in their body clock (circadian rhythm) between childhood and adulthood. This is their daily sleep–wake cycle, that primary urge we have to be awake when it's light and asleep when it's dark. As children that urge to sleep comes on in the early evening, and as adults at around 10pm or 11pm in general. However, in puberty the brain shifts its onset of sleepiness dramatically to about 1am. For girls, the shift will likely happen between the ages of 11 and 13, and for boys a little later.[2] With the teenage need for approximately nine hours' sleep you can see how they then might want to sleep until late morning. While this can be accommodated by an understanding and supportive parent at weekends, our society is (unfortunately for teenagers) run by adults not adolescents, so we force them to get up at 7am or earlier, which would be the equivalent of 4am or 5am every weekday for us! They feel groggy, exhausted and irritable, with good reason. Such feelings are known as 'social jetlag', and can occur in anyone forced to be awake for work or social reasons, when they would normally be asleep.[3] Anyone thinking that teens should just go to bed earlier, should bear in mind that you can't force them to sleep sooner, as their brain literally can't 'switch off' until the early hours of the morning. You are setting yourself up to fail if you try to force them to do this. They are trapped in their teenage brains in an 'adult-adjusted' society, until eventually, in their mid-twenties, their rhythm (body clock) shifts back again, just in time for entry to the workplace for some.

In case you are wondering how evolution got this so wrong, it didn't. It is thought that this generational difference is another possible example (along with finding their parents excruciatingly embarrassing) of how evolution encourages young people to separate from their family, creating a time during which all the teenagers of the 'tribe' would have been awake together without parents or children around, allowing them to develop their self-identity. It may also explain (partially) why teenagers are often so grumpy!

PARENT POINTERS

- As parents we can perhaps use this knowledge to help us take a deep breath and remain calm next time we struggle to get our young adult ready in time for school in the morning, can't raise them from bed before lunchtime or hear that they missed their first morning lecture again. And young people sleep more deeply than adults, which may be another reason you are defeated when trying to wake them early.

- Being tolerant of their dramatically different body clocks will be helpful, but we have yet to see if society will be as tolerant or adapt to them, though some schools in the US are starting to trial later start times.[4]

The problem with sleep is that young people often view it as, at best, neutral or boring and, at worst, something to be cut as short as possible, in order to do more fun things. They will often try to get away with as little sleep as possible, unaware, as many of us are, of how important sleep is for our health and well-being. Missing sleep can be particularly calamitous for the still-developing brain. A good night's sleep isn't just great for improving our energy levels and mood, but it is vital for good mental and physical health, processing learning, memory and weight management!

Brain development

Sleep is the time when our teens' brain pathways are shaped and pruned, creating the brain that they will have as an adult. It is therefore essential to allow the brain the time it needs for this evolutionary process. This is one reason why adolescents need more sleep than adults, allowing their brains to develop and mature zone by zone.

Knowledge and learning

Most students go to uni to get a degree. They hope and expect to have some fun doing it and to learn new skills and meet some great people along the way, but for most their primary aim is to study and get the best degree that they can. Understanding how important sleep is to that aim, and how they can maximise its benefits, may be of interest to them. A healthy regular sleep habit will be *more effective* than taking study drugs and less stressful than revising all hours, and can potentially allow them to work more efficiently throughout their course.[5]

They need to know that sleeping well *before* learning new information is very helpful. As Matthew Walker explains, sleep helps to prepare your brain for laying down new memories, so a good night's sleep before *and* after lectures is sensible as it increases retention of memories by up to 40 per cent![6,7] This could be particularly impactful for university tests or exams of course. Curtailed sleep reduces the brain's ability to process memories and make room for new ones. School pupils will also find this relevant.

PARENT POINTERS

- If you can persuade your young adult to get the sleep they need (ideally 8–10 hours a night, especially around exam time, and also when learning new topics), you will be helping them to manage their moods and metabolism, and improve their memory.
- For textbook, fact-heavy learning it has been shown that the early part of the night is most important in terms of when to prioritise sleep. So whether they are learning lists of verbs for Modern Languages, anatomical names for Medicine or dates for History, they should try to sleep from as soon as they feel sleepy (midnight or 1am), to 'seal in' the learning they have done earlier that day. Sleep will then file away those memories and make room for new ones.

Interestingly, sleep also 'seals in' learning from practical skills such as playing the piano, or sports and athletic technique. That hard-to-master melody or basketball skill which eludes them on one day can come easily after practice and a good night's sleep. Walker's research has also identified that it is the *last* two hours of sleep that are most useful for this particular benefit. Getting up early to practise therefore may *reduce* the prior day's gains and be counterproductive.[8] Depending on what your child is studying (say Chemistry or Music) this may influence their sleep time.

Relationships

It may also interest young adults to consider the emotional impact on their social lives of 'sleep deprivation' (which anything less than seven hours is considered to be). Their relationships with friends and significant others are hugely important to them, so knowing that a lack of sleep will affect how they react and respond to friends, or under pressure, may influence them in ensuring that they get enough sleep. Being sleep-deprived makes us emotionally hyper-reactive and irrational, and we can mood swing rapidly. In extreme cases, lack of sleep can heighten the risk of self-harm and suicidal thinking and behaviours, much as alcohol can, as we become disinhibited and irrational in how we act.[9] If all that wasn't thought-provoking enough, there is evidence that lack of sleep leads to increased anxiety and weight gain (we put on weight when we don't sleep well, no matter what we do in the daytime).[10,11]

THINKING POINTS

Sleep is not a luxury. It is in fact a bit of an underappreciated 'wonder drug', so you can help by talking to your young adult about what happens during sleep (memories stored and put away, knowledge and learning sealed in, emotions processed) and ensuring that they are aware of its life-enhancing properties. As parents you can also tolerate their body clock shift (evolution again!), encourage nine hours' sleep when possible and stop screens one hour before sleep. Dr Anderson says,

'Light is a "wake-up drug" so switch to listening activities (audio) or real books at night, and turn screens off, as they will keep you awake. Ideally leave all screens outside the bedroom, as teenagers are more sensitive to light than adults.' She also encourages keeping the bed for sleeping, not for revising or chilling out on, instead using a beanbag if they choose to be in their bedroom in the daytime.

If your teen has tried the following 'sleep hygiene' recommendations and they are still struggling with sleep after a week or two, encourage them to talk to a healthcare professional.

- Sleep when it is dark and be up when it is light, broadly speaking, allowing for teenage body clocks. Don't sleep all day and work all night.
- Avoid daytime naps after 3pm.
- Go to bed and get up at the same time each day – routine and regular sleep times are essential if sleep has become disrupted.
- Avoid alcohol in the hours before bed, as well as heavy meals and hard exercise.
- Total caffeine per day is what matters for young people – no more than two cups of coffee or two cans of caffeinated soda per day are recommended for good sleep.
- Try not to pull 'all-nighters', as these impact response times and memory, as well as impair learning. Better to stop work and sleep on it to improve next day performance.
- Build regular exercise, fresh air and natural daylight into every day.
- Sleep in a dark room, and minimise noise disruption.
- Consider trying Cognitive Behavioural Therapy for Insomnia (CBT-I) on the NHS.[12] (If under 18, this might not be available, so consider apps for support and speak to a professional.)
- Avoid sleep medication (including from 'over the counter').

CHAPTER 12

Academic Pressure

We have traditionally considered university life to be the preamble to 'real life' – a time for finding ourselves, studying an area of interest, having philosophical discussions with our peers and gaining a network to set us up for gainful employment. Shouldn't students therefore feel *more* relaxed and confident about the future? Perhaps surprisingly, the answer is no. Students in the UK have been found to be less happy, less satisfied with life and more anxious than their non-student peers.[1] It would seem that being a student in the twenty-first century is more stressful than *not* going to university. Being a student is *not* protective of mental health. The main additional stressor seems to be academic pressure. As we discussed in Chapter 4, as parents you can help by preparing your young adult for the demands of academic study, supporting them to cope if things go wrong and listening when they need support. This underlines the need to be clear that they are not *letting you down* if things go wrong. This academic pressure is also relevant at school and so similar principles and issues will apply for younger teenagers. The world has become more competitive and target-driven, and the pressure has transferred to our youngest generation.

In our experience, the main issues that can spell doom for academic success are:

1. Fear of failure
2. Imposter syndrome
3. Procrastination
4. Perfectionism

These four psychological hurdles can trip up even the most able of students (and school pupils) if they are not prepared.

Fear of failure

One of the greatest worries for young people is *letting people down*, especially those that they love. Fear of failure can be a huge weight on young shoulders, as they bring the pressure of family, and sometimes the wider community, with them to school or university. This fear hovers like a cloud above them as they struggle from day to day, trying to do everyone proud. Carl Jung, the famous psychiatrist, once said, 'Nothing has a stronger influence psychologically on their children than the unlived life of the parent' and teaching staff are sadly very used to seeing young people living under the weight of their parents' expectations and dreams.[2]

Students are usually desperate to make their parents proud but also do themselves justice. They will have worked hard to win a place and may have sailed in on a wave of high expectations and optimism, only to see the reading list, academic texts or essay titles, which can cause them to wilt (or panic). Some of the university support professionals we spoke to had noticed a steady rise in students feeling a pressure to be at the top. This need to be the best and 'keep up with the Joneses' seemed ingrained in current students from an early age. One professional told us that a student had even recounted to him his parents' (somewhat shocking) view: 'My dad said "You're my pension – when the time comes you will need to look after us", which places a huge pressure on me to succeed, earn as much as I can, to be able to look after them later, because they have supported me financially till now.' We can only imagine the pressure this adds. These students feel unable to share their academic worries, despite the university staff strongly encouraging them to speak to their parents when life is difficult.

PARENT POINTERS*(THIS COULD SAVE THEIR LIFE)

- Tell them how proud you are (without going over the top) and really mean it. Avoid being the source of additional pressure; be their support instead.
- Let them know that whatever happens they can *always* talk to you. They are *not* their degree or their school grades, and it is them that you love, not their achievements.
- In our experience, this theme of letting loved ones down tragically runs through many student suicides, so this message *really* matters.

Imposter syndrome

It can be really hard for students to keep up the momentum academically and know how to pace themselves, and they can feel like a small fish in a big pond, when they have previously been the 'golden' girl or boy of their year. This scenario can lead to imposter syndrome, which makes them believe that they aren't clever or talented enough to be at university, despite the fact that they have been through a rigorous selection process or that universities have criteria for admissions. Fortunately, universities are ahead of them in dealing with academic stress and lay on 'academics skills' classes, which are a brilliant way for students to learn about time management or that they don't have to read *everything* on a subject before being able to sit down and write about it. Going along to these classes can be a fantastic experience as students realise that there are practical ways to manage and deal with all these new challenges.

Study skills and procrastination

Procrastination is also dealt with in these classes and top tips are given, such as starting by writing something, anything, even if they delete it at the end. Procrastination is common at all ages, when we can't quite face a task or don't know where to start. It can be easier to distract ourselves by editing a favourite playlist or tidying our room, but these displacement activities can also mean that we feel more stressed overall, as the task still hovers over us, demanding our attention. Recognising this behaviour in ourselves or in our young people, as well as discussing techniques to help focus the mind, such as 'elevator pitching' (being able to summarise your idea or concept in three or four simple points, in a way that engages your audience and makes them want to know more, in the 60 seconds it would take to ride an elevator), can be a helpful approach and such techniques are useful skills for future employment.

Paralysed by perfection

Procrastination itself is often driven by perfectionism of course, which, as we mentioned in Chapter 2, has risen dramatically in the student population in the last 30 years.[3] The young person driven by their perfectionist traits tries to produce work that is outstanding rather than 'good enough' for what is needed (they aim for *perfection* all the time), is highly self-critical and prone to exhaustion from redoing work multiple times. They even end up handing work in late, not because they didn't work hard enough but because they were doing *too much*. The perfectionist traits paralyse them and hinder their progress. Depending on how strong their perfectionist traits are they may benefit from attending perfectionism workshops laid on by the university support services or by trying cognitive behavioural therapy (CBT) approaches to manage it and rein it in. Learning to live with 'good enough' is the aim here, rather than risk the onset of mental health problems, which have been strongly linked with perfectionist traits (for example eating disorders, anxiety, depression, self-harm and OCD).

PARENT POINTERS

- Parents can do a lot to help with these academic-related stresses (whether at uni or at school), from telling their child that everyone gets things wrong or 'fails' at things sometimes (and that 'failure' is an essential part of learning) to sharing their own 'failures' or procrastination not just in youth but in everyday life, so that dealing with things when they go wrong becomes normal.
- Remind them that they can access academics skills classes/ perfectionism workshops or counselling as needed for free at university, or they can talk to professionals at school.
- One of our expert school teachers advised: 'If you are disappointed, be disappointed in the *behaviour*, not in the person, and protect your relationship with your child, as that is what really matters long term.'

EXAM STRESS

Exams are an obvious flashpoint for stress and not to be dismissed as 'just another worry'. The reality is that revision pressure often builds for weeks prior, and then the exams themselves crash over young people like a tidal wave of panic, bringing insomnia, palpitations and abdominal pain with it. There are, however, ways to remain calm, keep healthy and prepare thoroughly for exams, and other critical academic moments, and we will come to those shortly.

It is important to be aware, without wishing to cause alarm, that exam time may be associated with a higher risk of emotional distress in young people. For example, we know that suicides in children and young people peak in January, April/May and September/October.[4,5] While it is impossible to say exactly why they might peak at this time of year, it has been suggested that many school and university exams take place in January and April/May, and that associated revision as well as exams may be stressful enough to lead to suicidal behaviours. The third peak could be linked to exam re-sit time at university, overlapping with the time of year students arrive at university in October, which can be a trigger for distress.[6]

PARENT POINTERS

- If your young adult needs someone to talk to, and they don't seem keen to speak to the professionals just yet, you can encourage them to speak to trained peers, such as the university students who work for Nightline, which is a nocturnal helpline freely available in many universities. They just need to search for 'Find my Nightline' online and they can phone or use instant messaging if they prefer.

- Some schools have trained well-being peers as a first port of call for children, who can then connect them to a trained member of staff. School counsellors, if available, are also very helpful, and familiar with these issues. If school support is minimal there are many voluntary organisations offering children professional support, as they do university students.
- If your child suffers from exam stress it may be worth exploring university courses that don't have 'final' exams.

Exam preparation tips

If and when your young person is in a listening mood you may like to suggest the following tips to make their lives and revision easier. We can't guarantee that they will act on them, but it may be worth a try as the advice is rooted in science.

- It can be useful to remember that a little bit of anxiety is actually a good thing. We need a bit of adrenaline to help us focus and function, to be able to act and react, so young people should not be concerned if they feel a bit edgy and stressed, but they should seek help from a professional if it is overwhelming, for example if they can't sleep for several days or they stop eating or start losing weight.
- To deal with any short-term 'fight or flight' anxiety, such as sweaty hands, heart racing, feeling sick on the day itself or poor sleep the night before an exam, they may find it helpful to learn relaxation techniques such as mindfulness or meditation, or they could use a technique like 'shifting attention'.[7] The latter involves taking the attention away from their own anxiety by focusing on something else

around them, such as all the people wearing red or on inanimate objects on a shelf and naming them. This can also be done as 'sensory distraction', using each of their five senses to focus on something outside of themselves; what can they hear, see, smell, touch or taste? Shifting their focus in this way to external objects or sensations allows the mind to be distracted from its inner turmoil and the brain can then slowly refocus on what it is supposed to be doing. This can easily be done in an exam hall (or on the bus).

- Learning with images is particularly helpful, be it flow charts, diagrams or mind-mapping, as many people learn better visually.

- To really understand a topic, they should practise explaining it to people who don't know or understand it, such as their younger sibling (or you!). Or they could work in a group and explain it to each other.

- Varying the location of revision helps to prepare the brain for a new location on the day of the exam, and makes learning more effective, so it's worth moving to different rooms, libraries, study spaces and so on for revision sessions. *How We Learn* by Benedict Carey has some wonderful advice, and also mentions that for better long-term recall it is most effective to read through a topic then write down what you can remember, rather than copy out notes direct from the text.[8]

- Taking breaks every hour or so – for example 10 minutes of fresh air or a quick jog up and down the street – is great for allowing the brain to refresh.

- Healthy eating is one thing that can get lost in all the revision, but which is important not to forget about. A healthy breakfast on the day of the exam should not be missed if at all possible!

Personal tutors

One of the greatest sources of support for university students, though sometimes underused, is their academic, pastoral or personal tutor.[9] Tutors are receiving more training in welfare and well-being support in many institutions, as universities recognise the holistic needs of students, and that without good physical and mental health their students are unlikely to achieve their full academic potential. Many tutors are embracing the well-being agenda and are acting as liaison with welfare services, or participating in research on student well-being topics. Some have had mental health training, have taken an accredited online course in the topic of well-being or have a personal interest in welfare topics. Some do retain a more traditional view that well-being in any form is not their job and some are simply too busy to also take on this aspect of pastoral care.

The practical approach for a student needing support is to try talking to their own allocated personal tutor first, and if that does not appear to be a fruitful conversation, then it may be worth asking other students for recommendations. There may also be nominated well-being leads ('champions') or advisers who are not academics themselves but located in the academic department as a sort of 'outreach worker' from the main university student support services. By asking around or checking the website a student will be able to discover who exactly is in place within an institution to provide welfare support. There will always be somebody.

THINKING POINTS

Academic pressure is one of the most significant factors causing young people stress and is linked to mental health issues. While it is normal to be under some academic pressure at school and university, the rising drivers of perfectionism and competition in the modern world are potentially leading to heightened academic pressure compared with our own experiences. Alongside perfectionism you may notice greater procrastination in your children, and associated fear of failure or letting people down (family, friends, teachers and lecturers). They may doubt their ability to keep up with work, or be good enough for their school or university, and you can help greatly by reassuring them that they need only do their best, not be *the* best, that you are proud of them, that 'good enough' (not perfection) may be all that is required, and that sometimes things go wrong in life, and that you are there to support them while they figure things out, try again or try something different.

- Encourage healthy approaches to revision and exam time.
- Encourage them to attend teaching in person, and not to rely on lecture capture or online resources, as they will benefit both from the personal learning interaction and the regular social contact.
- Share your own 'failures' and bad days in a constructive way, to normalise the ups and downs of life and demonstrate how to cope pragmatically.
- Aim for 'good enough', not perfectionism, in your own life to model healthy standards.
- Remind your young adult that help is available: professional counsellors, trained volunteers/peers or online – the choice is up to them.
- If they are struggling, especially around exam time, don't ignore it. This is a vulnerable time and extra support may be needed; a listening ear, anxiety management techniques such as mindfulness, revision breaks, healthy food and just reminding them that all they can do is their best will all help to ease the pressure.

CHAPTER 13

The Mental Health 'Epidemic'

Mental health matters. We consider diet and exercise to be of fundamental importance to physical health, and fret if our kids spend too much time horizontal, snacking, in front of a screen. Understandably, many parents feel less well-prepared to advise on the emotional aspects of their child's well-being. Being a parent is challenging enough without worrying that you may miss a significant symptom of psychological distress or fearing that you may inadvertently be causing more issues. Teenagers in particular can be tricky to support at the best of times, so knowing what to watch out for and when to seek help may be very useful. Knowing what to say and what not to say to your child are equally important (see pages 267–9).

As teenagers grow up they will, all being well, leave home and, for parents, enabling them to do this successfully is a very rewarding achievement. However, whether at university or work, living at home or independently – even for the best-prepared young people – things can sometimes go wrong.

Many 16–25-year-olds say they have either suffered from a mental health problem themselves *or* have wanted to help a friend who is suffering. Leaving the safety net of home and friends for a town (or country) that may be hundreds of miles away can exacerbate any problems young people may have had earlier in their lives, and it can lead to new issues. So how can you prepare your children if mental health issues arise and what can you do to support your young adult?

IS THERE REALLY AN 'EPIDEMIC'?

When reading the news, it's hard to know what to believe about mental health and young people. The media is divided, with some outlets using the word 'crisis' liberally to catch attention, and others arguing that we are overreacting, and that the younger generation needs to 'man up' and stop being 'snowflakes'. Both are unhelpful and wrong. There is no epidemic, and the young are not (on the whole) overreacting, but they have been raised in a very different society, and this has led to very different outcomes for them (as we saw in Chapter 2).

The evidence

The facts are clear. In England, in 2014, 1 in 6 adults in the general population over 16 years of age was found to have a common mental health disorder (defined as depression, anxiety, phobia, OCD and panic disorder).[1] These disorders were more common in women (1 in 5) than men (1 in 8). The figures were obtained by a national large-scale population survey, which has been carried out in England since 1993, every seven years. Momentously, 2014 was the first year a significant rise had been seen in *any* demographic group in the survey, and that group was young women aged 16–24 years. We can therefore confidently assume that we are seeing a greater number of young women, in England at least, with clinically significant symptoms, *whether or not* they themselves recognise them as such. Countries all over the world have also noticed a rise in mental health issues in young adults. In the USA, a study published in 2017 showed a significant national increase in depression between 2005 and 2015, in particular in the youngest group in the study, aged 12–17 years.[2] In Australia they have seen similar rises, again more in young women than in young men, and in Malaysia, a report of young people's mental health in 2017 demonstrated a steady rise in problems over the previous 15 years, so it really does seem like it may be a worldwide trend.[3,4] However, it is certainly not an 'epidemic' or 'crisis', but may be a result of societal changes.[5] Some of the rise in mental health demand and awareness may also be due to our talking about it more (as suggested by Dr Stan Kutcher, an international adolescent mental health expert), which is no bad thing.[6]

We should resist feeling disheartened for the world's next generation, and focus instead on how we can best support and encourage our young adults to be resourceful in the face of challenge, to be open to talking about feelings, to avoid bottling things up and to know where they can get help if they need it.

WHEN DO MENTAL HEALTH PROBLEMS START?

Mental health disorders most commonly start in childhood and adolescence. The reasons behind this are complex, and include environmental, genetic and epigenetic factors. Epigenetic factors are factors that affect how a gene (a segment of DNA) is 'expressed' (operates), which will in turn affect how the brain develops, potentially leading to mental health disorders. In real life, these factors can include: sleep, diet, physical surroundings, stress, traumatic events, alcohol and drugs. This means that a huge variety of factors can affect how our genes operate, which affects how our brains develop, which influences whether or not we will have a mental health condition. Genetics *and* our environment both play a part in whether or not people develop mental health problems. This is the 'nature and nurture' that we always hear about, and both play a role.

JAMES'S STORY

James was a first-year university student but had been unwell since about the age of 11, when he first developed a tendency to be very careful about the presentation of his homework, and then his appearance. If the work did not meet his own exacting standards he would, as a child, cry and rip it up, starting again, with increasing frequency as the years passed. Rituals developed; the need to count in threes, and touch every third rung on his bedstead before going to sleep. By the time James went to see the doctor at the university clinic, he had reached the desperate daily scenario whereby if he did not complete the self-imposed rituals he had created for saying goodbye to departing flatmates before leaving the house, he would remain at the front door, all day, until they returned, not moving even to eat, drink or visit the toilet. He had finally reached a point at which he himself recognised that he needed help and was willing to be referred for talking therapy with a psychologist. He was diagnosed with OCD, medication was discussed and started, and a review doctor appointment made.

James's story illustrates a well-recognised fact. Three-quarters of mental health conditions start before the age of 24, and half show symptoms before the age of 14.[7] So it is very common for mental health problems to start in young people, with a peak between the ages of 16 and 24. In other words, at the age when emotional disorders most commonly start, we traditionally encourage teenagers to leave home, for university or the workplace. It is therefore no great surprise that at this transitional time of life, where biological destiny and challenging environment collide, mental health issues deteriorate. We are 'removing' young adults from their support networks and, in many cases, NHS or other therapists, just when they need it most, leading previous problems to worsen. James had kept his metaphorical OCD plates spinning until he left the familiarity of his home, when he had to move into university residences, attend lectures, manage deadlines and meet new people. When he couldn't keep his plates spinning any longer, he collapsed emotionally.

One of the things young people worry most about is if they are 'normal' or not when compared with their peers.[8] This pressure may be particularly obvious when young people might have mental health issues and for whom stigma, being different and standing out from the crowd in this specific way, is very stressful, and can be the reason many of them don't seek help until they reach crisis point, if they seek help at all.

A 'fresh start' or just wishful thinking?

It is common for young people to arrive at university having had a mental health problem at school or home and to hope that it will magically resolve itself, or be less of an issue, when they arrive, despite the fact that they are in an unknown environment, filled with academic pressure, new people and other stress. Senior clinical psychologist, Dr Ian Barkataki, explained it like this: 'We have hopes and expectations when we come to university, and very rarely do they include us being impaired or unwell in any way.' It is entirely understandable that the young adult is hopeful that the fresh start will mean they can embark on a new life without any associated stigma or labels. Unfortunately, the challenge with this kind of magical thinking is that mental health conditions don't have borders or boundaries, and are in fact likely to get worse at first in a stimulating but stressful environment. This can then be compounded by other changes, such as to sleep patterns or by drinking more alcohol.

If a young person has been having therapy before leaving, they should assume they will need to continue with it during the transition phase, even if they can then wean off it as they settle in. The same goes for medication. Countless students arrive at university having suddenly stopped medication for mental health conditions, in the hope that the new surroundings will be enough to sort out their problems. Very sadly, and sometimes with tragic consequences, this approach rarely works.

PARENT POINTERS

- We may not be able to influence all of the factors that can lead to our child having mental health problems (if they have any), but we can definitely influence some.
- We can't fight biology and genetics, but we can absolutely *minimise* risk.
- We can make sure that the environment ('nurture') part of the equation is as positive as possible.

WHAT TO LOOK OUT FOR

It can be hard to know what to watch for and which behaviours to worry about. Below is a list of things you may notice and want to discuss with your young adult or read more about if they seem persistent. If you are worried about any of these speak to a healthcare professional for advice.

Symptoms ('What people complain of')	Behaviours ('What others might notice')
Low mood, tearfulness	Isolating self
Feeling hopeless, helpless or trapped, with the feeling that there is no way out	Mood swings
	Self-harming
Anger	Irritability
Low self-esteem	Paranoia
Feelings of guilt or shame	Talking to self
Poor sleep (various changes), focus, concentration, memory	Secret behaviours e.g. vomiting after eating, secret eating or drinking alcohol, hiding/ stealing food
Cloudy thinking, 'brain fog'	
Feel empty/numb/'outside' of themselves	Panic attacks, an 'overwhelming sense of doom' leading to hyperventilation, shaking, dizziness, feeling out of control
Lost interest in usual activities, stopped doing preferred activities	
No pleasure or enjoyment in usual activities	Phobic or avoidant behaviours
Can't make decisions	Reckless behaviour, out of character risk-taking
Excessively and disproportionately happy (euphoric) or energetic	Extremes of behaviour
	Inappropriate thoughts, behaviour, disinhibited
Racing thoughts	Spending a lot of money
Appetite changes, more or less	Nonsensical speech, disjointed thoughts
Weight changes, up or down	
Agitation/can't sit still	Grandiose thinking
Anxious, worrying, ruminating, fear and excessive vigilance	Excessive drinking/drug misuse
	Self-medicating
Repetitive thoughts, actions, behaviours that are unwanted and disruptive	Failing academically (beware perfectionists who will let health deteriorate preferentially to work) or in relationships/losing friends
Physical symptoms, e.g. heart racing, chest pain, headaches, fatigue, 'fight or flight' reaction	
Auditory or visual hallucinations	
Flashbacks and unwanted images	

MENTAL HEALTH AND LGBT+ YOUNG PEOPLE

LGBT+ (lesbian, gay, bisexual, transgender, plus others such as questioning their gender or asexual) young people need extra care, support and understanding as they navigate a world that is not always tolerant and kind towards them. It is a sad fact that they are more likely to suffer poor well-being and are more at risk of mental health problems throughout life. They are more likely than non-LGBT+ young people to suffer from depression, anxiety, post-traumatic stress disorder and self-harm, as well as being more likely to misuse alcohol and drugs, possibly to cope with some of the stresses of being in a minority demographic.[9] Their loved ones therefore have a huge role to play in boosting their resilience, and one of the most effective ways you can do this is to be positive, encouraging and comforting when they need someone to lean on.

Support and acceptance from family and close friends is a significant *protective* factor for the mental health of LGBT+ young people.[10] It is so important to be compassionate, open, tolerant and loving of your child, whatever their sexuality.

WHAT TO DO

What we say matters

As the Instagram quote says: 'Mental health is not Fight Club, we *can* talk about it!' A rule of thumb when talking to young people about their feelings, emotions and mental health is to start with *open* questions. Try to find a time when they are relaxed or when you are doing something else together, such as driving or walking the dog, and ask something like, 'Is there anything you want to talk about?' or ' How are you feeling at the moment?' and be guided by their response. Even if they are not keen to talk right then, they will know that you are open to talking when they feel ready. Don't force them to talk, but leave it open and with them to raise when they feel ready.

> ### PARENT POINTER
>
> - Some teachers we spoke to recommended making time for your young person on a *regular* basis – going for a coffee, having a chat and catching up – accepting that most of the time it might be quite a low-key conversation, but that 1 in 10 'coffee chats' might perhaps suddenly lead to a revelation or discussion of a more difficult topic. Having this routine in place would allow your child to know that they can talk to you when they feel ready.

The wonderful YoungMinds UK website has some great examples of 'Questions I wish my parents had asked me', such as 'What are you worried about when you lie in bed and can't sleep?' or 'It's okay to keep stuff private but did you want to tell me more about … ?' which may be useful for introducing tricky topics.[11] If your young person starts to tell you something important, make time for them, be *curious* and reflect with them on what is happening, but remember that you don't have to have all the answers – you can find them together.

Really listen

When your child does start to talk it's really important to let them speak and just listen. Try not to interrupt. Hear what they are saying and try to see it from their point of view, *without* all your years of experience; or the insight that feelings go up and down, and difficult times usually pass; or that getting through those difficult times actually makes us the people we are (and often stronger for it). Try not to use phrases that could sound dismissive such as 'This time next week you'll feel fine', 'It's a phase' or 'You'll get over it', even if you think that might be the case. Your young adult needs to feel believed, understood and validated, which means their feelings need to be taken seriously and valued, so these conversations can be critical moments in your relationship.

Be present

As one school counsellor told us:

> Parenting is inconvenient. Parents will sometimes have to stop what they are doing, rearrange their day, or even take time off work if their child needs them for something important, especially related to well-being. You can't 'outsource' parenting. You have to do your bit, but you don't need to *know* everything.

She told of one young adult who liked hearing her mum 'pottering about' the house in the holidays, needing no more than that to feel reassured that her mum was there, but not needing a conversation or constant contact. As your teenager grows up, they may need you less often but they need to know you are there; they need to hear you in their lives.

REDUCING THE RISK OF MENTAL HEALTH ISSUES

In a sense, this whole book hopes to reduce the risk of longer term mental health and well-being issues in your child, as we hope it will help you to build their resilience, deal with things when they go wrong in a healthy way, reduce perfectionism, learn about life's ups and downs, understand that bad times pass, and that we are built to survive adversity but that sometimes it can be really hard.

There will be some things you can control and some things you can't. You can only do the best you can with the resources available to you at the time. Being aware of the factors that affect the likelihood of mental health problems developing, and which you can influence, may help you to feel more able to minimise the risk of future problems.

Areas you can usefully focus on include:[12]

- Your child's physical health and nutrition.
- Your own mental health and well-being (this is vital – see pages 256–8).
- Issues with bullying or isolation.
- Providing a stimulating environment and avoiding neglect are both effective in preventing mental illness, so the fact that you are reading this book, taking an active interest and looking for ways to support your child is really positive.
- Taking the 'authoritative' approach to parenting (loving, with boundaries around behaviours – see pages 58–9), which is the most protective parenting strategy for well-being. 'Authoritarian' and 'helicopter' parenting have actually been shown to be harmful to well-being.
- Minimising use of drugs (by educating your child about risks and informed decision-making).
- Encouraging their school to discuss topics related to well-being and reducing stigma.

These are very effective ways to decrease the likelihood of problems developing in their teens and early twenties.[13]

Population approaches, such as teaching all children mindfulness at school (or CBT techniques) for example, have been disappointing in not yet showing a reduction in mental health issues (anxiety, depression or eating disorders in particular) in young people, but may still be useful techniques for some on an individual level.[14]

Self-care and staying well

There are many ways for young people to look after themselves and stay as well as they can. A brief but brilliant model of ways we can all look after ourselves is the 'Five Ways to Wellbeing', which you may have come across in your own life.[15] It is a set of five evidenced-based actions to improve mental health and wellbeing in the population. The premise is simple: if we follow these five actions in our everyday lives we will feel better and live happier lives. You can think of it as an emotional health version of your 'five-a-day fruit and veg' for physical well-being!

The Five Ways to Wellbeing are:

1. Connect: be engaged in positive relationships and with your community.
2. Be active: by physically exercising and moving.
3. Take notice: be engaged and aware of the world around you and of your own experiences.
4. Keep learning: challenge and stretch cognitively by engaging with new learning and discovering new things.
5. Give: help others.

In other words, if your young adult has good relationships with others, exercises, looks up at the world around them occasionally, tries new things and helps others, they are very likely to flourish.

Role-model good behaviour

You can help by talking openly about feelings, sharing when things go wrong for you too, and how you cope when that happens, and role-modelling good behaviours, such as asking for help when you need it, giving yourself downtime and eating, sleeping and exercising well. These may help your child to follow your example, even if it takes a while for them to feel confident in doing so.

The Rev Ed Davis has supported many young people in over a decade as Co-ordinating Chaplain at the University of Bristol and he told us:

> Seeing their parents cope with difficulties, such as health issues or conflict, will give young people a template of how to react themselves when things are challenging. It is really important to know as a parent, therefore, that if they see you cope, they are more likely to cope well too.

We have to teach young people to be able to bear what life brings and, as Dr Vik Mohan, a doctor with 15 years' experience caring for students, puts it: 'the young person in front of you is their own solution, we just have to help them see and understand that'.

DON'T OVERSHARE!

You should probably not share everything with your child; they are, after all, still young, and may not have the skills to cope with your distress too. We have heard of parents talking to their children about work stress, financial problems and even their sex lives. Parents are occasionally oversharing or being over-heard by their children when on the phone or in the car. Your teenagers or young adults do not need to know everything, so if you are stressed, try to ensure you have your own support set up and prioritise your well-being for a while. Your children should *not* be your main support.

Cat Taylor, an occupational therapist who works with young people with mental health issues, has frequently supported parents coping with very difficult scenarios. She told us:

> Parents need to look after themselves. I recall one parent feeling very down so I asked her, 'What have you done for yourself this month? Have you been out with friends, or sat with a cup of tea talking to other adults?' Try to accept that your child is not well, and make sure you attend to your own needs too, while they take time to recover. People are more than just parents, so don't feel guilty about needing time for yourself. Support your friends and ask for their support too. Then you can better support your young person.

Be grateful

In life, we navigate between a constant continuum of either feeling 'blessed' or feeling that we are entitled to what we possess in life. In short, we oscillate between gratitude and entitlement. Gratitude is said to have emotional and interpersonal benefits.[16] Research has also demonstrated that using the power of gratitude and appreciation lastingly reduces depressive symptoms and increases happiness levels.[17]

Practise mindfulness

What if we started viewing our emotions (positive or negative) as our inner compass or guidance system telling us how we perceive an external situation or judging a person?

PARENT POINTER

- A simple exercise to introduce on a daily basis is to encourage your child (and everyone in the family) to begin and finish the day with three things they are grateful for. When we start the day appreciating being alive or being healthy, or being grateful for breakfast, it sets the tone for the day.

Positive emotions indicate that we view an event as good and negative emotions as bad. It enables us to know how we are feeling about the situation. We should resist stifling or getting rid of our emotions but rather notice them, acknowledge and pay attention to them and see them as a gift. We can then process them and let them go, rather than trying to push them away or pretend they are not there. This is one of the principles of mindfulness, which has demonstrated that it can help individuals to process the emotions they experience differently in the brain and decreases our emotional reactivity to situations and events.[18]

PARENT POINTERS

- Encourage your young adult not only to become curious about their emotions but to not fear them, by openly expressing how they are feeling rather than building up a facade.
- You may want to consider introducing mindfulness into your family life, but note that, just like other tools, mindfulness is far from being the answer to all problems and it does not help everybody.
- Trying mindfulness apps to help your child sleep at night can be a nice way to see if it works for them, but it can take time to settle into, and needs practice.

Although mindfulness can be seen as a tool, it can also become an approach to life. It means that we develop awareness of the present moment, of our emotions, feelings and sensations, and that we are able to observe these without judgement (neither positive nor negative). A recent trial by the University of Surrey in the UK looked at the effect of the *online* Mindfulness-Based Cognitive Therapy (MBCT) Be Mindful course on depression, anxiety and perceived stress.[19] The results showed that participants who completed the course reported significantly lower levels of perceived stress, depression and anxiety. These effects were maintained at three- and six-month follow-ups. These outcomes rival those of studies which employed a group face-to-face mindfulness-based intervention.

MINDFULNESS AND MENTAL HEALTH

Mindfulness has been previously reported as having negative effects on certain people and, although it might be suitable for young people who are only facing some normal and daily challenges, it might not be suitable for those experiencing mental health problems or mental ill health.[20] For example, research shows that it could be risky to use mindfulness meditation with students experiencing mental disorders or trauma.[21] We would therefore recommend consulting a professional if in doubt.

THINKING POINTS

We have considered how important good mental health is for young people, and that the number of young people having difficulties with their mental health is unfortunately rising. Positive and compassionate parental support and openness to talking about well-being is instrumental to recovery for many young adults. The important thing to remember when times are challenging is that they can get better and you can be highly influential in making that happen.

Here are a few things to consider:

- Be present when your young person needs you and be prepared to talk. Use open questions.
- Find the answers to the problems they bring you together, or help them to discover their own solutions. Encourage self-care.
- LGBT+ young people are at higher risk of well-being issues so will need support and compassion, but, most of all, your acceptance.
- Watch out for worrying or persistent symptoms and behaviours and ask for help if you need it.
- Discourage sudden changes to therapy when they leave home.
- Look after yourself; you are more than just a parent. Try to 'role-model' healthy behaviours.
- You can't fight biology, but you can minimise the risk of mental health issues.
- Use positive psychology practices to find contentment and joy with your family.

If you are worried about your child's mental health or if they are struggling with their emotions, make sure that you seek professional advice.

CHAPTER 14

A Short Guide to Common Mental Health Conditions

S ome of the most common disorders are described below, but for the less common ones you will find loads of fantastic resources, many of which are listed on page 307. We will cover suicidal thinking and behaviours, and mental health crises and how to manage them in the next chapter.

ANXIETY

A nxiety is a very common disorder, often starting in childhood, and is rooted in control, or lack of it, over daily events. The young person may always have been a 'worrier' but it becomes significant if school or family activities are disrupted. Anxiety itself can feel like being on edge all of the time, causing irritability, exhaustion, poor appetite and poor sleep. The mouth can feel dry, and abdominal aches and cramps are not unusual.

There are many forms of anxiety:

• Generalised anxiety: daily, affecting almost everything, for example worrying about homework, the cat or the bus being late.

- Social anxiety: affecting social interactions and communication with others, worrying about going to parties or walking into classes or lectures.
- Specific phobias of different situations or objects: 'fear that is disproportionate to the threat posed', such as fear of spiders, flying or birds.
- Health anxiety: excessive worrying about physical health or symptoms. This is being increasingly recognised by doctors but can often be missed. Such symptoms might include frequent pains, headaches, sensory disturbances (tingling), tiredness and diarrhoea.

Anxiety can lead to panic attacks, where the feelings can become intense or overwhelming and may be described as having a feeling of 'impending doom', that something terrible is about to happen or that they might die. Panic attacks can be very frightening, occur suddenly, often without warning, even wake them at night, and cause sweating, a racing heart, shaking and overbreathing which leads to tingling in the hands and around the mouth. If your child is having a panic attack, try to get them to breathe in through their nose and out through their mouth, while counting the breath in and out slowly with them. Remain calm, use a soothing tone and teach them breathing exercises in the longer term.

Treatment for all types of anxiety is usually through talking therapies. The type and cause of the anxiety will dictate the type of therapy, but medication can also be useful for some.

PARENT POINTERS

- You can teach your child simple distraction techniques, or they might like mindfulness, which involves focusing on the present moment while being aware of how we feel at that moment.

- Distraction techniques can also be useful for anxiety, exam stress or panicky feelings, as we described on page 242.

Unfortunately, anxiety is often a co-conspirator with several other mental health conditions, for example being present in the vast majority of those who have Asperger's Syndrome, as well as commonly occurring alongside depression, eating disorders, OCD and self-harm. So, if your young adult has one of these conditions, they are very likely to have anxiety too.

Student anxieties

University students worry about their academic work, their other (sporting/activity) commitments and they often worry about trying to balance all of these demands on their time. They can sometimes worry that they might be sabotaging themselves by trying to do too much, never giving any one area the time and attention it really needs. They then worry about telling their parents about these worries, because they don't want to stress them or because they feel that their parents are so invested in their university career.

OBSESSIVE COMPULSIVE DISORDER (OCD)

OCD often starts as anxiety. Young people with OCD (like James, who we met on page 248) can feel very anxious if they are unable to complete certain rituals or behaviours, and will often demonstrate perfectionist tendencies. They may believe that something terrible will befall a loved one if their rituals are not completed, and this can be extremely distressing. Control, in particular the need to regain control over difficult and challenging circumstances, is a powerful drive for those with OCD. OCD is much more complex than simply being a 'neat freak' and liking to have things tidy, and will interfere with normal life. It took over the life of one student who roamed the streets of a city at night, collecting rubbish, unable to sleep until she had collected as much as she could, and of a young man who had persistent intrusive thoughts about harming those he loved, which made him feel desperate. Both of these young people recovered well with treatment.

More common OCD behaviours include repeated washing of hands, checking of light switches or saying every fifth word out loud when reading. Effective treatment is available in the form of psychological talking therapies and, in some cases, medication, but asking for help is frequently delayed by the individual's guilt and shame over their thoughts and behaviours, and, all too often, like James's case, only addressed when it reaches crisis point.

DEPRESSION

Depression in young people can be difficult to detect as they may not feel 'sad' but may instead feel angry, irritable or as though they have 'brain fog'. They may lose interest in their usual activities, have low self-esteem and feel flat or numb, but if reasonably able at school or uni, or reasonably resilient, they may continue with their normal life despite their symptoms, compensating as best they can while masking their low mood and poor concentration. You might be tempted to dismiss their mood swings as part of 'teenage behaviour' and sleep or appetite changes could similarly be explained away, when in fact they are suffering from the sleep disturbances and loss of (or excess) appetite that often accompany clinical depression. Being overweight is also often associated with depression.[1]

A depressed teen may withdraw into themselves or pick fights and argue constantly, and they may have anxiety as well as the mood issues. Left unaddressed, depression can lead to self-harm (see pages 269–71) and in some cases suicidal thoughts or behaviours (see Chapter 15). Knowing what to say and when to intervene can be really hard, so read on for useful advice.

PARENT POINTER

- If you are not sure how to differentiate between teenage angst and depression, take note of how persistent and pervasive the behaviours are, whether they are daily and whether they are directed towards everyone or just you. Has your teen stopped doing the things they like, such as going out and seeing people they normally seem happy with? If so, it is important to talk to them about it and show your concern, and seek help if you need to. The more pervasive the issues, the more likely it is to be depression.

How to talk with your child if they are depressed

No special skills are needed to talk to a young person who is feeling depressed, or so low that they believe their life is not worth living (we will cover suicidal thoughts in more detail in the next chapter). You just need to be kind, compassionate and sensitive, taking a direct approach with open questions.

It's helpful to start by asking how they are feeling ('I can see you're not yourself. Can we talk about it?') or, if you already know things are bad, asking if things have got so bad that they think they might harm themselves, but try to avoid 'negative questions'. This means avoiding questions that start, 'You're *not* thinking of harming yourself, are you?' or 'You're *not* depressed, are you?' which are much more likely to get an answer designed to reassure you, rather than reveal their genuine emotional state.

Try to normalise their feelings without being dismissive. There's a subtle difference between saying, 'Lots of people sometimes feel like this, it's okay, we can sort this out together' and saying, 'Don't worry, it's completely normal, nothing to worry about.' Try to err on the side of the former so that although you are feeling worried yourself, you demonstrate hope and a belief that, although you take their feelings seriously, the situation is not so impossible that it can't be sorted out.

Avoid guilt trips

Guilt trips are really unhelpful at times like these. Depressed young people already feel dreadful, so telling them how sad they are making you feel is not going to help. It may be true, but when they've hit rock bottom it doesn't make things better.

If you can, try not to make it about you or your feelings ('This is making me feel so sad, I can't bear to see you like this' or 'I feel really down sometimes too'), although it is fine for them to be aware that you empathise and feel pain when you see them like this, through hugs and kind gestures.

Try to ensure that your young adult is part of the decision-making about next steps if at all possible, agreeing together what to do next, one step at a time.

Bear in mind that it will take time to sort out – think of any support you offer to your children for mental health issues as a marathon, not a sprint.

PARENT POINTERS

- Tell them how much you love them, that it's not their fault, that you want to help, that you are happy to be guided by them about how you can help and that you are there to listen. Emphasise that there is hope, that things can get better and that you will help them. And, importantly, make it clear that you believe them.
- Remember: listen, believe, give hope.

SELF-HARM

For many young people self-harm is like lifting the lid from the boiling pot of their emotions. It provides relief and an escape; a dissipation of pent-up energy and a feeling of calm may descend. Replacing emotional pain with physical pain distracts from the distressing feelings and creates something tangible or different to worry about. Some young people also use 'non-physical' self-harm such as 'digital self-harm', where they post mean things about themselves anonymously, either to purge themselves of their feelings or to receive comments (including negative ones) from others, whether for support or 'self-flagellation'.

Self-harm is a complex and difficult behaviour and warrants compassion. Coping with stress is something humans do in many different ways, and for some the choice is to harm themselves. Some young people self-harm to punish themselves, because they believe they deserve to suffer, while others do it to make visible their pain.

For parents, self-harm can be frightening, something that they don't understand and seems very risky. This is not entirely unreasonable and self-harm in all its forms is risky. When we talk about self-harm we can mean cutting, burning, scratching and hair pulling or hitting oneself, or we can mean taking an overdose of substances (substances that would not normally be toxic but are by definition in overdose) or ingesting poisons such as bleach. Self-harm can mean punching walls or banging heads, or in some cases we see it in the way a young person may repeatedly pick fights to enable others to hurt them. And it is reasonable to think of a lot of behaviours, such as regular binge drinking, restricting food or using drugs, as 'self-harm' if they are done to distract from overwhelming pain and distress.

What self-harm isn't

What self-harm *isn't* is 'attention seeking', a 'phase', something only done by young people or something people do because they 'like pain'. To understand why a young person might be self-harming it is crucial to really listen to what they are telling you about their *underlying* distress. The self-harm is a symptom of another problem, and only by dealing with that will the self-harm stop. This is why it is not helpful to tell someone who self-harms to 'just stop it'. If you recall the boiling pot analogy with its lid firmly on, you can imagine what might happen if you don't take the lid off (through self-harm). The pressure will build and build and something much worse might happen.

A safer and more supportive approach is to recognise the self-harm as a sign of internal torment and address that, carefully and with empathy, accepting that the self-harm behaviour will take time to stop.

How to react to self-harm

Self-harm is one of the things that worries parents most. But there is plenty you can do to be helpful and to reduce the risks.

Try *not* to overreact, don't tell or plead with them to stop, apply first aid carefully if needed, or seek medical attention for overdoses and ingestion of poisons, and together talk about longer term approaches to help your child, via your family doctor, the school counsellor or a therapist.

A very experienced teacher told us that when he talks to pupils about their self-harm and they are feeling overcome by guilt or shame, he reassures them with words such as, 'It's okay. The self-harm helped, it might not be ideal, but it helped.' He then tries to talk to them about healthier coping mechanisms for next time. These might include doing a fast 'on-the-spot' workout with star jumps, drawing red lines on the skin instead of cutting, sticking on fake tattoos instead of burning or hurting the skin, and rubbing a lovely scented cream into the skin for comfort.

Addressing the self-harm compassionately early on could avoid a much more serious outcome later. A rather heart-warming study from the USA recently showed that by 'training' three nominated adults (nominated by the young person who self-harmed) in how to support the young person with kindness, the risk of future suicide was massively reduced (suicide is more common in those with a history of self-harm).[2,3]

EATING DISORDERS

Eating disorders are another of the conditions that parents worry about, and with good reason. Strange as it may seem, eating disorders are less about food than they are about control.[4] Try to remember this if you are struggling with your child's eating behaviours. They may initially have been an anxious child and then, when a change occurred in their life which they felt unable to control, like a family upset or moving to university, they turned to controlling their eating as a coping mechanism. It can sometimes be missed or overlooked if parents and professionals worry that the weight loss is from a physical condition (such as coeliac disease) or that the behaviours are related to other issues such as depression, which can appear at the same time. In general, it is not possible to tell if someone has an eating disorder simply by looking at them, as although those with anorexia tend to be underweight, many with bulimia, and some with binge eating disorder, have a normal body mass index (BMI).

It is really important not to delay seeking help from professionals, ideally via your family doctor, if you suspect your child has an eating disorder. The NHS guidance does *not* say that you have to lose a certain amount of weight, or be below a certain weight, to be able to get help.[5] If a young person is thought to have eating issues they can be assessed and receive treatment. Recovery can then take months or years, as the therapy can take significant time to have beneficial effects, aiming to help the sufferer give up their control slowly and start to eat normally again.

Anorexia

In anorexia nervosa in particular, young people are often trying to control one thing they feel that they *can* control (what they eat or their body shape) when everything else in their lives may feel out of control. Eating issues can appear in all sorts of families, so it is helpful to be aware of how it may first start. 'Control' may initially start out quite subtly – a biscuit denied or food pushed to one side – but the feeling becomes intoxicating to the stressed young person, and so it continues, spiralling slowly downwards. They can view their eating disorder as a 'special power' or their secret friend. It can be completely uncontrollable.

The insidious and all-consuming nature of eating disorders makes them very high-risk and this is one of the reasons that they should not be dismissed as a 'phase' or 'experimentation', nor should sufferers simply be advised to 'just eat a bit more' (they may see that as a challenge to eat less) or 'give it a few months to see what happens'.[6] In fact, a study by the charity Beat discovered that on average people with eating disorders had had symptoms for a year and nine months before becoming aware that they had a problem, and they then waited on average another year before seeking professional help, after which there was a wait of about six months before starting therapy.[7]

Orthorexia

If your young adult has started obsessing about 'healthy' foods and only eats those that are free from additives, or are vegetarian/vegan (for reasons not based on animal ethics but because they are viewed as 'healthy'), then they may have 'orthorexia'.[8] This is an obsession about eating 'correctly'. Other variations include deciding to be gluten-free when they don't have coeliac disease or avoiding certain types of foods *rigidly*. They may call it 'clean eating' and view some foods as 'dirty'. Their thinking is driven by dissatisfaction with their bodies or perfectionism, and can be a precursor to other eating disorders.

It's important to be aware that veganism can be a way for young people to legitimise an eating disorder. By saying you are vegan you have an immediately 'worthy' and socially respected way to avoid several major food groups and dramatically reduce your calorie intake if you so wish.

PARENT POINTER

- Bear this in mind if your child no longer seems to be eating a balance of nutrients, is losing weight or is avoiding meals but saying they are 'vegan'. A calm discussion may be needed.

Dr Hugh Herzig is a psychiatrist specialising in eating disorders, praised in the *BMJ* by a colleague for 'his ability to understand the battle that goes on inside a patient's head and then guide them through this, towards a place of peace'.[9] We asked him what advice he had for parents worried about their child's eating behaviours. He told us:

> Don't be afraid to have early conversations about eating issues. This may head off future deterioration and long-term problems. Parents may need to manage their own anxieties, and not be put off if initial efforts to discuss things are rebuffed – don't give up. Leave it and come back to the topic at another, calmer time. Parents worry they are going to make things worse, which, provided that they are genuinely thinking about their child, and not just reassuring themselves, will not be the case.

He also had advice about good questions to ask:

> Just say that you've 'noticed things and is it okay to talk about it'. Ask them who they would like to speak to, if not you. Ask them what they are frightened of. Usually they fear losing control, so let them know you can face fears together. Share your concerns. You might say 'I know you think I'm being silly, but I'd really like to talk to our doctor about this and I'd like you to come too.' As a family you need to plan over time. You might suggest, 'Let's eat lunch together or, once a week, let's spend a meal together.' Even if they hate it, stick with it. Don't avoid food issues. Just like with alcoholism, you need to address alcohol intake as well as have therapy for underlying issues.

Dr Herzig's message is of compassionate inquiry and being *alongside* your child as they struggle or need support, rather than being confrontational in style, although families should not shy away from engaging their child in difficult conversations. He hopes families will feel empowered to tackle eating issues, not 'tread on eggshells', and will address the problem early, because, as he says, 'There's no way around it.'

Bulimia

Bulimia nervosa is similarly defined by control, but additionally by bouts of *lack* of control, as sufferers eat uncomfortably large amounts of food, such as carbohydrate-rich bread or biscuits, in a single sitting, then 'compensate' for the calorie intake by the use of certain behaviours, classically vomiting (purging) or exercising excessively to get rid of the calories. Other methods used to compensate can include use of diuretics (water tablets to make them pass urine a lot), laxatives or diet pills. (Binge Eating Disorder is defined as bouts of excessive eating, as with bulimia, but without the compensatory behaviours to 'get rid of' the calorie intake, so weight gain is much more likely.)

ARTI'S STORY

Arti had started throwing her lunch away at school when another girl had told her she was 'too chubby' to audition for the school dance show. Taking this comment to heart, and feeling unable to tell her family, she had started to restrict her food, as the bullying got worse. She concentrated on her academic work, and on her dream of going to university and helping others, by becoming a psychologist. Her weight dropped and initially she was pleased, but she did not want to stop, as it made her feel strong and in control. On arrival at university, she continued her 'disciplined' approach to eating, but over the months was surprised by a sudden urge to binge, which she eventually gave into (eating a packet of biscuits in one sitting), but then, overcome by guilt, she forced herself to vomit. So began her spiral downwards, culminating in her appointment with a doctor who was able to refer her to a local eating disorder team to consider CBT.

WHEN AND HOW TO GET HELP

As a parent you are likely to need to seek help if your young person is showing psychological symptoms that are interfering with their daily life, or with family life, on a regular basis. It is perfectly normal for any one of us to have anxious moments, an occasional bad day or feel worried about specific events, but if those feelings are happening most days or for most of the day most of the time, then help is needed. You then have lots of options.

The starting point for mental health care is often with your child's doctor. School and university counsellors and private therapists can be accessed without a doctor's referral, but keeping the family or university doctor informed is helpful for creating a clear picture of what is happening, should the need for referral arise. In the UK, doctors can refer directly to adult services or Child and Adolescent Mental Health Services (CAMHS), as can many schools. Waiting lists can be very frustrating, and expert third sector (charity) support in the meantime may be helpful to bridge the gap. However, don't be put off asking for help because of waiting lists.

Their doctor

You (or your child if they are over 16) should book a doctor's appointment for an assessment and discussion if you feel worried about their mental health. Doctors are perfectly placed to put things into context, give advice, signpost to support and refer if necessary. Try to go with an open mind and be prepared to listen as well as clearly saying what's worrying you, as they see mental health problems every day and are keen to help and have a practical discussion with you. It should hopefully be a two-way conversation between the doctor and your child, but include you if relevant of course, and with your young person's well-being at the centre of the discussions.

If your child would prefer to speak to their doctor alone, that may be a way to engage them in getting better, and the doctor can ask for their permission to share information with you afterwards. Doctors are familiar with seeing teenagers alone, and have guidance to follow about how and when to share confidential information with parents (see page 296).

PARENT POINTER

- When you or your young person phone to book a doctor's appointment, mention their age and that it is for mental health, as this helps the team prioritise the appointment and ensures that you see the most appropriate clinical member of staff.

Online help

If you are worried about specific symptoms you may wish to look up more information on a reliable website, such as the

NHS website or a charity that specialises in the behaviour you are worried about. Alternatively, you can check out a website like YoungMinds (in the UK, see page 315) which has info about lots of different well-being topics and parent-specific advice.

Charities

Many charities have young-person-specific mental health and well-being support available directly through drop-ins, groups and even parent support groups, so check out what is available near you. In Bristol, the organisation Off the Record (OTR) is a fantastic resource, providing a variety of free services for 11–25-year-olds, including parent support. The worksheets OTR produces, for example to manage anxiety in a young person, are a wonderful and practical way for parents to work through issues with their children. Examples of these resources are produced with their generous permission on pages 305–06.

School counsellor

Not all schools have counselling support, but if they do these dedicated experts can be a fantastic comfort and safe place for young people to turn to, as well as providing expert care.

MOVING FROM PRIVATE TO NHS SERVICES

A particular challenge arises when young people have been seeing private specialists at home and then move into NHS services when away, and the expectation of what the doctor or NHS service will be able to offer may be unrealistic, such as expecting certain medications to be prescribed immediately. Planning ahead and discussion with the specialist should smooth this over.

MEDICATION FOR MENTAL HEALTH

'But they're addictive.'

'I don't want to feel like a failure, by needing medication.'

'They'll make me fat.'

'They'll make my acne worse.'

'My parents won't approve.'

'I'll be on them forever.'

Doctors caring for young people, and managing their mental health issues, have heard all of these concerns, and more, when they bring up the topic of medication. Very occasionally a person will ask for medication to help them, but it is rare. In most cases the doctor, or sometimes a therapist, will raise the topic, usually when symptoms are severe or talking therapies are taking a while to work, or the person is actually too unwell to engage with therapy effectively.

Medications for mental health are varied and can include:

- anti-anxiety pills
- antidepressants
- sleeping tablets
- mood stabilisers (such as for bipolar disorder)
- pills for attention deficit hyperactivity disorder (ADHD)
- antipsychotic tablets and injections

Medication can transform a desperate situation and it can save lives, though it also has potential risks and side effects, and needs to be used carefully and appropriately, and reviewed regularly by a doctor. Many healthcare professionals, especially those working in universities or with a lot of young people, have a special interest in mental health, and so are very familiar and comfortable with prescribing and managing these medications, though there are a few that *only* psychiatrists prescribe (in the UK).

It is reasonable for parents and young people to ask about a doctor's experience with mental health, before discussing options for treatment. All doctors should discuss therapy and medication choices with every patient, and include them in the decision-making process. Medication is rarely a solution on its own. The main aim of treatment should be to address the underlying issues and young people should have a say in whether or not they take medication. The vast majority of mental health care in the UK (for 9 out of 10 people) is carried out in general practice, without ever involving a psychiatrist, but if a specialist is considered to be of potential benefit, the doctor will suggest a referral, perhaps for a second opinion about diagnosis, for complex medication advice or for an overview of treatment options.[10]

While young people are often reluctant to start tablets it is very common for them to return for their doctor review at three or six weeks commenting that they 'wish they had started them sooner' as their symptoms start to improve. Within eight to twelve weeks a situation may have transformed from suicidal thinking, crippling anxiety or six hours a day of obsessive thoughts, to more stable moods, less anxiety and manageable thoughts, and the person is able to engage effectively with talking therapies. However, if by six weeks no benefit is being noticed, it is completely reasonable to consider different medication.

PARENT POINTER

- Keeping an open mind about medication is helpful, and allowing it time to work is vital. Supporting your child's decision to try medication is very positive as they often stop taking it or decline to start it if they believe their parents won't approve.

THINKING POINTS

Intervening early will improve your child's health in the longer term, so it is important to know what behaviours to watch out for, when to bring it up with them, what to say and when to get help. Starting with open questions, gently mention that you have noticed that they are not themselves and you are concerned. Try to understand why they might be feeling like this, why they self-harm or restrict or binge eat food. It is only by tackling the reasons underlying the behaviours, not just addressing the behaviours themselves, that progress and recovery will eventually be made.

It can take a long time to recover so be prepared for one step forwards and two steps back, but stick with them, be their constant and be supportive (but don't do everything for them). They may need to go to doctor's appointments without you, depending on their age, or decide about medication or therapy, or whether to take time out from school, university or work. Your role is to listen to them, believe them and stay optimistic, giving them hope that they *can* do this and get better.

- You can make a transformational difference to your young adult when they are at a low point in their lives by guiding them compassionately.

- For specific conditions, consider how to bring up your concerns, when help might be needed and don't delay seeking advice, especially for eating disorders.
- Let the doctor's receptionist know your concern is for a mental health problem as they can ensure you see the right professional first time.
- Be open-minded about treatment options and medication – they can be life-changing.
- Plan any transition of care in advance, for example from child to adult services, private to NHS or from home to university/ abroad.

CHAPTER 15

Mental Health Crises

What do we mean by a mental health crisis? Have we (and in particular the media) overused the 'crisis' word and therefore minimised its importance and impact when we talk about mental health? Might 'crisis' include feeling stressed because of exam pressure or having a panic attack in the town centre? Should it only apply when someone is feeling desperate and planning their suicide, or if they are a threat to the safety of others? Officially, it is defined as follows:

> When people – of all ages – with mental health problems urgently need help because of their suicidal behaviour, panic attacks or extreme anxiety, psychotic episodes, or behaviour that seems out of control or irrational and likely to put the person (or other people) in danger.[1]

Mental health crises occur when situations reach 'red' level on a 'green/amber/red' scale of life events. They include not only life-and-death situations, but also very high-risk scenarios, and should be taken extremely seriously and dealt with as such. They should be recognised for what they are and where they can lead if ignored (accidental or suicidal death). Your gut instinct in such situations can be life-saving.

One senior university doctor we spoke to, who has more than two decades of experience caring for students, recalled such a life-saving gut instinct experienced by the mother of one of her patients. The student was a young woman in her early twenties, with significant depression, but keen to live her life independently at university. Her mother supported her by visiting once a month, driving several hours each way to check on her, though her daughter rarely called her in between times, and showed little appreciation of the care. One day, the mum's phone rang. It was her daughter, but she hardly spoke. There was something in her voice and manner though that alerted the mother, and she knew that she had to go to see her immediately, so she drove straight to her daughter's room, all those miles away. On arrival, she found the door locked, and as there was no response to her calls, she called the police who swiftly broke down the door. They found the young woman in the room, unconscious, having taken a large overdose, and immediately called an ambulance, which provided life-saving care. The mother had known instinctively that something was wrong when the phone call came, and her response had saved her daughter's life. Parental gut instinct can form an important part of the assessment by professionals, when young people are unwell.

Parents or others may need to raise concerns with a professional if a crisis occurs, and explain the specific context of that situation, for example, that this *particular* scenario has never happened before or that the situation has escalated in a specific way. You may be able to share that your child has harmed themselves before but on *this* occasion, they have given away their pet, for example, signifying an escalation in their suicide planning and risk level.

Unfortunately, you cannot assume that very busy, hard-working professionals will have had time to gather every last detail about your child, and this could be the 'red flag' that shifts their perception from 'self-harm risk' to 'impending suicide', and therefore save your child's life. You should never be afraid to check that the professionals have all the information that they need. Better to tell them something twice, than regret not mentioning it or assuming that they would have known.

PARENT POINTER

- The message here is simple: tell the professionals everything that you feel may be relevant – it could save the life of your loved one.

PSYCHOSIS

One of the mental health conditions that can create real worry in parents is psychosis, a condition that involves the young person experiencing altered perceptions and delusional beliefs or thoughts, often alongside hallucinations, with a loss of insight or understanding that they are unwell. This may or may not distress them, but becoming aware of such symptoms in your child can lead to a crisis situation. The commonest age for psychosis to start is 18–24 years, and the symptoms can be made rapidly worse by a change in environment, such as leaving school, moving to university or starting work. A young person who may have been having unusual thoughts for a while, keeping them hidden from family, may then suddenly be unable to maintain normal behaviour when they move away.

ELI'S STORY

Eli arrived at university after a summer spent hanging out with friends and gaming in his room. He was dropped at his new halls of residence by his parents and left to settle in. Very quickly his behaviour started to cause concern to his corridor mates and the staff in the residence. He moved the furniture around his room to create 'barricade-like' structures and drew intricate patterns on his walls in pen. When asked he said that he was 'being watched' and he was preparing in case someone tried to come and cause him harm. The patterns were to 'ward off evil'. He also started to comment that his corridor mates were listening to his conversations, and he suggested that they were using the pipes through the walls to spy on him. The staff in the residence gently enquired how long he had been worried about such things and it transpired that over the summer when he had had such thoughts he would go to his room and distract himself with games and other activities to block out the thoughts. He was encouraged to go with a staff member to see a medical professional on campus, and was agreeable to doing so, where he was referred to the local NHS Early Intervention in Psychosis team for assessment and a plan of treatment. Eli recovered well, and with treatment and support he did not have another episode of psychosis at university.

Psychosis symptoms can be frightening for both the sufferer and their loved ones, and can feature in bipolar disorder and schizophrenia, and occasionally certain types of depression. Such young people may be paranoid, and believe that authority figures are pursuing them, or plan to do them harm. It can therefore be very difficult to offer help, as they may be highly suspicious even of those they love and know well. But don't be put off or ignore such symptoms. Instead seek advice, talk to mental health professionals and your family doctor, and get support to allow you to approach the situation carefully, sensitively and compassionately. The sooner they receive help the better for young people with psychosis, and most areas in the UK will have an Early Intervention in Psychosis team for this very reason, focused on helping those experiencing their first episode or those who have recently become unwell.[2] Psychosis is treatable and manageable, but those who are affected will need a lot of support and care to recover, and to continue to stay well.

SUICIDAL THOUGHTS AND BEHAVIOURS

Many parents reading or hearing about suicides in young people will experience responses that swing from terror that it will happen to their child, through to reassuring themselves that it could never happen to them as they would just 'know' if something was wrong. The difficult truth of such tragic (and rare) occurrences is that the reality sits somewhere in the middle. Thinking about suicide is something that 1 in 5 students admit to in studies, with it being more likely in those who are LGBT+ or have had difficult childhood experiences, for example.[3] The vast majority will not act on these distressing thoughts, though some might self-harm. Seeking help and support is an important step for any young person who feels this way. The evidence is that in young people (in contrast with older adults) the final straw leading to suicide is often what we might consider quite small or trivial.[4] It can therefore be very difficult to predict, and being alert to warning signs is important.

A young person might have dealt quite well with failing an exam or the breakdown of a relationship, but as the pressures pile up, the final straw might be a badly worded text or a difficult interaction with family, which would never normally have been a trigger on its own.

This relatively trivial nature of final straws, coupled with the fact that young people are still very impulsive in their behaviour because their brains are still developing the 'handbrake' of the risk control zone (the prefrontal cortex: 'mission control'), means that when they suddenly feel 'That's it, I can't take anymore' they may act on it, when an older adult would be less likely to do so. The final straw comes along and they have less of an in-built ability (brake) to stop impulsive behaviours. So unfortunately, *no one* could have predicted it, because there was no way of knowing what the final straw would be to tip them over the edge.

'Trivial' trigger + high impulsivity + no 'handbrake' can = tragedy.

PARENT POINTERS

- While this may seem worrying, and we as professionals and parents may stress about how to spot those final straws, a pragmatic and preventative approach may be to instil in your child an understanding of the importance of talking about how they are feeling, normalising the fact that we all have bad days sometimes, that life will be bumpy and how to deal with the downs (and failures) as well as the ups, and that there is no shame in asking for help, especially when a situation is escalating.
- It's so important to emphasise that they will not be letting you down, and that you are there for them. Don't assume that they know this – be explicit.

We will never know exactly what is going on in the mind of a young person who chooses to take their own life, but perhaps we can minimise the risk by taking this approach from when they are young. In this way they might be much less likely to reach the edge in the first place and certainly less likely to react so catastrophically to potential final straws.

At-risk groups

Some groups of people in society are more isolated, bullied or stressed by their circumstances than others. At-risk groups include young men, who are at much higher risk of suicide than women, and those who identify as LGBT+ as they tend to suffer much more from bullying and discrimination. Other groups at increased risk are:[5]

- those with autism spectrum disorder
- those with caring responsibilities
- those bereaved by suicide
- eating disorder sufferers
- those leaving the care system, often called 'looked after children'

Other life experiences that can increase the risk of suicide are recent discharge from psychiatric care, Adverse Childhood Experiences (family discord/stressful life events/history of neglect and abuse/violence), academic pressure or exams, substance and alcohol misuse, and chronic pain.[6] To effectively protect and look after your child it can be helpful to be aware of these perils that they may have to deal with in the course of their life. Forewarned is forearmed.

Suicidal thoughts

Hearing that our children are *thinking* about suicide is something that can be very distressing for parents, but is in fact quite common. The commonest age for suicidal thinking is between 16 and 24. In the UK, 1 in 10 young women aged 16–24 have had suicidal thoughts in the previous year, and slightly fewer (1 in 14) similarly aged young men.[7]

PARENT POINTERS

- Suicidal thoughts do not, of course, have to translate into action, but they are a red flag of distress and should always be taken seriously, listened to calmly and acknowledged with kindness and without overreaction or unnecessary drama.
- If you do nothing else, following our 'listen, believe, give hope' approach may in itself avert a crisis (see page 369).

For many people, suicide may appear to be a solution to insurmountable problems, not because they actively wish to die, but because they no longer wish to exist. They believe that others would be better off without them. Sometimes they just want to go to sleep and 'not wake up'. They are exhausted by life and its demands on them, or by traumas such as bullying or abuse. According to the World Health Organization (WHO), suicide is the second leading cause of death worldwide (after accidents) for young people aged 15–29 years old, and in the UK suicide accounts for approximately 1 in 6 deaths of those between the ages of 10 and 34 years.[8,9] Three-quarters of those who die by suicide are male. (Of note, the language around suicide is changing, with a move away from using 'commit suicide', as that relates to when the act of killing oneself was a crime in the UK, before 1961, and thus it is perhaps less stigmatising in the twenty-first century to refer to 'dying by suicide' or 'taking one's life').

Suicide-related Internet use

A relatively newly identified warning sign in the last couple of years has been suicide-related Internet use prior to suicide or attempted suicide. According to a 2017 University of Manchester report, up to a quarter of young people who died by suicide were noted to have been searching for information about suicide methods or had been posting suicide-related content online.[10] The increased involvement of the Internet in suicide prevention approaches has led to clear media guidance being developed by the WHO, and the Samaritans in the UK, to try to ensure that journalists follow safe practice and minimise risk of suicide clusters, copycat behaviours ('contagion') and distress to bereaved families.

However, such excellent media guidance is not always followed and there has been considerable concern about social media's role in suicidal thoughts and behaviours, for example with images of self-harm on Instagram. Additionally, the portrayal of suicide in film and television can have significant impact on impressionable or vulnerable young adults. For example, a significant amount of debate was generated after the release of the Netflix US drama *13 Reasons Why* in 2017 which was felt by some commentators in the psychology field to 'glamorise' suicide and frame it as an acceptable behaviour, and a significantly increased Internet search volume for 'suicide' (up by 25 per cent) was noted in the three weeks following the premiere.[11] Research has previously shown a link between significant media coverage of celebrity suicide and suicide attempts or thinking. Therefore, it is generally felt by experts in suicide prevention and related charities to be good practice to keep media coverage of suicides to an absolute minimum wherever possible. Where this guidance is ignored, the results on our young people could be devastating.

GETTING HELP IN A CRISIS

Senior university clinical psychologist Dr Barkataki has some words of advice for incredibly emotionally charged times:

> Stay calm. It's hard to do if it's your child talking about suicide, but panicking is not a good reaction, or helpful, to the person who is distressed. Really listen. It's helpful to normalise and validate them. These thoughts can be common, don't dismiss them, don't tell them they're being silly, don't shut it down. Listen.

MARTHA'S STORY

Martha was an extremely bright girl who had sailed through school academic milestones, but had endured some nasty bullying around her sexuality from a few classmates. She had become anxious and her mood was low but, as university approached, she was keen to start a new life and meet some open-minded people with whom she could spend time and study.

Arriving at university she started to make friends, but as the weeks passed she realised that the workload was quite different from school, with less contact time in lectures or tutorials, and more time spent alone. She hadn't been able to completely shake the bullies either, as they had contacted her on social media and were undermining her new-found confidence, causing her to avoid new social situations to prevent teasing or other difficult conversations. She retreated to her room and self-harm returned to her life, much as she had used it for release of distress when she was younger. The second term passed in isolation, and Martha felt unable to speak to anyone about her sadness or self-harm, and guilt and shame overwhelmed her.

On returning home at Easter she spoke to her parents. They noticed the change in her appearance – she had lost weight and looked tired. They listened and sat with her as she told them that she couldn't go on feeling like this, that every day she wondered 'What's the point?', that she felt 'trapped' in her course, with few friends and too depressed to socialise and make new ones. She disclosed the self-harm, and they tried to stay calm, showing concern and warmth, but, aware that self-harm was a significant risk factor for suicide, they asked how they could help her. Martha was exhausted, depressed and unsure if anyone could help her anymore, but she agreed to their suggestion of making an appointment to speak to a doctor, and they offered to go with her, either to sit in the waiting room while she had her appointment or to go in with her.

HOW MARTHA'S PARENTS HELPED

- They listened to her, they believed her and they gave her hope.
- They didn't dismiss her thoughts or feelings, they didn't minimise or brush away the despair, and they didn't overreact or become distressed in front of her, though a few tears were shed together.
- They took her seriously and met her despair with compassion.

Phrases that should ring alarm bells

'Feeling trapped', 'unable to see the point in going on' and 'I can't do this anymore' as well as feeling a 'burden to others' should all ring alarm bells. They imply that the person is 'giving up' or justifying a reason for dying by suicide. Your child may feel isolated, alone and that they have 'lost control' over their own life or future.

Encouraging young people to seek help

We know that the majority of young people who die by suicide have not had recent contact with frontline medical services or university counselling services.[12] We all need to address this together. If we could encourage more young people to seek help, rather than taking tragic, often impulsive, action to end their lives, we could avoid some of the crises and devastating suicides that occur every year.

Talking about suicidal thoughts reduces the risk of suicide

All the evidence clearly and reassuringly demonstrates that talking about suicidal thoughts with your child does not increase their risk or likelihood of suicide. In fact, it has been shown to reduce the pressure and drive to harm themselves.[13] Talking about suicidal thoughts may actually *reduce* suicidal thinking and improve the mental health of those seeking treatment and help. If someone feels unable to talk because it is too painful or they can't find the words, it may be helpful to encourage them to *write down* how they are feeling, and share that with you if they feel able to.

MANAGING A CRISIS (SOMETIMES FROM A DISTANCE)

If your young person is living in a different geographical area, it may be necessary to engage the support of local well-being teams or to enlist the help of local health contacts. For universities there will be details of the well-being teams on the institution's website. You may need to intervene, while trying to respect your child's personal space, and get their consent wherever possible to involve professionals.

PARENT POINTERS

- It may reassure you to make a note of emergency contacts before you ever need them, just in case, once you know where your young adult is going to be.
- If they are going on a placement, a year abroad or a year in industry, or moving to a new area for work, it can be reassuring to know who you should contact if you are concerned about them.

In the UK the main sources of help for ongoing suicidal thoughts should be via their doctor. If they have no doctor, call NHS 111. If the situation is a crisis or emergency scenario requiring medical care, call 999 for an ambulance and the police if they are a danger to themselves or others, or are in a public place. If your child is known to a mental health team, that should be your first port of call for support and advice. Internationally there are suicide helplines in many countries (see page 310).

How to raise a concern about your adult child

Trying to liaise with the health service or a university about your adult child can be very challenging. It is important to remember that, while they cannot tell you anything without specific consent, they can still *receive* information and you can share your concerns with them. It is then their responsibility to consider the information and act appropriately.

If your child is at university, there should be information about 'who to contact if you are worried about a student' on the institution's website, so this is the best place to start. If this is not clear then look for a team who are responsible for student well-being and contact them – they will have their own webpage. Try to avoid contacting a variety of people all over the university as it might actually confuse things and muddy the situation, as a student who is feeling vulnerable might withdraw from help if it comes at them from too many different directions. Try to locate one team who can help and stick with them, build a relationship within the constraints of confidentiality and try to give them the space they need to do their job. In 'out of hours' scenarios or in emergencies the university will have a security team that you can contact, as well as the usual national emergency services.

MEDICAL CONFIDENTIALITY

The point at which doctors may break confidentiality is not black and white but there is clear General Medical Council UK guidance for them to follow, and every case is judged on its own merits.[14] Such decisions about breaking confidentiality and contacting parents should really be made by clinicians in health or education scenarios, as this ensures consistency and the following of professional guidance. Medical professionals and others are only likely to break confidentiality when they believe there is an acute risk of harm to a person or that they are a risk to others. Below that threshold they are unlikely to contact parents. Therefore, if you wish to be involved in decision-making, your young person will need to give consent if they are over 18.

Steps to take in an emergency situation

If you need to intervene and there is any possibility of aggression or violent behaviour it is important to first ensure your own safety and, if necessary, call for emergency services back-up. Similarly, if your child is physically hurt, don't hesitate to apply first aid or request medical help. If safety and physical well-being are ensured, it is then important to discuss professional support as the next step, such as seeing the doctor the same day or, if out of hours, calling NHS 111, or accompanying them to the Accident and Emergency department if the situation feels unsafe.

If it *is* out of hours and you think that your child can wait to see their own doctor or mental health professional the next day, that is the best option, as they will be known to the service and cared for in familiar surroundings. This will be less distressing to your child than having to attend the Accident and Emergency department, or meet new people. Once the acute crisis situation is over, it will be important for your young adult to continue engaging with support to minimise the risk of it happening again. Common problems include young people taking medication only for as long as the crisis lasts, then stopping it as soon as they feel better – 'I don't need it now, I'm fine' – so this might be a circumstance in which you can play an encouraging role (try using the LEAP approach mentioned below) if they seem reluctant to comply with medical advice.

What if your child rejects your help?

Sometimes young people who are ill do not want help. They may be in denial because of the condition itself, for example they have lost insight (the ability to see that they are ill) with psychosis or bipolar disorder, or they don't think they are that unwell and they want to be left alone, for example in severe depression. It can be a highly emotive subject to discuss, and parents can inadvertently and despite their best efforts sometimes feel like they are making things worse. If this is a situation you recognise and would like to understand more about, you might like to take a look at the book *I Am Not Sick I Don't Need Help!* by American psychologist Dr Xavier Amador. There are associated online resources and videos which could be very helpful. His LEAP approach is simple and is designed for use by families struggling with loved ones who are unwell but 'uncooperative' in getting themselves better.[15] LEAP stands for: Listen, Empathise, Agree, Partnership, and could be transformational in improving a very difficult situation for you. It takes an empathic approach, of negotiating while bearing in mind the point of view of the unwell person.

Hester, a 24-year-old student, put it very eloquently:

If parents are either approaching a topic regarding their child's mental health or trying to be supportive it is so important that they are not disheartened or put off if their child is defensive or reacts negatively towards them. It can be so easy to feel, as a parent, that you did the wrong thing or that your child doesn't want your help if they react negatively. However, mental health difficulties can be confusing, terrifying and overwhelming, and your child lashing out may actually reflect the fact that they don't understand or know how to feel about their struggles yet.

But don't be put off trying to help your child – it may just take time for them to feel safe to open up or to formulate the words they need to have that discussion with you. As a parent, try to maintain a quiet curiosity about your child's emotions and well-being. Continue to offer your support – accept that they may not take up your offer for a while but persevere. The important thing is to not push yourself on them – a quiet curiosity will let your child know that you are there for them whenever they feel ready.

Reducing student suicide risk

To reduce the risk of suicide heightened by university-related pressure, young people should not start university until they are well enough. We highly recommend that would-be students ensure that they take the time needed to recover, and to feel well and strong, before they attend university. University life is only likely to increase the pressure on them if they have had a mental health disorder.

There has only been a slight increase in the number of suicides in the full-time student population over the last few years.[16] This slight increase is not accounted for by an increase in total numbers of students, and studies are currently underway to clarify how much of this is a genuine increase in suicide in the student population and how much is related to other factors, such as coroners being more willing to record 'suicide' as an outcome, for example, although every single suicide is, of course, one too many.

It is likely, though, that something is happening to lead more students to take tragic action to end their distress. Factors such as changes in society, competitiveness, perfectionist traits, unrealistic expectations of themselves or from others, fear of letting people down, financial concerns, bullying and isolation, as discussed in Chapter 2, may go some way to explaining the pressure that young people live under, but each case is individual and, according to a 2017 University of Manchester report, it is 'rarely due to one thing, but to a combination of previous vulnerability and recent events'.[17]

Safety plans[18]

One practical thing you can do with your child if they self-harm or feel suicidal, when they are feeling calm and receptive, is to write a safety plan. You will find a basic safety plan template for tweens and early teens on page 306 (more adult ones are available online). The idea is to plan ahead for the next time your child might feel desperate and want to harm themselves, or is thinking of suicide, and to create a single side of A4 that they can refer to. When we feel distressed it can be hard to remember what we thought we should do next time, so having it written down (or on an app) can be really helpful. You could write one for yourself too – do it together, so that your young person feels less like they are in the spotlight. Safety plans are now considered good practice by professionals working in mental health and will give you a practical action to take with your child.

THINKING POINTS

This chapter may have been hard to read, but we hope that you will feel empowered to approach this difficult topic should it arise with your young adult, with both compassion and hope. You will also have a better idea of what to watch for, which phrases to be alert to and what to do next.

Caring for a young person who thinks about suicide can be draining, but you can play a key role in helping them through a difficult time and in their recovery. Watching your child suffer is unimaginably painful, but helping them to recover and move forwards in their life is both absolutely possible and life-affirming for a parent. **They can get better.**

Here are a few things to consider:

- Listen to your gut instinct in a crisis.
- Make a safety plan with your young adult as a proactive step.
- Tell professionals of your concerns, even if they are then bound by confidentiality.
- Know the local contacts for emergencies and for raising concerns if your young person has had issues.
- To avoid 'final straws', take a long-term approach to talking openly about feelings and share that life will always have ups and downs. Prepare them for dealing with life when things go wrong.
- Discourage attending university until a young person has been well and stable for a few months.
- Suicidal thinking is common; be compassionate and don't overreact.
- Listen, believe, give hope.

Conclusion

With this book we have tried to ease open the lid on your young adult's world and mind, and their experiences of living in the twenty-first century. We hope that we have shared with you some useful and practical advice for building a trusting and healthy long-term relationship with your child, while developing their skills for life, for resilience and for independence.

If they can create social networks of support, set themselves goals that stretch but don't overwhelm them, have a sense of purpose in life, overcome fear of failure or of letting people down, learn from mistakes, adapt to uncertainty and live with it, and learn too that bad times will pass, with your support and love, they will (as much as anyone can) grow into resourceful and strong adults. They will reduce their likelihood of having mental health difficulties, while learning the skills and having the resources to manage them should they occur.

As parents and carers, if you can resist the urge to do everything for your young adult, spend regular time with them, be open to talking and curious about their lives, provide boundaries within a loving and trusting relationship, and remember that, even when it doesn't seem like it, they are listening and you have influence, you should have the capacity and skills needed to raise a healthy, capable, creative, confident and self-sufficient adult.

Parenting is hard, and there will be many testing (and exhausting) as well as exhilarating times, but we very much hope that this book will have brought you some additional confidence, ideas and enthusiasm for the future grown-ups you are helping to grow.

Appendix
MANAGING ANXIETY

Challenge Your Negative Thoughts!

Examine your thinking. Be open-minded and test your thoughts!

Write a negative thought you have had below:

How does this thought make you feel or behave?

What is the evidence for the thought?

What is the evidence against the thought?

What would your best friend say if they heard your thought?

What would you say to your best friend if you knew they had this thought?

Is there a better alternative thought you could have now that doesn't leave you feeling bad? Write it here:

Reproduced with thanks from worksheets designed by Off the Record, Bristol

SAFETY PLAN TEMPLATE

Build Your SuperMe!

Think of a challenge or difficulty you faced in the past. What helped you get through it? Answering these questions will help you think about what you can do the next time you face something tough in your life.

Going to the gym

Writing a journal

Talking to a close friend

STRATAGIES – WHAT YOU DID
What did you do that helped you cope?

My best friend

My favourite book

My phone

Creative

Patient

RESOURCES – STUFF THAT HELPED
Were there any useful people, places
or things you used to help you?

STRENGTHS – WHO YOU ARE
When you look back on the situation what
positive qualities or strengths do you think
you used to get through it?

SUPER ME

INSIGHT – WHAT YOU LEARNT
Are there any insights or wisdom that you have now
when you look back on this that you could tell
yourself again? If you met someone else who was
now going through the same thing, what advice
would you give them?

Reproduced with thanks from worksheets designed by Off the Record, Bristol

Resources

APPS

Anxiety
Self Help for Anxiety Management (SAM)

Mindfulness/relaxation
Headspace

Self-care
Student Health – from Expert Self Care Social Enterprise (free)

Self-harm
Calm Harm
distrACT (free)

ARTICLES

Apprenticeship
https://www.allaboutschoolleavers.co.uk/articles/article/321/
what-do-parents-need-to-know-about-apprenticeships

Insomnia
How to access insomnia treatment on the NHS (UK):
https://www.sleepstation.org.uk/articles/sleep-clinic/nhs-
options-for-insomnia-treatments/

Underage drinking
Factsheet on underage drinking:
http://www.ias.org.uk/uploads/pdf/Factsheets/FS%20
underage%20drinking%20082016.pdf

Work versus uni
https://targetcareers.co.uk/careers-advice/work-v-uni/176-
work-v-uni-what-to-expect

BOOKS

An Unquiet Mind by Kay Redfield Jamison (bipolar disorder memoir)

Anxiety@University by Dr Dominique Thompson

Asperger's Syndrome: A Guide for Parents and Professionals by Tony Attwood

Bite Sized: A Mother's Journey Alongside Anorexia by Fiona Hamilton

Depression@University by Dr Dominique Thompson

Gen Z @ Work by David and Jonah Stillman

Generation Z Goes To College by Corey Seemiller and Meghan Grace

How to Survive the End of the World (When It's In Your Own Head): An Anxiety Survival Guide by Aaron Gillies (aka @ TechnicallyRon)

iGen by Jean Twenge

Inventing Ourselves: The Secret Life of the Teenage Brain by Sarah-Jayne Blakemore

How to Raise An Adult by Julie Lythcott-Haims

How We Learn by Benedict Carey

I Had a Black Dog by Matthew Johnstone (illustrated/cartoons on depression)

Left to Their Own Devices by Katharine Hill

Lighter Than My Shadow by Katie Green (eating disorder graphic/cartoon novel)

OCD: A Workbook for Clinicians, Children and Teens: Actions to Beat, Control & Defeat Obsessive Compulsive Disorder by Christian J Taylor

Reasons to Stay Alive by Matt Haig (depression)

Resourcefulness@University by Dr Dominique Thompson (how to cope when things go wrong)

Staying Well and Safe@University by Dr Dominique Thompson (surviving the first year and staying healthy and mentally well)

The Marshmallow Test by Walter Mischel

The Origins of Happiness by Andrew Clark, Sarah Flèche, Richard Layard, Nattavudh Powdthavee and George Ward

The Parent's Guide to Eating Disorders by Jane Smith

The Parent's Guide to Self-Harm: What Parents Need to Know by Jane Smith

We Are Generation Z by Vivek Pandit

Why We Sleep by Matthew Walker

SUICIDE HELPLINES

Australia 13 11 14
Brazil 188
Canada 1 833 456 4566
India 91 84229 84528
UK and Ireland 116 123
USA 1 800 273 TALK (8255)

VIDEOS

'Do schools kill creativity?', Sir Ken Robinson:
https://youtu.be/iG9CE55wbtY

Multiple useful short videos on mental health, Pooky Knightsmith:
https://www.youtube.com/channel/UCouKr8JeXinK6v_nf5d-WA1A

'Study drugs: Are they the smart choice?', What's Up TV:
https://www.youtube.com/watch?v=efkvtJ6i71A&feature=youtu.be

'Tea Consent', Blue Seat Studios:
https://youtu.be/oQbei5JGiT8

'The mysterious workings of the adolescent brain', Sarah-Jayne Blakemore:
https://youtu.be/6zVS8HIPUng

'Understanding the Why', Dr Dominique Thompson:
[Hyperlink to come]

'What I learnt from 78,000 GP consultations with university students', Dr Dominique Thompson:
https://youtu.be/gt-ToFPHCkI

'Why do we sleep?', Russell Foster:
https://youtu.be/LWULB9Aoopc

WEBSITES

Addaction
For drug/alcohol addictions.
www.addaction.org.uk/help-and-support/young-persons-services

Adfam
Information and support for the families of drug and alcohol users.
www.adfam.org.uk

ADHD Foundation
www.adhdfoundation.org.uk

Anorexia & Bulimia Care
www.anorexiabulimiacare.org.uk

Anxiety UK
www.anxietyuk.org.uk

Apprenticeships
www.apprenticeships.gov.uk

Asperger Syndrome
www.autism.org.uk/about/what-is/asperger.aspx

Big White Wall
(Paid) support for over 16s.
www.bigwhitewall.co.uk

Bipolar UK
www.bipolaruk.org

Campaign Against Living Miserably (CALM)
Leading a movement against suicide. For men aged 15–45.
www.thecalmzone.net

Connecting with People
For suicidal thoughts/behaviours.
www.connectingwithpeople.org/

Drugs and Me
A harm reduction guide to safer drug use.
www.drugsand.me/en/

Frank
Honest information about drugs.
https://www.talktofrank.com

GamCare
Free support and advice for anyone affected by problem gambling.
www.gamcare.org.uk

Kooth
Online support for young people.
www.kooth.com

LEAP Foundation
Science-based education and training and other support for organisations and individuals wishing to learn about mental health disorders.
https://lfrp.org/home

MeeTwo
A safe and secure forum for teenagers wanting to discuss any issues affecting their lives.
https://www.meetwo.co.uk/

Mermaids
Family and individual support for gender diverse and transgender children and young people.
www.mermaidsuk.org.uk

Mind
Help for mental health problems.
www.mind.org.uk

Mindspace
Mindful meditation training.
https://www.mindspace.org.uk/

My World of Work
Advice and information to help school leavers.
www.myworldofwork.co.uk

Net Aware
A guide to the social networks young people use: what parents need to know.
www.net-aware.org.uk

No Panic
Information for people who suffer from anxiety and phobic disorders.
www.nopanic.org.uk

Off the Record Bristol
Support and counselling for 11–25-year-olds.
http://www.otrbristol.org.uk

Papyrus
For suicidal thoughts/behaviours.
www.papyrus-uk.org

Release
In-depth descriptions, pharmacology, history, harm reduction and the law on over 50 drugs.
www.release.org.uk

Samaritans
https://www.samaritans.org/

Self-injury Support
Improving support and knowledge around self-injury.
www.selfinjurysupport.org.uk

Shambhala Publications
Mindfulness audio exercises for younger children (up to 12 or 13).
https://www.shambhala.com/sittingstilllikeafrog

Sleepio
Cognitive Behavioural Therapy for Insomnia (CBT-I).
www.sleepio.com

Students Against Depression
Information for people suffering the effects of depression and suicidal thinking. You can find useful safety plans here too.
www.studentsagainstdepression.org/

Student Minds
Mental health charity for students aged 16–25.
https://www.studentminds.org.uk

Stonewall Youth
To stay up to date with how you can make a difference for LGBT+ people everywhere. They share news, campaigns, events and ways you can support them.
https://www.youngstonewall.org.uk/

The Children's Sleep Charity
Supporting children with sleep issues.
www.thechildrenssleepcharity.org.uk

The Mix
Essential support for under-25s.
www.themix.org.uk

The Proud Trust
A life-saving and life-enhancing organisation that helps LGBT+ young people empower themselves to make a positive change for themselves and their communities.
www.theproudtrust.org

We're All Mad Here
Award-winning Blog on mental health (and book) by Claire Eastham.
www.allmadhere.co.uk/about-us/

YoungMinds
For parent resources (depression, anxiety, sleep, psychosis, etc.).
www.youngminds.org.uk/
UK university websites and resources

AccessAble
Accessibility information for thousands of venues, including universities.
www.accessable.co.uk/

Blackbullion
Helps young people develop financial skills for life.
www.blackbullion.com

National Union of Students (NUS)
www.nus.org.uk

Save the Student
The student money website for everything student finance.
www.savethestudent.org

Student Finance
Information on student finance, student loans or student grants for tuition fees and living costs, extra help and student loan repayments.
www.gov.uk/student-finance

Student Pad
Student accommodation and housing search.
www.studentpad.co.uk

The Student Room
The UK's biggest student community. Boost your grades, learn with free study tools, find your perfect uni place and get answers to any question on the forums.
www.thestudentroom.co.uk/

UCAS
www.ucas.com
www.ucas.com/money (information on financial support for students)

Acknowledgements

Many people have been incredibly supportive and enthusiastic as we have taken on the task of writing this book, which has been a passion project for both of us. Our families have tolerated our absence and 'Mummy's writing … again', and our friends have provided positive vibes and practical childcare, for which we are eternally grateful.

Jane Graham Maw, our agent, and Sam Jackson, our publisher, have kept the faith and provided encouragement to help us stay focused at tricky moments. Julia Kellaway, our brilliant editor, has been a silent superhero and guided us patiently through a sometimes painstaking process!

We also want to thank the significant number of generous and thoughtful professionals and friends (and parents!) who gave up their time to talk to us, to share their vast experience and expertise, and without whom this would be a very dry book! Cathy Robinson, Nusch Schofield, Steph Heasman, Romesh Vaitilingam, Jane Tappuni, Katrina Turner, Jo Williams, Annie Andrews, Jodie Zada, Kirstie Anderson, Rebecca O'Hare, Cat Taylor, Henry Bradley, Ian Barkataki, Ed Davis, Elaine Gibbs, Mike Jakubovic, Vik Mohan, Fiona Hayes, Oliver Stone, Sarah Richards, Jackie Head, Melissa Read, Aruna Gunawardana, Justin Harford, Fran Ripley, Niki Gibbs, Alan Percy, Alys Cole-King, Knut Schroeder, Sharmila

Choudhury, Hugh Herzig, Sumita Hutchison, Cathy A, Gareth, Ellie, Georgiana, Di, Hester, Selin, Shivali, Freya, Jacob, Steven, Martin, Amy, Penny, Mary, Ros, Mathilde Maccario, Charline Minet-Claret, Anna Muller Haas, Sophie, Anneline, Carla, Alison, Christine, Liza, Nicola Y, Lynn, Nicola Huelin, Antonia Troth, Frankie, Jules, Lorna, Stephen, Leia, Rob, Heather, Fiona, Louise, Serena and Emma, and finally the staff and pupils of BGS. Thank you all so much for the amazing belief you had in us, and for caring so much about young people's well-being. You are all fantastic!

References

CHAPTER 1

1   We Are Generation Z, http://wearegenz.com/, accessed 8 Jan. 2019.
2   'Vegan Demographics', Vegan Bits, http://veganbits.com/vegan-demographics/, accessed 10 Feb. 2019.
3   Horvat, S., 'The children skipping school aren't ruining the planet – you are', *The Guardian* (6 Feb. 2019), https://www.theguardian.com/commentisfree/2019/feb/06/children-skipping-school-ruining-planet-strike-climate-change, accessed 10 Feb. 2019.
4   'Generation Z – Beyond Binary: new insights into the next generation', Ipsos MORI (6 Jul. 2018), https://www.ipsos.com/ipsos-mori/en-uk/generation-z-beyond-binary-new-insights-next-generation, accessed 8 Jan. 2019.
5   Maybin, S., 'Busting the attention span myth', *BBC News* (10 Mar. 2017), https://www.bbc.com/news/health-38896790, accessed 8 Jan. 2019.
6   Kane, L., 'Meet Generation Z, the "millennials on steroids" who could lead the charge for change in the US', *Business Insider* (4 Dec. 2017), https://www.businessinsider.com/generation-z-profile-2017-9, accessed 8 Jan. 2019.
7   Collinson, P., 'One in three UK millennials will never own a home – report', *The Guardian* (17 Apr. 2018), https://www.theguardian.com/money/2018/apr/17/one-in-three-uk-millennials-will-never-own-a-home-report, accessed 8 Jan. 2019.
8   Stillman, D., and Stillman, J., *Gen Z@ Work: How the next generation is transforming the workplace* (HarperBusiness, 2017), p. 320.
9   'Opinions of Generation Z's ambitions and priorities differ greatly between the generations', Ipsos MORI (24 Sep. 2017), https://www.

ipsos.com/ipsos-mori/en-uk/opinions-generation-zs-ambitions-and-priorities-differ-greatly-between-generations, accessed 8 Jan. 2019.

10 Palley, W., 'April trend report examines the digital world of Gen Z', J. Walter Thompson Intelligence, (23 Apr. 2012), https://www.jwtintelligence.com/2012/04/april-trend-report-examines-the-digital-world-of-gen-z/, accessed 8 Jan. 2019.

11 Loudenback, T., 'People are paying $80,000 for "family architects" to fix their kids through 24/7 surveillance', *Business Insider* (22 Aug. 2017), https://www.businessinsider.com/family-architects-fix-kids-surveillance-2017-8, accessed 8 Jan. 2019.

12 'Generation Z – Beyond Binary: new insights into the next generation', Ipsos MORI (6 Jul. 2018), https://www.ipsos.com/ipsos-mori/en-uk/generation-z-beyond-binary-new-insights-next-generation, accessed 9 Jan. 2019.

13 'Opinions of Generation Z's ambitions and priorities differ greatly between the generations', Ipsos MORI (24 Sep. 2017), https://www.ipsos.com/ipsos-mori/en-uk/opinions-generation-zs-ambitions-and-priorities-differ-greatly-between-generations, accessed 8 Jan. 2019.

14 Fox, C., *I Find That Offensive!* (Biteback Publishing, 2016).

15 Durden, T., 'Generation Snowflake: Safe spaces, trigger warnings and the wussification of our young people', ZeroHedge (10 Jun. 2016), https://www.zerohedge.com/news/2016-06-10/generation-snow-flake-safe-spaces-trigger-warnings-and-wussification-our-young-people, accessed 9 Jan. 2019.

16 Tickle, L., 'Mental Health: the students who helped themselves when help was too slow coming', *The Guardian* (12 Feb. 2019), https://www.theguardian.com/education/2019/feb/12/mental-health-the-students-who-helped-themselves-when-help-was-too-slow-coming, accessed 16 Feb. 2019.

17 Chang, B., 'How four teenage girls organized this week's huge silent protest', *Chicago* (14 Jul. 2016), http://www.chicagomag.com/city-life/July-2016/Black-Lives-Matter-Chi-Youth-Sit-In-Rally/, accessed 8 Jan. 2019.

18 Horowitz, J., and Livingston, G., 'How Americans view the Black Lives Matter movement', Pew Research Center (8 Jul. 2016), http://www.pewresearch.org/fact-tank/2016/07/08/how-americans-view-the-black-lives-matter-movement/, accessed 8 Jan. 2019.

19 'I Heart Consent', NUS Connect, https://www.nusconnect.org.uk/liberation/women-students/lad-culture/i-heart-consent, accessed 8 Jan. 2019.

20 Fox, C., *I Find That Offensive!* (Biteback Publishing, 2016).

21 Haidt, J., and Lukianoff, G., *The Coddling of the American Mind: How good intentions and bad ideas are setting up a generation for failure* (Penguin UK, 2018).

22 'Elections: Turnout', House of Commons Library (9 Jan. 2014), https://researchbriefings.parliament.uk/ResearchBriefing/Summary/SN01467, accessed 8 Jan. 2019.

23 'Voter engagement and young people', The Electoral Commission (Jul. 2002), http://www.electoralcommission.org.uk/__data/assets/electoral_commission_pdf_file/0019/16093/youngpplvoting_6597-6188__E__N__S__W__.pdf, accessed 9 Jan. 2019.

24 '"Generation Sensible" in five charts', *BBC News* (19 Jul. 2018), https://www.bbc.co.uk/news/44880278, accessed 10 Jan. 2019.

25 'Motor vehicle deaths', Child Trends (27 Dec. 2018), https://www.childtrends.org/indicators/motor-vehicle-deaths, accessed 10 Jan. 2019.

26 Wang, D.D., Li, Y., Chiuve, S.E., Stampfer, M.J., Manson, J.E., Rimm, E.B., Willett, W.C. and Hu, F.B. (2016). 'Association of specific dietary fats with total and cause-specific mortality', *JAMA Internal Medicine, 176*(8), 1134–45, doi:10.1001/jamainternmed.2016.2417, accessed 10 Jan. 2019.

27 'Sensible, family-loving teens behind pregnancy rate drop', *BBC News* (18 Jul. 2018),https://www.bbc.co.uk/news/health-44860598, accessed 1 May 2019.

28 'People don't become "adults" until their 30s, say scientists', *BBC News* (19 Mar. 2019),https://www.bbc.co.uk/news/newsbeat-47622059, accessed 16 May 2019.

29 Blakemore, S.J., *Inventing Ourselves: The secret life of the teenage brain* (Penguin Books, 2018).

30 Somerville L. H., Jones R. M., Casey B. J. (2010). 'A time of change: behavioral and neural correlates of adolescent sensitivity to appetitive and aversive environmental cues', *Brain and Cognition, 72*(1), 124–33, doi:10.1016/j.bandc.2009.07.003, accessed 10 Jan. 2019.

31 Burnett, S., Bault, N., Coricelli, G., and Blakemore, S. J. (2010). 'Adolescents' heightened risk-seeking in a probabilistic gambling task', *Cognitive Development, 25*(2), 183–96, doi:10.1016/j.cogdev.2009.11.003, accessed 10 Jan. 2019.

32 Iqbal, N., 'Generation Z: "We have more to do than drink and take drugs"', *The Guardian* (21 Jul. 2018), https://www.theguardian.com/society/2018/jul/21/generation-z-has-different-attitudes-says-a-new-report, accessed 8 Jan. 2019.

33 Kane, L., 'Meet Generation Z, the "millennials on steroids" who could lead the charge for change in the US', *Business Insider* (4 Dec.

2017), https://www.businessinsider.com/generation-z-profile-2017-9, accessed 8 Jan. 2019.

34 'Getting Gen Z primed to save the world', *The Atlantic*, https://www.theatlantic.com/sponsored/allstate/getting-gen-z-primed-to-save-the-world/747/, accessed 8 Jan. 2019.

35 Scotti, M., 'Generation Z: What will be the legacy they leave behind?', *Global News* (24 Jun. 2018), https://globalnews.ca/news/4237033/generation-z-legacy/, accessed 8 Jan. 2019.

36 Pires, C., '"Young people are angry": the teenage activists shaping our future', *The Guardian* (13 May. 2018), https://www.theguardian.com/society/2018/may/13/young-people-are-angry-meet-the-teenage-activists-shaping-our-future, accessed 8 Jan. 2019.

CHAPTER 2

1 'Conceptions in England and Wales: 2016', Office for National Statistics, https://www.ons.gov.uk/peoplepopulationandcommunity/birthsdeathsandmarriages/conceptionandfertilityrates/bulletins/conceptionstatistics/2016, accessed 12 Feb. 2019.

2 'Being young in Europe today – family and society', European Commission (Dec. 2017), https://ec.europa.eu/eurostat/statistics-explained/index.php/Being_young_in_Europe_today_-_family_and_society, accessed 16 May 2019.

3 Stetka, B., 'Extended adolescence: when 25 is the new 18', Scientific American (19 Sep. 2017), https://www.scientificamerican.com/article/extended-adolescence-when-25-is-the-new-18/?redirect=1, accessed 22 May 2019.

4 Twenge, J., and Park, H. (2017). 'The decline in adult activities among U.S. adolescents, 1976–2016', *Child Development, 90*(2), 638–54, doi: 10.1111/cdev.12930, accessed 16 Feb. 2019.

5 Sawyer, S.M., Azzopardi, P.S., Wickremarathne, D., and Patton, G.C. (2018). 'The age of adolescence', *The Lancet Child and Adolescent Health*, 2(3), 223–8, doi: 10.1016/S2352-4642(18)30022-1, accessed 17 Jan. 2019.

6 'Vaping in England: An evidence update February 2019', Public Health England (Feb. 2019), https://assets.publishing.service.gov.uk/government/uploads/system/uploads/attachment_data/file/781748/Vaping_in_England_an_evidence_update_February_2019.pdf, accessed 3 May 2019.

7 'Smoking, drinking and drug use among young people in England – 2014', NHS Digital (23 Jul. 2015), https://digital.nhs.uk/data-and-information/publications/statistical/smoking-drinking-and-drug-use-among-young-people-in-england/2014, accessed 12 Feb. 2019.

8 Kirkham, C., 'FDA to impose severe restrictions on e-cigarette flavours', *Independent* (9 Nov. 2018), https://www.independent.co.uk/news/health/vape-ecigarette-flavours-vaping-fda-juul-age-types-teenagers-a8627151.html, accessed 28 Jan. 2019.

9 'The Scottish Health Survey', Scottish Government (2016), https://www.gov.scot/resource/0052/00525472.pdf/, accessed 12 Feb. 2019.

10 'Conceptions in England and Wales: 2016', Office for National Statistics, https://www.ons.gov.uk/peoplepopulationandcommunity/birthsdeathsandmarriages/conceptionandfertilityrates/bulletins/conceptionstatistics/2016, accessed 12 Feb. 2019.

11 '2017 KIDS COUNT Data Book', The Annie E. Casey Foundation (13 Jun. 2017), https://www.aecf.org/resources/2017-kids-count-data-book/, accessed 12 Feb. 2019.

12 'Campaign to protect young people from STIs by using condoms', Public Health England (15 Dec. 2017), https://www.gov.uk/government/news/campaign-to-protect-young-people-from-stis-by-using-condoms, accessed 12 Feb. 2019.

13 'Average age to start driving now 26, as younger adults put off learning and car buying', Journalism.co.uk (22 Jul. 2016), https://www.journalism.co.uk/press-releases/average-age-to-start-driving-now-26-as-younger-adults-put-off-learning-and-car-buying-/s66/a657725/, accessed 12 Feb. 2019.

14 Adams, R., 'Almost half of all young people in England go on to higher education', *The Guardian* (28 Sep. 2017), https://www.theguardian.com/education/2017/sep/28/almost-half-of-all-young-people-in-england-go-on-to-higher-education, accessed 19 May 2019.

15 'Youngsters fear for future job prospects', *Sky News* (24 Jan. 2018), https://news.sky.com/story/youngsters-fear-for-future-job-prospects-11220433, accessed 4 Jan. 2019.

16 'The WHO World Mental Health International College Student (WMH-ICS) Initiative', Harvard Medical School, https://www.hcp.med.harvard.edu/wmh/college_student_survey.php, accessed 16 May 2019.

17 'First-class honours for a quarter of UK graduates', *BBC News* (11 Jan. 2018), https://www.bbc.com/news/education-42649381, accessed 12 Feb. 2019.

18 'What impact is technology having on student cheating?', The NYU Dispatch (26 Feb. 2018), https://wp.nyu.edu/dispatch/2018/02/26/what-impact-is-technology-having-on-student-cheating/, accessed 12 Feb. 2019.

19 Swansea University, 'Sharp rise in essay cheating globally, with millions of students involved', retrieved from ScienceDaily (31 Aug. 2018), www.sciencedaily.com/releases/2018/08/180831110347.htm, accessed 12 Feb. 2019.

20 Praderio, C., 'Trying to be perfect has become an "epidemic" among young people, and it's taking a toll on their health', Insider (27 Nov. 2018), https://www.thisisinsider.com/perfectionism-definition-depression-anxiety-mental-health-2018-11, accessed 12 Feb. 2019.

21 Curran, T., and Hill, A.P. (2019). 'Perfectionism is increasing over time: A meta-analysis of birth cohort differences from 1989 to 2016', Psychological Bulletin, 145(4), 410, http://dx.doi.org/10.1037/bul0000138, accessed 12 Feb. 2019.

22 'Understanding Stress', Headstrong (19 Dec. 2017), https://headstrong.life/2017/12/19/understanding-stress/, accessed 12 Feb. 2019.

23 Rideout, V.J., Foehr, U.G., and Roberts, D.F., 'Generation M^2: media in the lives of 8- to 18-year-olds', Kaiser Family Foundation (Jan. 2010), retrieved from http://www.le-blog-de-mathieu-janin.net/attachment/279760/, accessed 12 Feb. 2019.

24 Frith, E., 'Social media and children's mental health: a review of the evidence', Education Policy Institute (30 Jun. 2017), https://epi.org.uk/publications-and-research/social-media-childrens-mental-health-review-evidence/, accessed 12 Feb. 2019.

25 Coughlan, S., 'Loneliness more likely to affect young people', BBC News (10 Apr. 2018), https://www.bbc.co.uk/news/education-43711606, accessed 12 Feb. 2019.

26 Callaghan, G., 'How micro social interactions with strangers can benefit our wellbeing', Sydney Morning Herald (19 May 2018), https://www.smh.com.au/lifestyle/health-and-wellness/how-micro-social-interactions-with-strangers-can-benefit-our-wellbeing-20180516-p4zfn1.html, accessed 10 Mar. 2019.

27 'People don't become "adults" until their 30s, say scientists', BBC News (19 Mar. 2019), https://www.bbc.co.uk/news/newsbeat-47622059, accessed 16 May 2019.

28 'The Good Childhood Report 2018', The Children's Society (Aug. 2018), https://www.childrenssociety.org.uk/good-childhood-report, accessed 3 May 2019.

29 Mischel, W., The Marshmallow Test: Mastering self-control (Back Bay Books, 2015).

30 Kidd C., Palmeri H., and Aslin R.N. (2013). 'Rational snacking: young children's decision-making on the marshmallow task is moderated by beliefs about environmental reliability', *Cognition, 126*(1), 109–14, doi: 10.1016/j.cognition.2012.08.004, accessed 10 Jan. 2019.

31 Clear, J., '40 years of Stanford research found that people with this one quality are more likely to succeed', https://jamesclear.com/delayed-gratification, accessed 10 Jan. 2019.

CHAPTER 3

1 Google Books Ngram viewer, https://books.google.com/ngrams/graph?content=parenting&corpus=15&direct_url=t1%3B,parenting%3B,c0&share=&smoothing=3&year_end=2008&year_start=1900, accessed 25 Nov. 2018.

2 Sterley, T.L., Baimoukhametova, D., Füzesi, T., Zurek, A.A., Daviu, N., Rasiah, N.P., Rosenegger, D., and Bains, J.S. (2018). 'Social transmission and buffering of synaptic changes after stress', *Nature Neuroscience, 21*(3), 393, doi: 10.1038/s41593-017-0044-6, accessed 12 Feb. 2019.

3 Meaney, M.J. (2001). 'Maternal care, gene expression, and the transmission of individual differences in stress reactivity across generations', *Annual Review of Neuroscience, 24*(1), 1161–92.

4 Hillman, M., Adams, J., and Whitelegg, J. (1990). 'One False Move … A study of children's Independent mobility', Policy Studies Institute.

5 'Paranoid Parenting by Frank Furedi', *The Guardian* (26 Apr. 2001), https://www.theguardian.com/education/2001/apr/26/highereducation.socialsciences, accessed 18 Feb. 2019.

6 Thelwell, E., 'How common are child abductions in the UK?', *BBC News* (29 Sep. 2016), https://www.bbc.co.uk/news/uk-37504781, accessed 18 Feb. 2019.

7 'Homicide in England and Wales: year ending March 2018', Office for National Statistics (7 Feb. 2019), https://www.ons.gov.uk/peoplepopulationandcommunity/crimeandjustice/articles/homicidein englandandwales/yearendingmarch2018, accessed 18 Feb. 2019.

8 'The Good Childhood Report 2017', The Children's Society, https://www.childrenssociety.org.uk/what-we-do/resources-and-publications/the-good-childhood-report-2017, accessed 18 Feb. 2019.

9 Clarke, K., Cooper, P., and Creswell, C. (2013). 'The parental overprotection scale: associations with child and parental anxiety',

Journal of Affective Disorders, 151(2), 618–24, doi:10.1016/j.jad.2013.07.007, accessed 18 Feb. 2019.

10 Ungoed-Thomas, J., 'Obesity rate in UK children doubles during primary school years to top US figure', *The Times* (20 May 2018), https://www.thetimes.co.uk/article/obesity-rate-in-uk-children-doubles-during-primary-school-years-to-top-us-figure-jz0d9txvs, accessed 18 Feb. 2019.

11 Louv, R., (2005). *Last Child in the Woods: Saving our children from nature-deficit disorder* (Algonquin Books of Chapel Hill, 2005).

12 Press Association, 'Children spend only half as much time playing outside as their parents did', *The Guardian* (27 Jul. 2016), https://www.theguardian.com/environment/2016/jul/27/children-spend-only-half-the-time-playing-outside-as-their-parents-did, accessed 18 Feb. 2019.

13 Carrington, D., 'Three-quarters of UK children spend less time outdoors than prison inmates – survey', *The Guardian* (25 Mar. 2016), https://www.theguardian.com/environment/2016/mar/25/three-quarters-of-uk-children-spend-less-time-outdoors-than-prison-inmates-survey, accessed 18 Feb. 2019.

14 'Reported road casualties in Great Britain: 2017 annual report', Department for Transport (27 Sep. 2018), https://assets.publishing.service.gov.uk/government/uploads/system/uploads/attachment_data/file/744077/reported-road-casualties-annual-report-2017.pdf, accessed 18 Feb. 2019.

15 'Home alone', Child Law Advice, https://childlawadvice.org.uk/information-pages/home-alone/, accessed 16 May 2019.

16 Baumrind, D. (1966). 'Effects of authoritative parental control on child behavior', *Child Development, 37*(4), 887–907; Baumrind, D. (1967). 'Child care practices anteceding three patterns of preschool behavior', *Genetic Psychology Monographs, 75*(1), 43–88.

17 Hesari, N.K.Z., and Hejazi, E. (2011). 'The mediating role of self esteem in the relationship between the authoritative parenting style and aggression', *Procedia-Social and Behavioral Sciences, 30*, 1724–30.

18 Matejevic, M., Todorovic, J., and Jovanovic, A.D. (2014). 'patterns of family functioning and dimensions of parenting style', *Procedia-Social and Behavioral Sciences, 141*, 431–7.

19 'Parenting styles: an evidence-based guide', Parenting Science, https://www.parentingscience.com/parenting-styles.html, accessed 3 May 2018.

20 Zuquetto, C. R., Opaleye, E. S., Feijó, M. R., Amato, T. C., Ferri, C. P., and Noto, A. R. (2019). 'Contributions of parenting styles and parental

drunkenness to adolescent drinking', *Brazilian Journal of Psychiatry*, https://www.ncbi.nlm.nih.gov/pubmed/30994851, accessed 3 May 2019.

21 'Parenting styles: an evidence-based guide', Parenting Science, https://www.parentingscience.com/parenting-styles.html, accessed 3 May 2018.

22 Segrin, C., Woszidlo, A., Givertz, M., Bauer, A., and Taylor Murphy, M. (2012). 'The association between overparenting, parent-child communication, and entitlement and adaptive traits in adult children', *Family Relations*, 61(2), 237–52, doi:10.1111/j.1741-3729.2011.00689.x, accessed 30 Jan. 2018.

23 Ibid.

24 Bandura, A., *Self-efficacy: The exercise of control* (WH. Freeman and Company, 1997).

25 LeMoyne, T., and Buchanan, T. (2011). 'Does "hovering" matter? Helicopter parenting and its effect on well-being', *Sociological Spectrum*, 31(4), 399–418, doi: 10.1080/02732173.2011.574038, accessed 30 Jan. 2018.

26 Schiffrin, H., Liss, M., Miles-McLean, H., Geary, K., Erchull, M., and Tashner, T. (2013). 'Helping or hovering? The effects of helicopter parenting on college students' well-being', *Journal of Child and Family Studies*, 23(3), 548–57, doi: 10.1007/s10826-013-9716-3, accessed 30 Jan. 2018.

27 Locke, J., Campbell, M., and Kavanagh, D. (2012). 'Can a parent do too much for their child? An examination by parenting professionals of the concept of overparenting', *Australian Journal of Guidance and Counselling*, 22(2), 249–65, doi: 10.1017/jgc.2012.29, accessed 31 Jan. 2018.

28 Ryan, R., and Deci, E. (2000). 'Self-determination theory and the facilitation of intrinsic motivation, social development, and well-being', *American Psychologist*, 55(1), 68–78, doi: 10.1037/0003-066x.55.1.68, accessed 30 Jan. 2018.

CHAPTER 4

1 Gunderson, S., Roberts, J., and Scanland, K. (2004). 'The jobs revolution: changing how America works', Copywriters Incorporated.

2 'National curriculum in England: framework for key stages 1 to 4', Department for Education (2 Dec. 2014), https://www.gov.uk/government/publications/national-curriculum-in-england-framework-for-key-stages-1-to-4/the-national-curriculum-in-england-framework-for-key-stages-1-to-4, accessed 3 May 2019.

3   Bass, R., and Good, J. (2004). 'Educare and educere: Is a balance possible in the educational system?', *The Educational Forum, 68*(2), 161–8, accessed 3 Mar. 2018.

4   Land, G., and Jarman, B., *Breakpoint and Beyond: Mastering the future today* (HarperCollins, 1992).

5   Robinson, K., 'Changing education paradigms' [video], TED (Oct. 2010), https://www.ted.com/talks/ken_robinson_changing_education_paradigms, accessed 31 Oct. 2017.

6   Dweck, C., 'Developing a growth mindset' [video], *YouTube* (9 Oct. 2014), https://youtu.be/hiiEeMN7vbQ, accessed 22 Feb. 2019.

7   Ibid.

8   Weale, S., 'Stress and serious anxiety: how the new GCSE is affecting mental health', *The Guardian* (17 May 2018), https://www.theguardian.com/education/2018/may/17/stress-and-serious-anxiety-how-the-new-gcse-is-affecting-mental-health, accessed 31 Oct. 2017.

9   'Graduate recruitment report: employer perspectives', Kaplan (2014), https://kaplan.co.uk/docs/default-source/pdfs/graduate_recruitment_report83B89056472C.pdf?sfvrsn=4, accessed 4 Jan. 2019.

10 McCloskey, M.J., Behymer, K.J., Papautsky, E.L., Ross, K.G., and Abbe, A. (2010). 'A developmental model of cross-cultural competence at the tactical level, technical report 1278', US Army Research Institute for the Behavioral and Social Sciences.

11 'School revenue funding', Department for Education (Mar. 2016), https://consult.education.gov.uk/funding-policy-unit/high-needs-funding-reform/supporting_documents/Current_funding_system.pdf, accessed 30 Jan. 2018.

12 Britton, J., 'The degrees that make you rich … and the ones that don't', *BBC News* (17 Nov. 2017), http://www.bbc.co.uk/news/education-41693230, accessed 30 Jan. 2018.

13 Butler, P., 'No grammar schools, lots of play: the secrets of Europe's top education system', *The Guardian* (20 Sep. 2016), https://www.theguardian.com/education/2016/sep/20/grammar-schools-play-europe-top-education-system-finland-daycare, accessed 30 Jan. 2018.

CHAPTER 5

1   Prensky, M., 'Digital natives, digital immigrants' (Oct. 2001), https://www.marcprensky.com/writing/Prensky%20-%20Digital%20Natives,%20Digital%20Immigrants%20-%20Part1.pdf, accessed 4 Jan. 2019.

REFERENCES

2 White, D.S., and Le Cornu, A., 'Visitors and Residents: A new typology for online engagement', First Monday (5 Sep. 2011), https://firstmonday.org/article/view/3171/3049, accessed 25 Feb. 2019.

3 Petter, O., 'Multitasking inhibits productivity, research claims', *Independent* (13 Mar. 2018), https://www.independent.co.uk/lifestyle/multitasking-productivity-levels-research-psychology-david-meyer-a8254416.html, accessed 13 Mar. 2018.

4 'Multitasking undermines our efficiency, study suggests', American Psychological Association (Oct. 2001), http://www.apa.org/monitor/oct01/multitask.aspx, accessed 13 Mar. 2018.

5 Young-Powell, A., 'How serious is essay plagiarism?', *The Guardian* (30 Dec. 2017), https://www.theguardian.com/education/2017/dec/30/is-plagiarism-really-a-growing-problem-in-universities, accessed 27 Feb. 2019.

6 Evans, J., '15% of students admit to buying essays. What can universities do about it?', The Conversation (18 Oct. 2018), http://theconversation.com/15-of-students-admit-to-buying-essays-what-can-universities-do-about-it-103101, accessed 27 Feb. 2019.

7 Ward, V., 'Speedo's daring Racerback swimsuit that caused moral outrage is to go on display at tge V&A', *Telegraph* (6 May 2018), https://www.telegraph.co.uk/news/2018/05/06/speedos-daring-racerback-swimsuit-caused-moral-outrage-go-display/, accessed 25 Feb. 2019.

8 Thompson, D., 'Screen time – a moral panic for the 21st century?' [blog], OnMedica (5 Feb. 2019), http://www.onmedica.com/BlogView.aspx?blogid=c26c6a90-102f-443a-974d-8b249f65ae2b&postid=2fa9cd41-b2d5-4413-8521-395c90b4c7b8, accessed 26 Feb. 2019.

9 'Matt Hancock warns of dangers of social media on children's mental health', Department of Health and Social Care (2 Oct. 2018), https://www.gov.uk/government/news/matt-hancock-warns-of-dangers-of-social-media-on-childrens-mental-health, accessed 4 Jan. 2019.

10 Smyth, C., 'Mental health risk of screens "no greater than wearing glasses"', *The Times* (15 Jan. 2019), https://www.thetimes.co.uk/article/mental-health-risk-of-screens-no-greater-than-wearing-glasses-5bkh0cdbn, accessed 2 Feb. 2019.

11 'The health impacts of screen time: a guide for clinicians and parents', Royal College of Paediatrics and Child Health, https://www.rcpch.ac.uk/sites/default/files/2018-12/rcpch_screen_time_guide_-_final.pdf, accessed 4 Feb. 2019.

12 Twenge, J., and Campbell, W. (2018). 'Associations between screen time and lower psychological well-being among children and

adolescents: Evidence from a population-based study', *Preventive Medicine Reports, 12,* 271–83, doi: 10.1016/j.pmedr.2018.10.003, accessed 4 Feb. 2019.

13 'The health impacts of screen time: a guide for clinicians and parents', Royal College of Paediatrics and Child Health, https://www.rcpch.ac.uk/sites/default/files/2018-12/rcpch_screen_time_guide_-_final.pdf, accessed 4 Feb. 2019.

14 Davies, S.C., Atherton, F., Calderwood, C., and McBride, M., 'United Kingdom Chief Medical Officers' commentary on "Screen-based activities and children and young people's mental health and psychosocial wellbeing: a systematic map of reviews"', Department of Health and Social Care (7 Feb. 2019), https://assets.publishing.service.gov.uk/government/uploads/system/uploads/attachment_data/file/777026/UK_CMO_commentary_on_screentime_and_social_media_map_of_reviews.pdf, accessed 25 May 2019.

15 'Discipline strategies for teenagers', Raisingchildren.net.au (10 Jan. 2019), https://raisingchildren.net.au/teens/behaviour/behaviour-management-ideas/discipline, accessed 3 May 2019.

16 'Good apps, games, TV shows, movies and YouTube for teenagers', Raisingchildren.net.au (24 Apr. 2019), https://raisingchildren.net.au/teens/entertainment-technology/media/good-apps-games-movies-teens, accessed 3 May 2019.

17 'Teens are using Google Docs as a sneaky messaging app right under their parents' (and teachers') noses', Creative Blog News (15 Mar. 2019), https://creativeblognews.blogspot.com/2019/03/teens-are-using-google-docs-as-sneaky.html, accessed 16 Mar. 2019.

18 Chandler-Wilde, H., 'Video games can reduce violence as well as cause it, researchers say as they launch pilot in schools', *Telegraph* (16 Sep. 2018), https://www.telegraph.co.uk/news/2018/09/16/videos-games-can-reduce-violence-cause-researchers-say-launch/, accessed 4 Jan. 2019.

19 'Online gaming', Childline, https://www.childline.org.uk/info-advice/bullying-abuse-safety/online-mobile-safety/online-gaming/, accessed 27 Feb. 2019.

20 Conrad, B., 'Ten video game addiction risk factors', TechAddiction, http://www.techaddiction.ca/video-game-addiction-risk-factors.html, accessed 27 Feb. 2019.

21 Xiuqin, H., Huimin, Z., Mengchen, L., Jinan, W., Ying, Z., and Ran, T. (2010). 'Mental health, personality, and parental rearing styles of adolescents with internet addiction disorder', *Cyberpsychology, Behavior, and Social Networking, 13*(4), 401–6, doi:10.1089/cyber.2009.0222, accessed 27 Feb. 2019.

22 'The hidden dangers of online gambling', UK Rehab, https://www.uk-rehab.com/blog/the-hidden-dangers-of-online-gambling/, accessed 27 Feb. 2019.

23 'Video game loot boxes declared illegal under Belgium gambling laws', *BBC News* (26 Apr. 2018), https://www.bbc.com/news/technology-43906306, accessed 10 Mar. 2019.

24 Dolan, E.W., 'Two large studies have found a link between look box spending and problem gambling', PsyPost (18 Mar. 2019), https://www.psypost.org/2019/03/two-large-studies-have-found-a-link-between-loot-box-spending-and-problem-gambling-53341, accessed 17 May 2019.

25 'Gambling addiction and problem gambling', HelpGuide (13 Feb. 2019), https://www.helpguide.org/articles/addictions/gambling-addiction-and-problem-gambling.htm/, accessed 27 Feb. 2019.

26 Peskin, M.F., Markham, C.M., Shegog, R., Temple, J.R., Baumler, E.R., Addy, R. C., and Emery, S.T. (2017). 'Prevalence and correlates of the perpetration of cyber dating abuse among early adolescents', *Journal of Youth and Adolescence: A Multidisciplinary Research Publication,* 46(2), 358–75, doi:10.1007/s10964-016-0568-1, accessed 28 Feb. 2019.

27 'Sexting', NSPCC, https://www.nspcc.org.uk/preventing-abuse/keeping-children-safe/sexting/, accessed 28 Feb. 2019.

28 Smith, S., 'Study of self-generated sexually explicit images & videos featuring young people online', Internet Watch Foundation (Nov. 2012), https://www.iwf.org.uk/sites/default/files/inline-files/IWF_study_self_generated_content_online_011112.pdf, accessed 27 Feb. 2019.

29 'Sexting', NSPCC, https://www.nspcc.org.uk/preventing-abuse/keeping-children-safe/sexting/, accessed 28 Feb. 2019.

CHAPTER 6

1 Smith, A., and Anderson, M., 'Social media use in 2018', Pew Research Center (1 Mar. 2018), https://www.pewinternet.org/2018/03/01/social-media-use-in-2018/, accessed 19 May 2019.

2 Parnell, B., 'Is social media hurting your mental health?' [video], *YouTube* (22 Jun. 2017), https://www.youtube.com/watch?v=Czg_9C7gw0o&feature=share, accessed 31 Jul. 2018.

3 Parnell, B., 'The dark side of social media' [video], SlideShare (1 Apr. 2015), https://www.slideshare.net/BaileyParnell/dark-side-of-social-media-46550955, accessed 15 Feb 2019.

4   'Half of UK girls have experienced some form of online harassment', Childnet International (15 Aug. 2017), https://www.childnet.com/blog/half-of-uk-girls-have-experienced-some-form-of-online-harassment, accessed 27 Feb. 2019.

5   Cross, D., Shaw, T., Hearn, L., Epstein, M., Monks, H., Lester, L., and Thomas, L. (2009). 'Australian Covert Bullying Prevalence Study (ACBPS)', Child Health Promotion Research Centre, Edith Cowan University, Perth, https://docs.education.gov.au/system/files/doc/other/australian_covert_bullying_prevalence_study_executive_summary.pdf, accessed 17 May 2019.

6   'Online abuse: facts and statistics', NSPCC, https://www.nspcc.org.uk/preventing-abuse/child-abuse-and-neglect/online-abuse/facts-statistics/, accessed 27 Feb. 2019.

7   'Keeping children safe on social networks', Net Aware (16 Apr. 2018), https://www.net-aware.org.uk/news/keeping-children-safe-social-networks/, accessed 27 Feb. 2019.

8   Sampasa-Kanyinga, H., and Lewis, R. (2015). 'Frequent use of social networking sites is associated with poor psychological functioning among children and adolescents', Cyberpsychology, Behavior, and Social Networking, 18(7), 380–5, doi: 10.1089/cyber.2015.0055, accessed 28 Feb. 2019.

9   'Instagram ranked worst for young people's mental health', Royal Society for Public Health (19 May 2017), https://www.rsph.org.uk/about-us/news/instagram-ranked-worst-for-young-people-s-mental-health.html, accessed 19 May 2019.

10 'Briefing 53: Social media, young people and mental health', Centre for Mental Health (3 Sep. 2018), https://www.centreformentalhealth.org.uk/sites/default/files/2018-09/CentreforMentalHealth_Briefing_53_Social_Media.pdf, accessed 28 Feb. 2019.

11 Buss, D. (2000). 'The evolution of happiness', American Psychologist, 55, 15–23.

12 Suls, J., and Wheeler, L., Handbook of Social Comparison: Theory and Research (Kluwer Academic, 2000).

13 Michalos, A. (1985). 'Multiple discrepancies theory (MDT)', Social Indicators Research, 16, 347–413.

14 Parkin, S., 'Has dopamine got us hooked on tech?', The Guardian (4 Mar. 2018), https://www.theguardian.com/technology/2018/mar/04/has-dopamine-got-us-hooked-on-tech-facebook-apps-addiction, accessed 1 Apr. 2018.

15 Brooks, D., 'How evil is tech?', The New York Times (20 Nov. 2017), https://www.nytimes.com/2017/11/20/opinion/how-evil-is-tech.html, accessed 1 Apr. 2018.

16 Sample, I., 'Bedtime social media use may be harming UK teenagers, study says', *The Guardian* (22 Feb. 2019), https://www.theguardian.com/media/2019/feb/22/bedtime-social-media-use-may-be-harming-uk-teenagers-study-says?CMP=Share_iOSApp_Other, accessed 23 Feb. 2019.

17 'Blue light filters for Android, iOS, PC and Mac', Moona (29 May 2018), https://en.getmoona.com/blogs/mission-sleep/blue-light-filters-for-android-ios-pc-and-mac, accessed 28 Feb. 2019.

18 Memon, A., Sharma, S., Mohite, S., and Jain, S. (2018). 'The role of online social networking on deliberate self-harm and suicidality in adolescents: A systematized review of literature', *Indian Journal of Psychiatry*, 60(4), 384–92, doi:10.4103/psychiatry.IndianJPsychiatry_414_17, accessed 28 Feb. 2019.

19 'Self-harm online support networks', Suicide Prevention Resource Center (1 Jun. 2012), http://www.sprc.org/news/self-harm-online-support-networks, accessed 28 Feb. 2019.

20 'What are pro-ana sites and why are they so dangerous?', Healthline (24 Apr. 2017), https://www.healthline.com/health/why-pro-ana-sites-are-so-dangerous, accessed 28 Feb. 2019.

21 Thompson, D., 'Boys and men get eating disorders too', Wiley Online Library, https://onlinelibrary.wiley.com/doi/pdf/10.1002/tre.568, accessed 28 Feb. 2019.

22 '#StatusOfMind: Social media and young people's mental health and wellbeing', Royal Society for Public Health (18 Jun. 2012), http://www.infocoponline.es/pdf/SOCIALMEDIA-MENTALHEALTH.pdf, accessed 28 Feb. 2019.

23 Keyes, C. (1998). 'Social well-being', *Social Psychology Quarterly*, 61, 121–40.

CHAPTER 7

1 Wiley, 'Social connectedness may help victims of cyberbullying', Medical Xpress (21 Feb. 2019), https://medicalxpress.com/news/2019-02-social-connectedness-victims-cyberbullying.html, accessed 28 Feb. 2019.

2 Buss, D., *Evolutionary Psychology: The new science of the mind* (Allyn & Bacon, 2007), third edition.

3 Pinker, S., 'Susan Pinker: Why face-to-face contact matters in our digital age', *The Guardian* (20 Mar. 2015), https://www.theguardian.com/books/2015/mar/20/secret-long-happy-life-mountain-villages-sardinia, accessed 23 Feb. 2019.

4   Adams, T., 'John Cacioppo: "Loneliness is like an iceberg – it goes deeper than we can see"' [interview], *The Guardian* (28 Feb. 2016),https://www.theguardian.com/science/2016/feb/28/loneliness-is-like-an-iceberg-john-cacioppo-social-neuroscience-interview, accessed 23 Feb. 2019.

5   Cacioppo, J.T., Hawkley, L C., and Thisted, R.A. (2010). 'Perceived social isolation makes me sad: 5-year cross-lagged analyses of loneliness and depressive symptomatology in the Chicago health, aging, and social relations study', *Psychology and Aging, 25*(2), 453–63, https://doi.org/10.1037/a0017216, accessed 23 Feb. 2019.

6   Seemiller, C., and Grace, M., *Generation Z Goes to College* (John Wiley & Sons, 2016).

7   Levine, A., and Dean, D.R., *Generation on a Tightrope: a Portrait of today's college student* (Jossey-Bass, 2012).

8   Seemiller, C., and Grace, M., *Generation Z Goes to College* (John Wiley & Sons, 2016).

9   Bland, B., and Stevenson, J., 'Family Matters: An exploration of the role and importance of family relationships for students in UK higher education', StandAlone, https://www.standalone.org.uk/wp-content/uploads/2018/06/FamilyMatters.-Final.pdf, accessed 4 May 2019.

10 Lavis, P., 'Why relationships are so important for children and young people', Mental Health Foundation (20 May 2016), https://www.mentalhealth.org.uk/blog/why-relationships-are-so-important-children-and-young-people, accessed 4 May 2019.

11 Bourg Carter, S., '6 reasons you should spend more time alone', Psychology Today (31 Jan. 2012), https://www.psychologytoday.com/us/blog/high-octane-women/201201/6-reasons-you-should-spend-more-time-alone, accessed 23 Feb. 2019.

12 Long, C., and Averill, J. (2003). 'Solitude: An exploration of benefits of being alone', *Journal for the Theory of Social Behaviour, 33*(1), 21–44, doi:10.1111/1468-5914.00204, accessed 23 Feb. 2019.

13 Larson, R. (1997). 'The emergence of solitude as a constructive domain of experience in early adolescence', *Child Development, 68*(1), 80–93, doi:10.1111/j.1467-8624.1997.tb01927.x, accessed 23 Feb. 2019.

14 Gillett, R., '6 scientific benefits of being bored', *Independent* (28 Jan. 2016), https://www.independent.co.uk/news/science/6-scientific-benefits-of-being-bored-a6839306.html, accessed 23 Feb. 2019.

15 Kauflin, J., 'How Match.com's founder created the world's biggest dating website – and walked away with just $50,000', *Business Insider* (16 Dec. 2011), https://www.businessinsider.com/match-gary-kremen-2011-12?r=US&IR=T, accessed 23 Feb. 2019.

16 Emerging Technology from the arXiv, 'First evidence that online dating is changing the nature of society', MIT Technology Review (10 Oct. 2017), https://www.technologyreview.com/s/609091/first-evidence-that-online-dating-is-changing-the-nature-of-society/, accessed 19 May 2019.

17 Goodnough, A., 'Reported cases of sexually transmitted diseases are on rise', *The New York Times* (19 Oct. 2016), https://www.nytimes.com/2016/10/20/us/reported-cases-of-sexually-transmitted-diseases-are-on-rise.html, accessed 23 Feb. 2019.

18 Rowsell, J., 'Love Island terms translated and the social media guide to dating', BirminghamLive (7 Jul. 2018), https://www.birminghammail.co.uk/whats-on/music-nightlife-news/love-island-terms-translated-social-14877002, accessed 23 Feb. 2019.

19 Morin, A., '10 ways to help your teen deal with a breakup', Verywell Family (19 Oct. 2018), https://www.verywellfamily.com/how-to-help-your-teen-deal-with-a-breakup-4047445, accessed 10 Mar. 2019.

20 'Suicide risk factors', The Trevor Project, https://www.thetrevorproject.org/resources/preventing-suicide/suicide-risk-factors/#sm.0000rzy91qfo1fikutl1nthapkzr5, accessed 4 May 2019.

21 Wolak, J., Mitchell, K.J., and Finkelhor, D. (2006). 'Online victimization of youth: 5 years later (No. 07-05-025)', National Center for Missing & Exploited Children.

22 Parker, I., 'Young people, sex and relationships: the new norms', IPPR (27 Aug. 2014), http://www.ippr.org/read/young-people-sex-and-relationships-the-new-norms#, accessed 19 May 2019.

23 Margolies, L., 'Teens and internet pornography', PsychCentral (8 Oct. 2018), https://psychcentral.com/lib/teens-and-internet-pornography/, accessed 23 Feb. 2019.

24 Parker, I., 'Young people, sex and relationships: the new norms', IPPR (27 Aug. 2014), http://www.ippr.org/read/young-people-sex-and-relationships-the-new-norms#, accessed 23 Feb. 2019.

25 Wolak, J., Mitchell, K.J., and Finkelhor, D. (2006). 'Online victimization of youth: 5 years later (No. 07-05-025)', National Center for Missing & Exploited Children.

26 'Healthy sexual behaviour', NSPCC, https://www.nspcc.org.uk/preventing-abuse/keeping-children-safe/healthy-sexual-behaviour-children-young-people/, accessed 7 Mar. 2019.

27 Thames Valley Police, 'Tea and consent' [video], *YouTube* (16 Nov. 2015), https://www.youtube.com/watch?v=pZwvrxVavnQ, accessed 7 Mar. 2019.

28 'Changing the culture', Universities UK (Oct. 2016), https://www.universitiesuk.ac.uk/policy-and-analysis/reports/Documents/2016/changing-the-culture.pdf, accessed 8 Jan. 2019.

29 Ibid.

30 'Consent Matters: boundaries, respect, and positive intervention', Epigeum (Jul. 2016), https://www.epigeum.com/courses/support-wellbeing/consent-matters-boundaries-respect-and-positive-intervention/, accessed 7 Mar. 2019.

CHAPTER 8

1 Williams, L., 'The "sober generation": Australian teens snubbing alcohol and cigarettes thanks to parents, researchers say', *ABC News* (12 Jan. 2018), https://www.abc.net.au/news/2018-01-12/australian-teenagers-turning-away-from-alcohol-research-says/9323858, accessed 17 May 2019.

2 'Adult drinking habits in Great Britain: 2017', Office for National Statistics (1 May 2018), https://www.ons.gov.uk/peoplepopulation-andcommunity/healthandsocialcare/drugusealcoholandsmoking/bulletins/opinionsandlifestylesurveyadultdrinkinghabitsingreatbrit-ain/2017, accessed 23 Jan. 2019.

3 NUS Press Team, 'New survey shows trends in student drinking', National Union of Students (24 Sep. 2018), https://www.nus.org.uk/en/news/press-releases/new-survey-shows-trends-in-student-drink-ing/, accessed 23 Jan. 2019.

4 Berglund, M., and Ojehagen, A. (1998). 'The influence of alcohol drinking and alcohol use disorders on psychiatric disorders and suicidal behavior', *Alcoholism: Clinical and Experimental Research*, 22, 333s–45s, doi:10.1111/j.1530-0277.1998.tb04388.x, accessed 24 Jan. 2019.

5 Boden, J.M., and Fergusson, D.M. (2011). 'Alcohol and depression', *Addiction*, 106, 906–14, doi:10.1111/j.1360-0443.2010.03351.x, accessed 24 Jan. 2019.

6 'The connection between anxiety and alcohol', American Addiction Centers (26 Nov. 2018), https://americanaddictioncenters.org/alco-holism-treatment/anxiety, accessed 24 Jan. 2019.

7 Walker, M., *Why We Sleep: The new science of sleep and dreams* (Penguin Books, 2018).

8 Davis, N., 'Cannabis smoking in teenage years linked to adulthood depression', *The Guardian* (13 Feb. 2019), https://www.theguardian.

com/society/2019/feb/13/cannabis-smoking-in-teenage-years-linked-to-adulthood-depression, accessed 16 Feb. 2019.

9 'The law on alcohol and under 18s', drinkaware, https://www.drinkaware.co.uk/alcohol-facts/alcohol-and-the-law/the-law-on-alcohol-and-under-18s/, accessed 8 May 2019.

10 Selleck, A., 'Teenage parties – a parents' guide', *The Guardian* (5 Sep. 2014), https://www.theguardian.com/lifeandstyle/2014/sep/05/teenage-parties-a-parents-guide, accessed 8 May 2019.

11 Frood, A., 'Use of "smart drugs" on the rise', *Nature* (5 Jul. 2018), https://www.nature.com/articles/d41586-018-05599-8, accessed 28 Jan. 2019.

12 'Taking the hit: student drug use and how institutions respond', NUS Connect (26 Apr. 2018), https://www.nusconnect.org.uk/resources/taking-the-hit-student-drug-use-and-how-institutions-respond, accessed 28 Jan. 2019.

13 'Get the facts about young people and drugs', Mentor UK, https://mentoruk.org.uk/get-the-facts/, accessed 4 May 2019.

14 Noisey, 'No smoking in the booth: a film about skunk, grime and mental health' [video], *YouTube* (9 May 2017), https://www.youtube.com/watch?v=CeJFKFE3lCM, accessed 12 Feb. 2019.

15 MacLaren, E., 'History and statistics of "study drugs"', DrugAbuse.com (3 Dec. 2018), https://drugabuse.com/adderall/history-and-statistics-of-study-drugs/, accessed 28 Jan. 2019.

16 Dallek, R., 'The medical ordeals of JFK', *The Atlantic* (5 Nov. 2013), https://www.theatlantic.com/magazine/archive/2013/08/the-medical-ordeals-of-jfk/309469/., accessed 28 Jan. 2019.

17 Nicholas, E., 'Hitler's suicide and new research on Nazi drug use', *Time* (28 Apr. 2017), http://time.com/4744584/hitler-drugs-blitzed/, accessed 28 Jan. 2019.

18 Thompson, D., 'Not so "smart" drugs' [blog], OnMedica (20 Aug. 2018), https://www.onmedica.com/BlogView.aspx?blogId=c26c6a90-102f-413a-974d-8b249f65ae2b&postId=0b748fdf-52d3-476a-9602-13334e7f1a1b, accessed 28 Jan. 2019.

19 Newham, T., 'Smart drugs: would you try them?', *The Guardian* (24 Oct. 2012), https://www.theguardian.com/education/mortarboard/2012/oct/24/smart-drugs-would-you-try-them, accessed 28 Jan. 2019.

20 'Bristol to become first UK city to provide drug safety testing', Bristol247 (14 May 2018), https://www.bristol247.com/news-and-features/news/bristol-become-first-uk-city-provide-drug-safety-testing/, accessed 28 Jan. 2019.

21 Lakhan, S.E., and Kirchgessner, A. (2012). 'Prescription stimulants in individuals with and without attention deficit hyperactivity disorder: misuse, cognitive impact, and adverse effects', *Brain and Behavior*, 2(5), 661–77.

22 'Ritalin side effects center', RxList (21 Jan. 2019), https://www.rxlist. com/ritalin-side-effects-drug-center.htm, accessed 28 Jan. 2019.

23 'Ritalin side effects by likelihood and severity', WebMD, https:// www.webmd.com/drugs/2/drug-9475/ritalin-oral/details/list-sideeffects, accessed 28 Jan. 2019.

24 Ma, J., Pender, M., and Welch, M., 'Education Pays 2016: The benefits of higher education for individuals and society', CollegeBoard (Dec. 2016), https://trends.collegeboard.org/sites/default/files/education-pays-2016-full-report.pdf, accessed 7 Jan. 2019.

CHAPTER 9

1 Adams, R., 'Almost half of all young people in England go on to higher education', *The Guardian* (28 Sep. 2017), https://www.theguardian.com/education/2017/sep/28/almost-half-of-all-young-people-in-england-go-on-to-higher-education, accessed 7 Jan. 2019.

2 'Alternatives to university', UCAS, https://www.ucas.com/alternatives-to-university, accessed 10 Jan. 2019.

3 Bullock, A., 'How to write a personal statement: 10 things to put in yours', Which? University (10 Jan. 2018), https://university.which. co.uk/advice/personal-statements/10-things-to-put-in-your-personal-statement, accessed 8 May 2019.

4 Comaford, C., 'This is what Generation Z wants from the workplace', Forbes (22 Apr. 2017), https://www.forbes.com/sites/christinecomaford/2017/04/22/what-generation-z-wants-from-the-workplace-are-you-ready/, accessed 8 Jan. 2019.

5 Tapo Institute, *The Great Global Check Out: Millennials, iGens, and the growing epidemic of disengagement* (CreateSpace, 2017).

6 Bulman, M., 'Number of young adults living with parents reaches record high', *Independent* (8 Nov. 2017), https://www.independent. co.uk/news/uk/home-news/young-adults-live-parents-at-home-property-buy-homeowners-housing-market-a8043891.html, accessed 19 Jan. 2019.

7 Lightfoot, L., 'Commuter students: locked out, left out and growing in number', *The Guardian* (30 Jan. 2018), https://www.theguardian.

com/education/2018/jan/30/commuter-students-debt-universities-live-home, accessed 16 Feb. 2019.

8 'Young people are the loneliest age group, according to new survey', The University of Manchester (1 Oct. 2018), https://www.manchester.ac.uk/discover/news/loneliest-age-group/, accessed 28 Jan. 2019.

CHAPTER 10

1 'From student grants to tuition fees', *The Guardian* (23 Jan. 2003), https://www.theguardian.com/politics/2003/jan/23/uk.education, accessed 13 Jan. 2019.

2 'Undergraduate applications offers and acceptances publications', Australian Government, https://www.education.gov.au/undergraduate-applications-offers-and-acceptances-publications, accessed 7 May 2019.

3 'Enrollment [sic] in elementary, secondary, and degree-granting post-secondary institutions, by level and control of institution: Selected years, 1869–70 through fall 2027', National Center for Education Statistics, https://nces.ed.gov/programs/digest/d17/tables/dt17_105.30.asp, accessed 7 May 2019.

4 Anderson, E., 'Graduates earn £500,000 more than non-graduates', *Telegraph* (16 Jul. 2015), https://www.telegraph.co.uk/finance/jobs/11744118/Graduates-earn-500000-more-than-non-graduates.html, accessed 13 Jan. 2019.

5 'The Leap', Unite Group, http://www.unite-group.co.uk/campaign/the-leap, accessed 15 Jan. 2019.

6 'University for students with special needs', The Good Schools Guide, https://www.goodschoolsguide.co.uk/special-educational-needs/learning/university-for-special-needs, accessed 28 Jan. 2019.

7 'Guide to university for disabled students', The Complete University Guide, https://www.thecompleteuniversityguide.co.uk/universities/disabled-students'-university-guide/, accessed 28 Jan. 2019.

8 'The Leap', Unite Group, http://www.unite-group.co.uk/campaign/the-leap, accessed 15 Jan. 2019.

9 Ibid.

10 'Resources', Buzz Consulting, https://www.buzzconsulting.co.uk/copy-of-about, accessed 23 Jan. 2019.

11 Inge, S., 'Minister renews call for universities to be "in loco parentis"', *Times Higher Education* (15 Jun. 2018), https://www.timeshigher-education.com/news/minister-renews-call-universities-be-loco-parentis, accessed 18 Jan. 2019.

12 Barden, N., 'Parents – partners or interference?', Wonkhe (28 Jun. 2018), https://wonkhe.com/blogs/parents-partners-or-interference/, accessed 18 Jan. 2019.

13 Thompson, D., *Staying Safe at University* (Trigger Publishing UK, 2019).

14 Rawlinson, K., 'Newcastle student died after initiation bar crawl, inquest told', *The Guardian* (22 Oct. 2018), https://www.theguardian.com/uk-news/2018/oct/22/newcastle-student-died-after-initiation-bar-crawl-inquest-told, accessed 23 Jan. 2019.

15 Thompson, D., *Staying Safe at University* (Trigger Publishing UK, 2019).

16 'Health and safety standards for rented homes (HHSRS)', Shelter (18 May 2018), https://england.shelter.org.uk/housing_advice/repairs/health_and_safety_standards_for_rented_homes_hhsrs, accessed 31 Jan. 2019.

17 Thompson, D., *Resilience @ University* (Trigger Publishing UK, 2019).

18 'Sexual offences in England and Wales: year ending March 2017', Office for National Statistics (8 Feb. 2018), https://www.ons.gov.uk/peoplepopulationandcommunity/crimeandjustice/articles/sexualoffencesinenglandandwales/yearendingmarch2017, accessed 27 Jan. 2019.

19 'The nature of violent crime in England and Wales: year ending March 2017', Office for National Statistics (8 Feb. 2018), https://www.ons.gov.uk/peoplepopulationandcommunity/crimeandjustice/articles/thenatureofviolentcrimeinenglandandwales/yearendingmarch2017, accessed 27 Jan. 2019.

CHAPTER 11

1 Walker, M., *Why We Sleep: The new science of sleep and dreams* (Penguin Books, 2018).

2 Hagenauer, M.H., Perryman, J.I., Lee, T.M., and Carskadon, M.A. (2009). 'Adolescent changes in the homeostatic and circadian regulation of sleep', *Developmental Neuroscience, 31*(4), 276–84.

3 Wittmann, M., Dinich, J., Merrow, M., and Roenneberg, T. (2006). 'Social jetlag: misalignment of biological and social time', *Chronobiology International, 23*(1–2), 497–509.

4 University of Washington, 'Teens get more sleep with later school start time, researchers find', ScienceDaily (12 Dec. 2018), https://

www.sciencedaily.com/releases/2018/12/181212140741.htm, accessed 18 May 2019.

5   What's Up TV, 'Study drugs: are they the smart choice?' [video], *YouTube* (8 May 2019), https://www.youtube.com/watch?v=efkvtJ6i 71A&feature=youtu.be, accessed 8 May 2019.

6   Walker, M., *Why We Sleep: The new science of sleep and dreams* (Penguin Books, 2018).

7   Jenkins, J., and Dallenbach, K. (1924). 'Obliviscence during sleep and waking', *The American Journal of Psychology, 35*(4), 605–12, doi:10.2307/1414040, accessed 26 Jan. 2019.

8   Walker, M.P., Brakefield, T., Seidman, J., Morgan, A., Hobson, J.A., and Stickgold, R. (2003). 'Sleep and the time course of motor skill learning', *Learning & Memory, 10*(4), 275–84.

9   Norra, C., and Richter, N. (2013). 'Sleep disturbances and suicidality: relationships and clinical', *Fortschritte der Neurologie Psychiatrie 81*(10), 561–9, doi: 10.1055/s-0033-1350473, accessed 26 Jan. 2019.

10 'How does anxiety affect sleep?', National Sleep Foundation, https:// www.sleepfoundation.org/sleep-disorders-problems-list/how-does-anxiety-affect-sleep, accessed 27 Jan. 2019.

11 Breus, M., 'Here's what really happens when you're sleep deprived', The Sleep Doctor (10 Apr. 2018), https://www.thesleepdoctor. com/2018/04/10/sleep-deprivation/, accessed 27 Jan. 2019.

12 'How to access insomnia treatment on the NHS', Sleepstation (13 Nov. 2018), https://www.sleepstation.org.uk/articles/sleep-clinic/nhs-options-for-insomnia-treatments/, accessed 8 May 2019.

CHAPTER 12

1   Thorley, C., 'Not By Degrees: Improving student mental health in the UK's universities', IPPR (4 Sep. 2017), https://www.ippr.org/publications/not-by-degrees, accessed 16 Mar. 2019.

2   'Carl Jung quotes', Goodreads, https://www.goodreads.com/ quotes/47721-nothing-has-a-stronger-influence-psychologically-on-their-environment-and, accessed 8 May 2019.

3   Curran, T., and Hill, A.P. (2017). 'Perfectionism is increasing over time: a meta analysis of birth cohort differences from 1989 to 2016', *Psychological Bulletin* [advance online publication], http://dx.doi. org/10.1037/bul0000138, accessed 27 Jan. 2019.

4   'Report: suicide by children and young people 2017', Healthcare Quality Improvement Partnership (13 Jul. 2017), https://www.hqip. org.uk/resource/report-suicide-by-children-and-young-people-2017/, accessed 19 Jan. 2019.

5   'Suicide by children and young people: National Confidential Inquiry into Suicide and Homicide by People with Mental Illness (NCISH)', University of Manchester (2017), https://www.hqip.org.uk/wp-content/uploads/2018/02/8iQSvI.pdf, accessed 8 May 2019.

6   Campbell, D., 'Suicides by young people peak in exam season, report finds', *The Guardian* (13 Jul. 2017), https://www.theguardian.com/ society/2017/jul/13/suicides-by-young-people-peak-in-exam-season-report-finds, accessed 1 Jan. 2019.

7   'CBT – basic attention shifting technique', Alice Boyes (12 Dec. 2011), http://www.aliceboyes.com/cbt-attention-shifting-technique-panic-disorder/, accessed 19 Jan. 2019.

8   Carey, B., *How We Learn* (Penguin Random House Books, 2015).

9   Vailes, F., 'Freshers' week: how tutors can help students cope', *The Guardian* (21 Sep. 2017), https://www.theguardian.com/higher-education-network/2017/sep/21/freshers-week-how-tutors-can-help-students-cope, accessed 18 Jan. 2019.

CHAPTER 13

1   'Adult psychiatric morbidity survey: survey of mental health and wellbeing, England, 2014', NHS Digital (29 Sep. 2016), https://digital. nhs.uk/data-and-information/publications/statistical/adult-psychiatric-morbidity-survey/adult-psychiatric-morbidity-survey-survey-of-mental-health-and-wellbeing-england-2014, accessed 12 Feb. 2019.

2   Weinberger, A.H., Gbedemah, M., Martinez, A.M., Nash, D., Galea, S., and Goodwin, R. D. (2018). 'Trends in depression prevalence in the USA from 2005 to 2015: widening disparities in vulnerable groups', *Psychological Medicine, 48*(8), 1308–15.

3   'Youth mental health report: youth survey 2012–16', Black Dog Institute, https://blackdoginstitute.org.au/docs/default-source/research/ evidence-and-policy-section/2017-youth-mental-health-report_mission-australia-and-black-dog-institute.pdf?sfvrsn=6, accessed 12 Feb. 2019.

4   'Malaysian Mental Healthcare Performance: Technical report 2016', Ministry of Health Malaysia: Putrajaya (pp. 1–67).

5   Twenge, J.M., 'Are mental health issues on the rise?', Psychology Today (12 Oct. 2015), https://www.psychologytoday.com/gb/blog/our-changing-culture/201510/are-mental-health-issues-the-rise, accessed 18 May 2019.

6   Kutcher, S., 'Feeling negative emotions is not a mental illness, say psychologists', *Independent* (2 Apr. 2018), https://www.independent.co.uk/life-style/health-and-families/healthy-living/negative-emotions-mental-illness-depression-health-crisis-pathologising-wellbeing-psychology-a8277251.html, accessed 16 Mar. 2019.

7   Kessler, R.C., Amminger, G.P., Aguilar–Gaxiola, S., Alonso, J., Lee, S., and Ustun, T.B. (2007). 'Age of onset of mental disorders: a review of recent literature', *Current Opinion in Psychiatry, 20*(4), 359.

8   Harvey, K.J., Brown, B., Crawford, P., Macfarlane, A., and McPherson, A. (2007). '"Am I normal?" Teenagers, sexual health and the internet', *Social Science & Medicine, 65*(4), 771–81.

9   Russell, S.T., and Fish, J.N. (2016). 'Mental health in lesbian, gay, bisexual, and transgender (LGBT) youth', *Annual Review of Clinical Psychology, 12*, 465–87.

10 Nodin, N., Peel, E., Tyler, A., and Rivers, I., *The RaRE Research Report: LGB&T mental health risk and resilience explored* (London: PACE, 2015).

11 'The #Take20 parents' hub', YoungMinds, https://youngminds.org.uk/take20/, accessed 8 Feb. 2019.

12 Breedvelt, J., 'Preventing mental health problems: what can we do?', National Elf Service (15 May 2018), https://www.nationalelfservice.net/treatment/mental-illness-prevention/preventing-mental-health-problems-what-can-we-do/, accessed 25 Feb. 2019.

13 Arango, C., Diaz Caneja, C.M., McGorry, P., Rapoport, J., Sommer, I.E., Vorstman, J.A., McDaid, D., Marin, O., Serrano Drozdowskyj, E., Freedman, R., and Carpenter, W. (2018). 'Preventive strategies for mental health', *The Lancet Psychiatry*, doi: 10.1016/S2215-0366(18)30057-9, accessed 25 Feb. 2019.

14 Tomlin, A., 'Prevention and early intervention for youth mental illness: how should we focus our limited resources?', National Elf Service (2 Feb. 2018), https://www.nationalelfservice.net/treatment/mental-illness-prevention/prevention-and-early-intervention-for-youth-mental-illness-how-should-we-focus-our-limited-resources-mqsciencemeeting/, accessed 25 Feb. 2019.

15 'Five ways to wellbeing: the postcards', New Economics Foundation (21 Oct. 2008), https://neweconomics.org/2008/10/five-ways-to-wellbeing-the-postcards, accessed 28 Jan. 2019.

16 McCullough, M.E., and Emmons, R.A. (2003). 'Counting blessings versus burdens: An experimental investigation of gratitude and subjective well-being in daily life', *Journal of Personality and Social Psychology, 84*(2), 377–89.

17 Seligman, M.E., Steen, T.A., Park, N., and Peterson, C. (2005). 'Positive psychology progress: empirical validation of interventions', *American Psychologist, 60*(5), 410.

18 Farb, N.A.S., Segal, Z.C., Mayberg, H., Bean, J., McKeon, D., Fatima, Z., and Anderson A.K. (2007). 'Attending to the present: Mindfulness meditation reveals distinct neural modes of self-reference', *Social Cognitive and Affective Neuroscience, 2*, 313–22; Ortner, C.N.M., Kilner, S.J., and Zelado, P.D. (2007). 'Mindfulness meditation and reduced emotional interference on a cognitive task', *Motivation and Emotion, 31*, 271–83.

19 Querstret, D., Cropley, M., and Fife-Schaw, C. (2018). 'The effects of an online mindfulness intervention on perceived stress, depression and anxiety in a non-clinical sample: a randomised waitlist control trial', *Mindfulness, 9*(6), 1825–36, doi: 10.1007/s12671-018-0925-0, accessed 27 Feb. 2019.

20 Foster, D., 'Is mindfulness making us ill?', *The Guardian* (23 Jan. 2016), https://www.theguardian.com/lifeandstyle/2016/jan/23/is-mindfulness-making-us-ill, accessed 23 Jan. 2019.

21 Russel, T.A.. and Siegmund, G. (2016). 'What and who? Mindfulness in the mental health setting', *British Journal Psychology Bulletin, 40*(6) 333–40.

CHAPTER 14

1 Jantaratnotai, N., Mosikanon, K., Lee, Y., and McIntyre, R. S. (2017). 'The interface of depression and obesity', *Obesity Research & Clinical Practice, 11*(1), 1–10.

2 King, C.A., Arango, A., Kramer, A., Busby, D., Czyz, E., Foster, C.E., and Gillespie, B.W. (2019). 'Association of the youth-nominated support team intervention for suicidal adolescents with 11-to 14-year mortality outcomes: secondary analysis of a randomized clinical trial', *JAMA Psychiatry* [published online 6 Feb. 2019], doi:10.1001/jamapsychiatry.2018.4358, accessed 9 Feb. 2019.

3 Beckman, K., Mittendorfer–Rutz, E., Waern, M., Larsson, H., Runeson, B., and Dahlin, M. (2018). 'Method of self–harm in

adolescents and young adults and risk of subsequent suicide', *Journal of Child Psychology and Psychiatry, 59*(9), 948–56.

4 'Eating disorders', Mental Health Foundation, https://www.mental-health.org.uk/a-to-z/e/eating-disorders, accessed 9 Feb. 2019.

5 'Eating disorders: recognition and treatment', National Institute for Health and Care Excellence (May 2017), https://www.nice.org.uk/guidance/ng69, accessed 2 Feb. 2019.

6 Arcelus, J., Mitchell, A.J., Wales, J., and Nielsen, S. (2011). 'Mortality rates in patients with anorexia nervosa and other eating disorders: a meta-analysis of 36 studies', *Arch Gen Psychiatry, 68*(7), 724–31, doi:10.1001/archgenpsychiatry.2011.74, accessed 2 Feb. 2019.

7 'Delaying for years, denied for months', B-eat Eating Disorders, https://www.beateatingdisorders.org.uk/uploads/documents/2017/11/delaying-for-years-denied-for-months.pdf, accessed 2 Feb. 2019.

8 Parra-Fernández, M.L., Rodríguez-Cano, T., Onieva-Zafra, M.D., Perez-Haro, M.J., Casero-Alonso, V., Fernández-Martinez, E., and Notario-Pacheco, B. (2018). 'Prevalence of orthorexia nervosa in university students and its relationship with psychopathological aspects of eating behaviour disorders', *BMC Psychiatry, 18*(1), 364, https://doi.org/10.1186/s12888-018-1943-0, accessed 10 Feb. 2019.

9 Rimmer, A. (2018). 'Role model: Hugh Herzig', *BMJ, 362*, k3289, https://doi.org/10.1136/bmj.k3289, accessed 14 Mar. 2019.

10 England, L., '90 per cent of people with mental health problems cared for within primary care', Royal College of General Practitioners, http://www.rcgp.org.uk/clinical-and-research/about/clinical-news/2017/december/90-per-cent-of-people-with-mental-health-problems-cared-for-within-primary-care.aspx, accessed 12 Jun. 2018.

CHAPTER 15

1 'Mental health crisis care concordat: Improving outcomes for people experiencing mental health crisis', Department of Health and Concordat signatories (18 Feb. 2014), https://www.crisiscareconcordat.org.uk/wp-content/uploads/2014/04/36353_Mental_Health_Crisis_accessible.pdf, accessed 9 Feb. 2019.

2 Shields, G., 'Early intervention in psychosis services: better outcomes, improved costs', National Elf Service (21 Dec. 2016), https://www.nationalelfservice.net/treatment/systems/early-intervention-in-

psychosis/early-intervention-in-psychosis-services-better-outcomes-improved-costs/, accessed 25 Feb. 2019.

3 O'Neill, S., McLafferty, M., Ennis, E., Lapsley, C., Bjourson, T., Armour, C., Murphy, S., Bunting, B., and Murray, E. (2018). 'Socio-demographic, mental health and childhood adversity risk factors for self-harm and suicidal behaviour in college students in Northern Ireland', *Journal of Affective Disorders, 239*, 58–65.

4 'Suicide by children and young people: National Confidential Inquiry into Suicide and Homicide by People with Mental Illness (NCISH)', University of Manchester (2017), https://www.hqip.org.uk/wp-content/uploads/2018/02/8iQSvI.pdf, accessed 8 May 2019.

5 Ibid.

6 Mughal, F., 'Mental health in young people: top tips for GPs', Royal College of General Practitioners, http://www.rcgp.org.uk/clinical-and-research/about/clinical-news/2018/february/mental-health-in-young-people-top-tips-for-gps.aspx, accessed 11 Jun. 2018.

7 'Adult psychiatric morbidity survey: survey of mental health and well-being, England, 2014', NHS Digital (29 Sep. 2016), https://digital.nhs.uk/data-and-information/publications/statistical/adult-psychiatric-morbidity-survey/adult-psychiatric-morbidity-survey-survey-of-mental-health-and-wellbeing-england-2014, accessed 3 May 2018.

8 'Suicide', World Health Organization (24 Aug. 2018), https://www.who.int/news-room/fact-sheets/detail/suicide, accessed 8 May 2019.

9 'Suicides in the UK: 2017 registrations', Office for National Statistics (4 Sep. 2018), https://www.ons.gov.uk/peoplepopulationandcommunity/birthsdeathsandmarriages/deaths/bulletins/suicidesintheunitedkingdom/2017registrations, accessed 8 May 2019.

10 'Suicide by children and young people: National Confidential Inquiry into Suicide and Homicide by People with Mental Illness (NCISH)', University of Manchester (2017), https://www.hqip.org.uk/wp-content/uploads/2018/02/8iQSvI.pdf, accessed 8 May 2019.

11 Ayers, J.W., Althouse, B.M., Leas, E.C., Dredze, M., and Allem, J.P. (2017). 'Internet searches for suicide following the release of *13 Reasons Why*', *JAMA Internal Medicine, 177*(10), 1527–9, doi:10.1001/jamainternmed.2017.3333, accessed 9 Feb. 2019.

12 Suicide by children and young people. National Confidential Inquiry into Suicide and Homicide by People with Mental Illness (NCISH). Manchester: University of Manchester, 2017. 'Suicide by children and young people: National Confidential Inquiry into Suicide and Homicide by People with Mental Illness (NCISH)', University of Manchester

(2017),https://www.hqip.org.uk/wp-content/uploads/2018/02/8iQSvI. pdf, accessed 16 Mar. 2019.

13 Dazzi, T., Gribble, R., Wessely, S., and Fear, N. (2014). 'Does asking about suicide and related behaviours induce suicidal ideation? What is the evidence?' *Psychological Medicine, 44*(16), 3361–3, doi:10.1017/ S0033291714001299, accessed 11 Jun. 2018.

14 'Confidentiality: good practice in handling patient confidentiality', General Medical Council, https://www.gmc-uk.org/ethical-guidance/ ethical-guidance-for-doctors/confidentiality, accessed 12 Jun. 2018.

15 'Why is LEAP needed?', LEAP Institute, https://lfrp.org/why-is-leap-needed, accessed 10 Feb. 2019.

16 'Estimating suicide among higher education students, England and Wales: experimental statistics', Office for National Statistics, https:// www.ons.gov.uk/peoplepopulationandcommunity/birthsdeathsand marriages/deaths/articles/estimatingsuicideamonghighereducation studentsenglandandwalesexperimentalstatistics/2018-06-25, accessed 18 May 2019.

17 'Suicide by children and young people: National Confidential Inquiry into Suicide and Homicide by People with Mental Illness (NCISH)', University of Manchester (2017), https://www.hqip.org.uk/wp-content/uploads/2018/02/8iQSvI.pdf, accessed 3 May 2018.

18 'Safety Plan', Getselfhelp.co.uk (2011), https://www.getselfhelp. co.uk/docs/SafetyPlan.pdf, accessed 9 Feb. 2019.

Index